D1064418

Managing the Team

DATE			

Human Resource Management in Action

Edited by Brian Towers

Successful Training Practice
Alan Anderson

Practical Employment Law
Paul Lewis

Managing the Team
Mick Marchington

The Japanization of British Industry
Nick Oliver and Barry Wilkinson

Handbook of Human Resource Management
Edited by Brian Towers

Managing Performance Appraisal Systems
Gordon C. Anderson

Managing the Team

A Guide to Successful Employee Involvement

MICK MARCHINGTON

First published 1992

Blackwell Publishers
108 Cowley Road
Oxford OX4 1JF
UK

238 Main Street
Cambridge, Massachusetts 02142
USA

ISBN 0-631-186778

British Library Cataloguing in Publication Data
A CIP catalogue record for this book is available from the British Library.

Library of Congress Cataloging-in-Publication Data
Marchington, Mick.
Managing the team: a guide to successful employee involvement /Mick Marchington.
p. cm. – (Human resource management in action)
Includes index.
ISBN 0-631-18677-8 (pbk.)
1. Management – Great Britain – Employee participation. I. Title.
II. Series.
HD5660.G7M333 1992
658.4'02 – dc20 92-15428 CIP

Typeset in 11 on 13 pt Plantin
by Best-set Typesetter Ltd., Hong Kong
Printed in Great Britain by TJ Press (Padstow) Ltd., Padstow, Cornwall
This book is printed on acid-free paper

Contents

Foreword

Good managers have long since decided that, whatever their natural inclinations, work relationships could not for long be conducted on the basis of simply giving orders to be obeyed. This has had little to do with morality or altruism: experience and research show that involving employees, beyond the cosmetic, can contribute to organizational success.

However, in current circumstances this has little to do with the redistribution of power (or even influence) towards employees and their trade unions. Industrial democracy – as an aspect of practical industrial relations – was buried with the Bullock Committee fifteen long years ago; and employee participation in its replacement by employee involvement is silent on power but noisy on getting work done more effectively.

Employee involvement has a long history even though it became a major fashion in the eighties. Its growth has been inevitably associated with the increasing weakness of trade unions, a development which has not been confined to the UK. This must largely explain the squeezing of the power dimension out of participation, rendering it employee involvement.

But these comments are analysis separated from regret. Furthermore, if employee involvement helps organizations to be more successful (even though much less than fully democratic) then employees can still judge it in terms of tangible benefits such as more secure jobs, better paid jobs and more interesting jobs.

There is therefore a rationale for entering the employee involvement restaurant. But if management decides to dine then it must carefully translate and understand the very long menu. This is the purpose of this book; to provide a comprehensive guide to the array of approaches, schemes and techniques available under the heading of employee involvement. Its style is also rooted in practice, assisting understanding and choice with numerous case studies.

Perhaps the most important quality of this guide is that it is even-handedly critical – as all the books selected for this series. Nothing is without blemish; everything has its cost. These remain important caveats if management is not to be slave of fads and fashions.

Brian Towers
Strathclyde Business School

Preface

This book was written during the early part of the 1990s after a decade in which employee involvement, especially of a direct and personal form, had increased in significance within Britain. For the most part, these schemes had been implemented by employers without any direct pressure from trade unions or legislation from the Conservative government. Rather more important had been other pressures, such as a need to compete in more difficult world markets, improve customer care and product quality, and make use of skills held by 'resourceful humans'. This means that, on one level, there is a multitude of different types of employee involvement on which to focus – from team briefing through to teamworking and total quality management (TQM), or from consultative committees through to employee share ownership. On another level, however, the schemes in operation at the beginning of the 1990s did not vary a great deal given that virtually all of them had been introduced and sustained by management – obviously with employer objectives at the forefront of their minds.

I am grateful to all those practitioners who have told me so much about employee involvement and participation over the last two decades, especially those working in the organizations from which the case studies are drawn. They have been given pseudonyms to protect their confidentiality, and I trust that this will be achieved. Other people have helped in a more direct manner. Adrian Wilkinson, a colleague of mine in the Manchester School of Management at the University of Manchester Institute of Science and Technology (UMIST), read the entire draft, and made many more comments than I was ever able to take on board; I am very grateful to him for all the effort he put into this. Other colleagues at UMIST also made comments on various parts of the text, in particular Professor

John Goodman and Peter Ackers (now at Loughborough University Business School). Some of the case study material has been derived from research funded by a number of organizations, in particular the Department of Employment and the Economic and Social Research Council, and I am grateful to these bodies for their financial assistance. The views expressed in this book, however, are those of the author alone and do not necessarily reflect those of either funding body. Professor Brian Towers also provided useful advice and encouragement as the Series Editor, especially about matters of style and presentation, and the eventual title was his suggestion. As ever, my family had to bear the major burden, although I think that they are now getting used to it. Any errors or misinterpretations remain my responsibility.

Mick Marchington

1 Employee Involvement and Human Resource Management

Introduction

Most commentators agree that there has been an increase in managerially-initiated schemes of employee involvement (EI) in Britain over the course of the last twenty years. Many of the surveys illustrate that different forms of EI have increased in coverage, and that managers are prone to pinpoint greater involvement and communications as one of the principal additions to their employee relations over this period. It is the purpose of this book to analyse the development of EI within the context of moves to a Human Resource Management (HRM) perspective, as well as increasing pressures from the European Community for action in this area. This will be done by drawing upon a wide range of case studies and published surveys, in addition to my own research in many organizations drawn from different sectors of industry.

Three important questions will be addressed in this book. First, *what* is the shape of EI in the early 1990s, and what different forms of EI are in existence? The remainder of the book analyses the nature of various different forms of EI, incorporating the range from one-way downward communications (such as house journals, employee reports, and team briefing), through upward problem-solving devices (such as quality circles or customer care committees) and consultative committees, to financial participation (such as profit sharing schemes or value-added bonus systems). Second, *why* is EI introduced into organizations, and what are the major reasons for its continuance in workplaces where it has existed for many years? At least six sets of reasons seem important, although it should be noted that many of these can operate at the same time in the same organization.

1 *information and education*: many of the direct forms of EI, such as team briefing and house journals, are introduced to communicate information to staff as part of an attempt to 'educate' them about the business position, to stress the importance of the customer, or pave the way for some new initiative which management is about to introduce. Equally, consultative committees aim to provide information to employee representatives about the current state of the business or future plans, a process designed in part to convince them of the 'logic' of management's actions as well as offering an opportunity for these to be questioned.
2 *gaining commitment*: to some extent, this is implicit in the previous set of reasons as employers seek higher levels of employee commitment to organizational goals and methods. However, it goes further in that commitment is sought not only via communications schemes but also through problem-solving techniques and financial involvement in which employees are encouraged to adopt a unitary/teamwork view of the organization.
3 *appropriating knowledge*: this describes the situation in which employers make use of schemes designed to tap into employee opinions, search for new ideas, or find ways of improving departmental or organizational performance as a whole. It is most apparent in relation to quality and customer care initiatives, suggestion schemes, and consultative committees. Depending upon the perspective of the observer, this is seen either as a good thing (everybody gains from greater involvement) or as a way in which employers find yet more subtle methods to subjugate employees.
4 *recruitment and retention*: EI is also introduced as a device to attract and retain staff, especially at times of labour market shortages and in specific skills. It is particularly apparent in relation to profit sharing and share ownership schemes. However, a strong commitment to EI is also seen as one of a number of factors which employers feel can enhance their reputation in the labour (and product) market, and in some cases this ethos is interwoven into the fabric of employee relations at an organization.
5 *stability and conformance*: there are a number of different factors which can be combined under this heading, but all are directed towards the objective of providing greater stability and order in the employment relationship. For example, joint consultative committees often have as one of their objectives the provision of a 'safety valve', an alternative channel for discontent rather than grievance procedures or industrial action. Similarly, greater order or conformance can also be an objective behind the introduction of regular communications schemes to overcome a previous problem of haphazard and incomplete passages of information.

6 *externally-driven*: not all EI initiatives have their source in either the establishment or the organization as a whole, and at least part of the rationale may be external to the workplaces which have to operate the schemes. EI may be enforced upon employers via legislation (UK or EC) or it may be part of a company-wide directive with which all establishments are required to comply.

The final question to be addressed in this book concerns the impact of EI, and *how* schemes operate in practice. In each chapter, there will be some discussion of how different systems actually operate and some assessment of their implications for the various parties at work. In particular, how does EI impact upon employees themselves (the supposed recipients of schemes), upon middle managers and supervisors, and upon trade union organization. The interrelationship between EI and each of these differing interest groups is often exceedingly complex, and much depends upon the motives behind the introduction or extension of EI. However, it must be stressed that the consequences of EI may be different from its objectives, that is, the motives behind the introduction of a particular technique may lead to a quite different impact in practice. In addition, although motive and impact have been distinguished here on analytical grounds, the reality is often more complex.

The context in which organisations operate also has important implications for the character which employee involvement exhibits in practice. At least six sets of factors are worth mentioning. These are:

1 the increasingly competitive nature of product markets within which organizations operate, some of which has been stimulated by the impact of Japanese firms on the world scene.
2 structural changes in patterns of employment have led to a decline in traditional areas of industry (e.g. manufacturing and the public corporations) and growth in the private service sector. With this has also come a growth in part-time and temporary employment.
3 the reduction in trade union power and influence at national level and in many cases also within employing organizations. This is most apparent in the decline of UK union membership since 1979 (13 million to less than ten) and union density (from 55 per cent to under 40 per cent).
4 the continuing impact of technological change at both a sectoral and individual job level, and its effects on organizational structures, cultures and tasks.
5 the political emphasis in the UK on deregulation, individualism and voluntarism, compared with a more dirigiste EC perspective.

6 adjustments to organization structure and culture, including greater moves to decentralization and the supposed shift in some organizations to human resource management.

Of course, these six sets of factors are not independent of one another, but are intertwined in ways which have the potential to reinforce developments in organizations. In addition, each has important implications not only for the context in which EI is being developed but also for the vocabulary which is used to describe these recent initiatives by employers. Of these factors, two (EC influences and HRM) are especially important for the remainder of this book, and these will now be analysed in more detail. This will include discussions about the relationship between British and EC views of employee involvement, as well as competing notions of HRM.

Employee Involvement: Britain and the EC Programme

Over the 1980s and early 1990s, three successive Conservative governments developed a free market approach to the economy, and attempted to remove restrictions on employers in the labour market, and elsewhere. A spirit of enterprise and of individualism has been promoted by government, explicitly encouraging employers to adopt arrangements which are designed to fit with their own specific environmental and organizational conditions. In this sphere, there has been a range of initiatives to promote links between industry and education, as well as those designed to increase training access and provision. Equally, there has been a body of legislation designed to increase union democracy and reduce the likelihood that employers will suffer from industrial action, and to reduce statutory and collective regulation in the field of employment. With regard to EI, the principal emphasis of the UK Conservative government in the 1980s was on voluntary measures undertaken by employers because they see that it makes sense to them.

This is set against repeated moves within the EC designed to produce a more coherent and uniform 'social' framework for the community, and to harmonize certain standards and aspects of employment and company law across the member states. Over the past two decades, there has been a number of attempts to introduce a 'social' element into Community affairs and to harmonize company law within the EC, both of which would have significant implications for employee involvement were these to be approved. These are summarized in a variety of publications [see for example European Industrial Relations Review (1990); Gold and Hall (1990); both these publications contain information about the structure of EI in the various member states as well. This commenced with the draft Fifth Directive back in 1972 which proposed to harmonize the structure of companies with 500 or more employees. In its initial form, the directive would have required these companies to adopt a two-tier board structure (executive and supervisory) with at least one-third of the members of the supervisory (lower) board being drawn from among employees. Having made no progress at all (apart from spawning the Bullock Committee of Inquiry in Britain in the mid-1970s), the Commission issued a more flexible set of proposals in 1983 which allowed member states to choose from three options for all companies which employed 1,000 or more employees. These were (a) employee directors constituting between one-third and one-half of the supervisory board, (b) works councils with equivalent rights to information as the employee directors on boards, plus the right of consultation on strategic plans, and (c) any other collective agreement which included employee participation corresponding to the principles and rights of the previous models. This also allowed for unitary (single) board structures as well. Further amendments were made in 1988, significantly to allow for Qualified Majority Voting (QMV) rather than unanimity, but there has still been no movement on this issue.

The Vredeling directive forms the second area in which there have been EC initiatives on employee participation; this was modified twice in the early 1980s. Vredeling outlined proposals for information and consultation in undertakings with complex structures, such as the major multinationals, and initially sought to provide a similar sort of role for employees in companies which had their headquarters outside of the EC. The initial directive required companies with over 100 employees to release information on an occasional basis to employees in subsidiaries, and to consult on issues which were likely to have a serious impact on employee interests. If local management failed to provide the requisite information, employee representatives would have the right to approach the parent company directly. This was modified in 1983 to allow exemptions for confidential information and to raise the size threshold to 1,000 employees. Again there has been no real movement in this area despite further attempts to gain progress in the late 1980s, and it is expected that this will now be withdrawn (Involvement and Participation Association EC Newsletter, Number 6; March 1991).

The third set of proposals which are relevant to EI are those relating to the European Company Statute. This has also been on the agenda since the early 1970s, but it re-emerged in 1989 with a directive to develop participation for specific companies which operated in at least two member states. Basically, any organization which corresponds to these conditions can choose to become an SE (a standard European company) and thus be eligible for tax and legal incentives provided it complies with the participation arrangements as well. These would be similar to those already outlined in the paragraph on the 5th Directive and its subsequent amendments. But, the decision to become an SE is voluntary, and it is difficult to believe that many British organizations would choose to do so at the current time.

Finally, there have been the relevant clauses in the Social Charter (the Community Charter of Fundamental Social Rights for Workers) which was adopted by eleven of the twelve member states in December 1989; the UK was the sole country which did not vote in favour of this social programme. One part of the Social Charter and several subsequent directives refer to attempts to harmonize employee participation throughout the EC, and the adoption of one of a set of proposals for implementing EI; again much in line with the details which have already been discussed in earlier parts of this section. In addition, there is an instrument on equity sharing. Within this, and to some extent similar in coverage though not in detail to the previous proposals, is the draft directive on information and consultation of employees in European-scale undertakings. In organizations with at least 1,000 employees, and at least two establishments in at least two member states – each of which employs at least 100 workers – representatives would be free to request the formation of a European Works Council (EWC). In this case, management must meet with representative (a special negotiating body) to establish an EWC to agree the nature and composition of the works council, its constitution, timing etc. If there were to be no agreement, certain minimum conditions would then automatically apply. Broadly, this would allow for an annual meeting with central management at which certain information would be provided to appointed employee representatives.

The British Conservative party is opposed to this, as it is to all other attempts to introduce EI on a statutory basis, but interestingly the Involvement and Participation Association (IPA) has given this proposal some support. They note that this is 'mild and conciliatory when compared to earlier attempts by the Commission to frame employee consultation legislation. The EWC will be set up at the request of employees and appears to cover all employees rather than only those represented by trades union agreements. It is much less prescriptive than previous proposals' (IPA EC Newsletter, March 1991). Nevertheless, the government is keen on pursuing the development of EI by voluntary means which employers feel are suitable for their own specific contextual circumstances. Apart from the legislative provisions requiring employers over a certain size to report on developments in EI (which is described in chapter 3), and that on employee share ownership (see chapter 8), during the 1980s encouragement has come via exhortation. In 1989, for example, the Department of Employment published *People and Companies; Employee Involvement in Britain* which reproduced a number of case studies of employing organizations which used different forms of EI. In the summary of the booklet, it is stated that:

> The Government believes that the EC proposals for compulsory legislation on worker participation would not be worthwhile for workers or their employers in the United Kingdom and could destroy what they were designed to build. Firms should be free to choose for themselves the policies and practices that they wish to develop. It will remain the Government's policy to give every encouragement to the voluntary development of employee involvement and participation.

Following the outcome of the Maastricht summit in December 1991, there is little likelihood of a future Conservative government adopting any elements of the Social Charter by the mid-1990s, especially in relation to employee participation, communications and consultation. On the other hand, the Labour Party is committed to embracing the main body of the Social Charter, and would accept a more regulatory framework for employee involvement – especially representative participation.

The Human Resource Management Puzzle

In recent years, there has been a considerable amount of debate in both Europe and North America about the nature of human resource management (HRM), and in particular whether or not it constitutes anything new in the management of people at work. Not surprisingly, the debate has generated much confusion, because the term HRM has been interpreted in a wide range of different ways. For example, some have merely used the term HRM as a substitute for personnel management, whereas others have argued that HRM represents a distinctively different approach to managing people. Similarly, some have suggested that the key characteristic of HRM is closer integration or 'fit' between corporate strategy and people-management, whereas others have seen its key feature as the treatment of employees as resources (rather than costs) on the assumption that such policies will contribute to competitive advantage in the market place; in other words, the distinction between 'hard' and 'soft' HRM (Storey, 1989, p. 8). Yet others have contrasted HRM, defined as the 'new' industrial relations, with the more adversarial, collectivist approach predominant in Britain in the 1970s. The whole debate is best summed up by Legge (1989, p. 29):

> The problem is that while 'fit' with strategy would argue a *contingent* design of HRM policy, internal consistency at least with the 'soft' human resource values associated with 'mutuality' – would argue an *absolutist* approach to the design of employment policy. Can this contradiction be reconciled without stretching to the limit the meaning of HRM as a distinct approach to managing employees? (my emphasis).

Below, the literature will be reviewed under four separate subheadings, the last of which – absolutist HRM – is of greatest relevance for the subject matter of this book.

Old wine in recycled bottles

At its most basic level, HRM has come into vogue as a new or more trendy name for personnel management, one which it is felt will give personnel departments/managers more power within the boardroom. This view is predicated upon the notion that personnel management is decidedly unstrategic, concerning itself with parochial issues or those of a short term nature. The history of personnel management gives some credence to this, in that the early roots of the occupation were in the welfare field and consisted of little more than improving the environment within which work was undertaken. Similarly, the view that the personnel department acts as a receptacle for jobs which no other manager wishes to undertake, a sort of dumping ground for everything from paying wages, organizing the social club, or dealing with outside bodies, reinforces the image of a rag-bag of activities which lack coherence. Although a large number of organizations now have experienced and professional personnel managers, the department is still seen in some companies as second-class, a place where other managers are put out to grass when they are no use elsewhere. Clearly, in such circumstances, a mere retitling of the personnel function as HRM will produce little change in practical terms or in the principal activities carried out within the department.

Personnel management plus

A second, and somewhat different, view can be found in the work of Torrington who views human resources management as the latest addition to the personnel role, thus following others such as social reformer, acolyte of benevolence, humane bureaucrat, consensus negotiator, organization man, and manpower analyst (1989, pp. 57–9). For Torrington, 'the human resources manager starts not from the organization's employees (how to find, train, pay them etc.) but from the organization's need for human resources; with the demand rather than the supply' (1989, p. 60). HRM incorporates the generally welcome (such as training) through to the generally unwelcome (such as dismissal), as well as arranging for subcontractors or consultants to meet the demand for labour. Unlike the final two categories dealt with below, HRM is not revolutionary in any respect, but rather a 'further dimension to a multi-faceted role' (p. 66). In other words, the title of 'personnel management plus' seems appropriate given the fact that HRM is added to the mix which is already in existence, with the precise composition of activities contingent upon the situation within which the organization is operating.

The strategic management of human resources

While the previous two categories can be seen as developing out of personnel management, the next two offer a distinctive break with previous theory and practice. The defining characteristic of this model – the strategic management of human resources – is the notion of strategy whereby the management of people is integrated into corporate plans/philosophies. The 'fit' works in two directions; on the one hand, people-issues are incorporated into the strategic decision making process, preferably though not necessarily via the presence of a senior human resource manager on the board or its equivalent. On the other hand, the most appropriate style for managing people is heavily influenced by the broader strategy of the business, and in particular the nature of the product markets within which the organization operates. This therefore implies that certain contextual conditions may prove less conducive to the development of EI than other more favourable circumstances.

This view of HRM has been most regularly put forward by a number of American writers, of which Baird and Meshoulam are the most explicit. They argue (1988, p. 117) that the effectiveness of HRM depends upon its ability to adapt to meet different stages in the life cycle of the organization, from initiation through to complete strategic integration. Similarly, the texts by Fombrun et al. (1984) and Beer et al. (1985) for the most part adopt a contingency perspective. Some UK writers (for example Miller, 1987; Purcell, 1989) have also suggested that the management of human resources is contingent upon corporate (or business unit) strategies. For example, with Purcell's attempt to apply portfolio planning to human resources issues (1989, pp. 77–88), the preferred approach for managing human resources varies between business units and over time depending upon circumstances. Accordingly, HRM is seen to differ from previous models for managing people at work because it has now become an issue of strategic concern to the organization which needs to be integrated into other plans at the same level.

Therefore, the essential feature of this form of HRM – the strategic management of human resources – is that it is related to the structures via which senior managers make decisions, rather than to a specific or distinct *style* for managing people which conforms to some absolute idea of best practice. Thus, HRM could take the form of direct control or responsible autonomy (Friedman, 1977), theory X or theory Y (McGregor, 1960) depending upon the dictates of the business situation. Additionally, of course, the way in which human resources are managed can vary significantly between establishments or businesses within the same organization, as well as over time. Consequently, there may be businesses for which any form of EI is seen as inappropriate by senior managers, or there may be times when its relevance is called into question. For others, conversely, EI may be viewed as an integral part of how to manage employees, given that the latter may be able to influence significantly the operation of the business or its contacts with customers.

The management of resourceful humans

Unlike the previous model, the approaches to be considered here conceive of HRM as a distinct way of managing people, one which emphasizes the value of employees as resources to be developed by the organization. This is not usually for any altruistic reason but because it is seen to make 'good business sense' and provide a source of competitive advantage. In broad terms, there are two essential features of this version of HRM, often somewhat misleadingly subtitled 'soft' HRM. First, in common with the previous models, the management of people is an important issue which *should* be the concern of senior management, either through a senior personnel practitioner or through some other manager with a specific responsibility for and interest in such affairs; in other words, the notion of strategic integration. Second, and this is where the difference appears, a specific form of people-management is viewed as superior to any other; depending upon the writer or the organization surveyed, this has been variously defined as an approach which fosters commitment, flexibility and adaptability, training and development, individualism and non-unionism, or employee involvement. As Storey suggests in his review of (soft) HRM, it 'becomes recognized as a central business concern; its performance and delivery are integrated into line management; the aim shifts from merely securing compliance to the more ambitious one of winning commitment' (1989, p. 6). Below, a number of alternative variants of this absolutist version of HRM can be outlined. Given that these perspectives are the most relevant for the subsequent analysis of EI, this will be dealt with in a little more detail than the previous versions.

The first variant is that HRM is a combination of strategic integration and a focus on human resource development/employee training. Pettigrew and his colleagues – who have had the most to say about this conceptualization – not (Hendry and Pettigrew, 1986, p. 4) that there are two themes which overlap in the definition of strategic HRM, the first contained in the term 'strategic' and the second in the philosophy of 'human resources'. The latter suggests that people are a valued resource, a critical investment in an organization's current performance, whereas the former has at least four meanings. These are (1) the use of planning, (2) a coherent philosophy for managing human resources, (3) matching HRM to business strategy, and (4) seeing people as a strategic resource for achieving competitive advantage. Having outlined their view of HRM, the authors then move on to consider how employees will be able to offer organizations competitive advantage, and they consistently focus on the importance of training and development as the solution to this problem. Referring to their research with a range of companies in different industries (for example, in retail, banking, computing and manufacturing), they reports that human resource development/training is an important feature of strategic HRM. This training can be either technical to improve job skills, or attitudinal (as with cultural change programmes) designed to increase employee awareness of and commitment to organizational goals. A major implication of this renewed interest in employee development would be a transformation of the standing of the training function within organizations, and this has been illustrated by both the quantity and the seniority of job advertisements within this area in recent years. Whilst there is little doubt that training/HRD has become more widespread (for example, the introduction of teamwork training sessions with process operators in some parts of the chemical industry), there remain suspicions about the extent of this 'transformation' throughout industry. Moreover, there are also doubts about the durability of this new-found commitment to training in less favourable business circumstances, especially if a recession puts even more pressure on companies to cut back on costs (Keep, 1989, pp. 117–21). For Keep (p. 125):

> The training effort is one useful litmus test of the reality of the adoption of HRM/HRD policies . . . if the training and development of its employees is not afforded high priority, if training is not seen as a vital component in the realization of business plans, then it is hard to accept that such a company has committed itself to HRM.

The second variant of absolutist HRM has a somewhat broader focus on the securing of *employee commitment* as the twin strand with strategic integration. This theme is apparent from the work of a number of American writers, for example Walton (1985, pp. 77–85) who analyses a shift in the USA from policies designed to exert tight control over employees to those aimed at eliciting commitment. The former rests on the assumption that employees have little interest in work, whereas the latter suggests that higher levels of commitment will lead to enhanced performance. The author points to practices in a variety of US organisations which demonstrate the value of initiating a strategy directed at eliciting high commitment. Kochan and Chalykoff also develop this line with their comparison of 'new' as opposed to 'traditional' HRM policies (1987, p. 185). New HRM comprises both strategic integration (as described above) and commitment-generating practices such as high compensation levels, employment stability for core workers, internal promotion wherever possible, extensive training and career development, and a range of techniques designed to increase employee involvement. Clearly, this is a much broader focus than the HRD models, and includes a multiplicity of devices to foster commitment: in recruiting the right people, in developing their commitment to the organization, in rewarding them at an appropriate level, and in encouraging them to remain with the organisation.

The model developed by Guest (1987) is also a variant of this, in that he identifies four dimensions of HRM. These are:

1 *integration*, which is defined as the inclusion of human resource issues in strategic plans, the coherence of all HR policies, line management commitment to the importance of human resources, and employee identification with company goals. The proposition is that the greater the degree of integration, the more likely the organization's plans are to be successfully implemented (p. 512).
2 *commitment*, both to job and organization. His theoretical proposition is that higher levels of commitment will result in higher satisfaction, better levels of performance, longer tenure and a willingness to accept change (p. 514).
3 *flexibility/adaptability*, and basically the need to avoid rigid structures, attitudes and job descriptions. The proposition is that more flexibility will result in a capacity to respond swiftly and effectively to changes, and so ensure the full utilization of human resources (p. 515).
4 *quality* of staff, performance, and reputation with customers and suppliers. The proposition is that high quality in all these spheres will lead to high performance levels (p. 515).

Guest's approach is useful because he puts forward a number of testable propositions about the link between absolutist HRM and performance in a way which can allow others to assess whether or not these hold in practice rather than just in theory. However, one of the problems with this model is that it tends to confuse process and output dimensions of HRM, those where a contingency approach is adopted versus those where an absolutist stance is taken; for example, under the goal of integration, he includes factors relating to decision making and organisation structure – such as the integration of human resources into strategic planning – with those relating to specific outputs of HRM – such as employee identification with the company. The latter could much more easily and appropriately be located under the second heading of commitment, as too could the other dimensions of flexibility and quality since both of these are inextricably linked with employee preparedness to identify with the aims of the company. For example, individuals who are committed to the organization are likely to be flexible and adaptable in their attitudes to work, as too are those employees who are selected via stringent criteria in the first place. In short, Guest's model, though different in some respects from people such as Walton and Kochan and Chalykoff, does reinforce the absolutist emphasis on commitment and strategic integration.

Similar views have been expressed by senior personnel practitioners in the UK such as Fowler and M. Armstrong. For Fowler (1987, p. 13), HRM comprises the integration of employee management with general business management as well as 'a dominant emphasis on the common interests of employer and employed in the success of the business (which) will release a massive potential of intitiative and commitment within the workforce'. A key part of this is employee involvement, 'but on the company's terms'. Armstrong supports this stance, arguing that human resources are the most important asset an organisation has, and their effective management is the key to success (1987, p. 33). On the other hand, he warns that HR policies must be relevant to the organization's circumstances, presumably indicating that, despite the fact that employees are supposedly the most valuable asset, there are occasions (perhaps many) when soft HRM can not be pursued because it does not 'fit' with other strategies; we shall return to this later.

Developing out of this second variant of absolutism is the third, in which soft HRM is seen to be equivalent to non-unionism because of its unitarist and individualistic underpinnings. This is in part supported by examples such as IBM and Hewlett Packard, companies which are of course non-union, and are what Keenoy describes as 'traditional' HRM (1990, p. 4); those organizations which treat people well, so that 'they will respond positively with loyalty and commitment, and of course will not find any particular attraction in joining a union'. A number of the American texts have implicitly or explicitly conflated HRM with non-unionism, and this has led to the argument as to whether HRM is only achievable in or suitable for an un-unionised establishment or organisation. Again, some of the American evidence suggests that HRM and non-unionism are likely to go together; the research of Foulkes (1980) indicates that HRM policies were introduced on greenfield sites, often encouraged by a powerful chief executive, and the union question was not explicitly considered. Only at a later date has non-unionism become a policy goal. Others have suggested that managements may introduce HRM in order to forestall unionism, although a more recent study by Ichniowski et al. (1989, p. 116) found that – in relation to manufacturing and production workers – 'progressive (soft) HRM policies are not confined to or predominant in the non-union sector'.

In Britain, according to Guest (1989, pp. 50–1), at 'a signficant proportion of foreign-owned, greenfield sites, management is pursuing some of the central features of HRM . . . there is either no role for trade unions or at best a limited one where unions are allowed to operate but only on management's terms.' This is not to say that these organisations are avowedly anti-union, but rather that unions are seen to be unnecessary or irrelevant – although the consequence of this for trade union membership remains much the same. The situation on established, as opposed to new, sites is rather more complex, and in many cases recognised trade unions have been able to limit the development of absolutist HRM, fearing that its emphasis on individual employee commitment will undermine their role in the workplace. On the other hand, some of the case study evidence presented by Marchington and Parker (1990) illustrates the way in which employee involvement techniques, especially those where communications about company prospects become a central feature of management attempts to generate commitment, may serve to de-emphasise the role of the union(s) within the workplace. It should be stressed that, apart from a number of notable exceptions, managers have not tended to introduce employee involvement/HRM with the prime objective of marginalizing unions. However, it is also apparent that the more success managements have in developing HRM, the harder it is for trade unions to maintain their position within the workplace.

Although there are differences between them, each of the absolutist versions of HRM focuses on the idea that employees are a valued resource which the organisation needs to develop in order to establish or retain competitive advantage in the market place. Of course, there may be features of each variant operating at the same time, with a stress on training and development, employee involvement, and a negligible (or no) place for trade unions. Equally, it should be remembered that not all non-union sites practise HRM; far from it, as reports on the working conditions experienced at Grunwick in the late 1970s made abundantly clear (Rogaly, 1977).

Summary of Forthcoming Chapters

The remainder of the book is structured as follows. In chapter 2, there is a short discussion of the participation and involvement literature which serves to place the later more detailed analysis in perspective. While it is difficult to do justice to the vast amount of material which has been published on the subject, the chapter aims to clarify the different vocabularies of participation and to isolate the key characteristics by which different forms of EI can be categorized. It also provides a glossary of terms which are used in the remainder of the book. Some readers may wish to skip the main part of this chapter and move on to those which deal in more detail with specific forms of EI. The next two chapters focus on one-way communications from management to other employees, with chapter 3 examining written and audio-visual media and chapter 4 concentrating on face-to-face verbal communications, such as team briefing. Both these forms of EI grew substantially during the 1980s, as employers sought to inform and 'educate' employees about the competitive position of the organization or establishment for which they worked. By contrast, chapters 5 and 6 examine the contribution which employees can make towards the operation of their own department or unit, and considers the perspective that employees are resourceful humans who have much to offer (and receive from) the effective management of organizations. The first of these chapters deals with involvement in problem-solving – such as quality circles, suggestion schemes, total quality management, and customer care initiatives. Whilst it is recognised that all these techniques are principally geared to the satisfaction of production or service criteria, they have also been associated with EI, and it is assumed that they will help to enhance the commitment of employees as well. Chapter 6 is concerned with task participation and the extended involvement of employees in their work via job redesign. This can take three forms; (a) the extension of jobs at the same skill level (horizontal job redesign), (b) the addition of tasks which have traditionally been undertaken by more skilled employees or supervisors (vertical role integration), and (c) teamworking, which in theory combines both horizontal and vertical job loading. In chapter 7, the emphasis shifts to an analysis of joint consultation, a form of indirect EI, and to the conditions under which JCCs assume different characters. Chapter 8 evaluates various forms of financial participation, including profit sharing, employee share ownership, profit-related pay, and value-added payment schemes. Finally, in chapter 9, we conclude with an overview of the material, and offer a few pointers to the future.

The principal purpose of the book is to provide a succinct analysis of the various EI schemes which have developed in the UK. On the one hand, it is important to describe how these different forms of EI operate in practice, and it is hoped that the book will be able to do this. At the same time, it is my intention to provide a text which critically appraises the impact of EI, and does not rely on superficial (and generally glossy, public relations-oriented) descriptions of the universal benefits of all varieties of managerially-initiated schemes for 'involving' employees. Where possible, I try to introduce case study material to illustrate general points. In addition, each chapter contains a rather longer case study (up to about 2,000 words) of particular forms of EI in practice.

Irrespective of any legislation from the EC, it is anticipated that all the forms of EI which are dealt with here will continue to be relevant to and appropriate for employing organizations in the UK. Any compulsory obligations on British employers, for example requiring the introduction of European works councils or employee directors, would merely add another chapter to the analysis. As Gold and Hall (1990, p. 29) note, 'direct and indirect forms of participation fulfil different *functions* at the workplace. A failure to take this point into account often leads employers and unions into talking past one another when discussing participation.' As if to illustrate this point, recent research by Marchington et al. (1992) has found that it is typical, especially in large organizations, for there to be a mix of EI techniques rather than an emphasis on just one or two.

2 The Nature of Employee Involvement

Introduction

'Employee involvement' – often referred to as EI – is a new term which has entered into the vocabulary of British practitioners and academics during the 1980s. It appears to represent the most recent manifestation of attempts by *employers* to find more participative ways in which to manage their staff, and to some extent, with the support of government and employers' organizations, it has replaced earlier variants such as industrial democracy and employee participation. EI is a phrase which is redolent of employer initiatives. The onus is on the employer to 'involve' or give employees opportunities to become involved in their work and the organization, beyond simple performance or the contractual wage/work bargain. It falls short of 'participation', certainly in terms of participation in decision making. Some EI practices do, however, give an opportunity to exercise influence – for example, joint consultation or quality circles – but most do not impact upon the decision-making structure of the business. In this way, EI differs from collective bargaining and industrial democracy, both of which are explicit forms of power sharing between management and employees – via their representatives. However, as we shall see, these terms are sometimes used interchangeably and there are no commonly-agreed definitions for any one of them.

In this chapter, the aim is briefly to review the substantial literature on the subject, as well as offer a number of definitions which have been adopted in this book. First, there is a short historical discussion of practical participation initiatives in the UK. This is followed by a section on definitions, which includes an attempt to deconstruct the terminology by reference to a variety of characteristics of involvement. Thirdly, the analysis is placed within the broader framework of four competing paradigms of participation. Finally, we conclude with a series of short definitions of each of the EI techniques which are analysed in the remainder of the book.

A Short History of Participation in Britain

Following Ramsay's historical analysis (1977), the first wave of interest in participation occurred towards the end of the nineteenth century, and this centred around a variety of initiatives in the area of profit sharing. Share schemes were often introduced by philanthropic employers as part of a policy to extend welfare provisions within the company, but many of these were soon dropped due to worsening economic conditions; this happened in one of the most widely-quoted examples (Henry Briggs and Company in the 1860s). In other cases, the introduction of profit sharing combined both altruistic and union-avoidance objectives; the most relevant example of this was the scheme at the South Metropolitan Gas Company around 1890, and this resulted in a period of severe industrial relations problems as splits emerged not only between union and non-union labour but also between the union and its members at the company (Poole, 1989, pp. 8–14).

The second surge of interest occurred during and just after the First World War in the period 1917–20, with the development of Whitley Councils. The origins of Whitleyism can be found in a mixture of external pressures and a desire to integrate workers more closely within the enterprises by which they were employed, and the Committee of Inquiry's terms of reference focused on how to achieve a permanent improvement in relations between employers and work(men). The Committee eventually proposed that a series of joint employer-union bodies should be set up to operate at three tiers, national, district, and workplace. Against the background of extensive industrial conflict, it was suggested that workers should have a greater opportunity of participating in the regulation and adjustment of all those aspects of their employment conditions of most concern to them. By the end of 1921, 73 Joint Industrial Councils had emerged with over 1,000 local committees, although it is significant that none had been introduced into mining or engineering where collective bargaining was already well established. Over the next few years, most of the new councils were scrapped, and it was only within parts of the public sector that Whitleyism survived (Marchington, 1980, p. 2; Brannen, 1983, p. 42). However, some consultative schemes which were introduced during the 1920s still remain in existence over 60 years later, for example those at ICI and Clark's Shoes.

During the Second World War, we find evidence of the third wave of interest in participation as employee representatives were offered some degree of shared control via Joint Production and Advisory Committees (JPACs). This was part of a war-time drive to stimulate productivity and reduce conflict with governmental encouragement for these factory-level committees. The JPACs were designed to deal with any issue relating to production or increased efficiency, but to exclude matters dealt with by the negotiating machinery. It has been estimated that by the mid 1940s there were over 4,000 committees in existence in engineering alone, covering in excess of 2.5 million workers, but their numbers waned during the post-war part of the decade. Brannen suggests that part of the reason for the decline related to the (ab)use of these committees by management – as a bolster for their power – but it also reflects the fact that JPACs were principally a union initiative to which management displayed little real commitment (1983, p. 44). Although interest in the JPACs declined, some surveys suggest that joint consultative committees (JCCs) remained in a large number of organizations at the end of the 1940s (Hawes and Brookes, 1980, p. 355). However, a number of surveys undertaken during the next two decades, despite being rightly criticized for their lack of comparability by MacInnes (1985), did indicate that JCCs had increasingly been abandoned (Marchington, 1989a, p. 380). The fact that the Donovan Commission in 1968 devoted just ten paragraphs to the subject of workers' participation illustrates that it was seen very much as subsidiary to collective bargaining as a form of employee participation in decisions which affected their working lives (Marchington, 1980, p. 3).

The fourth phase of interest in participation occurred during the 1970s. Much of this was stimulated by Britain's accession to the European Economic Community (EEC), and its concern with the harmonization of company law, industrial democracy and the presence of worker directors on the boards of companies in several European countries. In Britain there was evidence from a variety of surveys that consultation had also gone through a resurgence during this period. According to Clegg (1979, p. 439), the revival in interest emerged and intensified in the early 1970s because of a remarkable change of attitude on the part of the Trades Union Congress (TUC) towards the concept of employee representation at board level. This, coupled with entry to the EC and the election of a Labour government in 1974, led to the setting-up of the Bullock Committee of Inquiry which ensured that the debate about industrial democracy was never far from the centre of industrial relations at the time. The Committee was divided from the start because of its terms of reference, and ultimately two reports were published; the majority report supported the idea of worker directors on unitary boards, and in line with TUC thinking, suggested that these be based on union channels, while the minority report favoured representation on the supervisory element of two-tier boards. It should be recalled that the employer members of Bullock were deeply suspicious of employee representation at board level, even in any form. The subsequent White Paper in 1978 watered down the Bullock majority proposals, and there was a change of government before any further action was taken. Given the strong hostility of employers to this form of employee involvement, however, it is unlikely that any legislation would have been particularly effective (see Elliott, 1978). The debate about Bullock probably did help to raise the profile and extensiveness of JCCs though, as employers sought to find ways to develop 'bottom up' as opposed to 'top down' forms of participation, and to be seen to be taking initiatives which they regarded as more acceptable and appropriate for organisational needs (Marchington, 1989b).

The latest wave of interest commenced in the early 1980s, and is very different from most of those which have gone before it. The most recent manifestation of EI is individualist (as opposed to collective and conducted via representatives), it is championed by managements often without any great pressure from employees or trade unions (as opposed to previous incarnations where employee or union pressure was highly influential), and it is directed at securing greater employee commitment to and identification with the organization and its success. The terminology of EI is very apt in the sense that it relates to managers giving employees more information, or in some cases more influence. It contrasts well with the meaning of industrial democracy, which alters the structure of authority by giving employees a *right* to share in decision making with management. The forms which EI has taken, as we shall see below in rather more detail, include a greater willingness to communicate regularly with staff, as well as a much greater recognition of the contribution which employees can make to the successful operation of the enterprise. Each of the surveys indicate that forms of EI such as team briefing, quality circles, employee reports, suggestion schemes, and profit sharing and share ownership have all grown since the late 1970s, and that joint consultation has remained at broadly the same level (see, for example, Batstone, 1984; Millward and Stevens, 1986; Smith, 1986; Edwards, 1987; Confederation of British Industry (CBI), 1989; Advisory, Conciliation and Arbitration Service (ACAS), 1991). With the exception of share ownership, all the other mechanisms have grown without specific legislative support, although there have been repeated exhortations from government ministers to develop EI along voluntary lines. It is unlikely that the provisions in the 1982 Employment Act requiring certain companies to report on action taken to introduce, maintain or develop employee involvement has had a significant impact upon its growth throughout Britain.

Definitions and Characteristics

As would be expected from the large number of publications on the subject, a number of attempts have been made to define precisely what is meant by the terms 'workers' participation', 'employee involvement' and 'industrial democracy'. They vary considerably in detail, length, and central concept, but broadly these can be subdivided into three categories. The first series of definitions refers to employees taking part or having a say or share in decision making, with no attempt to quantify their impact on this process. For example, Clarke et al. (1972. p. 6) regard participation as 'any process whereby workers . . . have a share in the reaching of managerial decisions in the enterprise'. Fox (1985, p. 111) is more explicit and argues that participation in decision making 'through collective bargaining has become by far the most widespread and important form in Western Society'. Similar sorts of definition can be found in Walker (1975) and Schuller (1985).

The second set of definitions are more specific and refer to participation as concerned with the extent to which employees may influence managerial actions. For example, Wall and Lischeron (1977, p. 37) define participation as 'influence in decision making exerted through a process of interaction between workers and managers and based upon information sharing'. In a similar vein, Heller (1983, p. xxxvi) notes that organizational democracy 'is meant to describe a considerable variety of interpersonal and/or structural arrangements which link organisational decision making to the interests and influence of employees at various levels'. Both of these, and other attempts at definition (see, for example, French et al., 1960; Hebden and Shaw, 1977) seem to coincide with Pateman's notion of 'partial participation', which is regarded as influence without having equal power to decide (1970, p. 70). [Note that this is distinct from Pateman's other categories of 'pseudo-participation' – which includes 'techniques used to persuade employees to accept decisions which have already been taken by management' – and 'full participation' which is where all members have equal power to decide.]

The third set of definitions link together participation and control over decision making. Thus, for Guest and Fatchett (1974, pp. 10–11), participation is 'any process through which a person or group of persons determines (that is, intentionally effects) what another person or group of persons will do', and they make use of a continuum developed by Tannenbaum to illustrate this. At least with these sorts of definition, it is easier to evaluate the degree of impact which is made by employees on management decisions, although there remain substantial methodological and theoretical problems with the definition of control (see Lukes, 1974, for example). The notion of control is also central to Ramsay's (1977, 1983) conception of the subject but, for him, practical examples of participation have only served to strengthen rather than weaken *management* control.

Perhaps the problem of definitional complexity is best typified by Brannen (1983, p. 13) who suggests that the notion of participation implies that 'individuals or groups may influence, control, be involved in, exercise power within, or be able to intervene in decision making within organizations.' Added to this is the fact that different terms are used interchangeably by many authors. For example, Poole's first book on the subject (1975) was entitled *Workers' Participation in Industry* whereas his update (1986), with much the same content, is *Towards a New Industrial Democracy; Workers' Participation in Industry*. Similarly, Schuller's reader (1985) is titled *Democracy at Work*, but in the first chapter of this book he admits that he will use the terms participation and industrial democracy almost interchangeably (p. 4). This is not a problem which is easily overcome, but a simple distinction between the terms will be helpful for the remainder of this report. For our purposes, therefore, the term *participation* will be used as an umbrella to define the subject as a whole. *Industrial democracy* will be used to describe those practices whose principal aim is to increase the rights of employees (or their representative organizations) to participate in decision making: in one sense collective bargaining falls in this category. *Employee involvement*, conversely, will be used to describe those practices which are initiated principally by management, and are designed to increase employee information about commitment to the organization [see also the IPA/IPM Code, 1990, p. 11]. EI therefore does not involve and *de jure* sharing of authority or power with employees, though some forms of EI *may* give employees channels through which their influence is enhanced.

An alternative way to help understand the subject is to deconstruct the different components of EI, so that any technique can be located within a four-dimensional matrix comprising *degree of involvement*, the *form* which involvement takes, the *level in the organizational hierarchy* at which individuals are involved, and the *range of subject matter* dealt with. A similar exercise to this has been undertaken by various writers on participation over the last twenty years (Schuchman, 1957; Blumberg, 1968; Guest and Fatchett, 1974; Poole, 1975; Wall and Lischeron, 1977; Loveridge, 1980; Marchington, 1980; Schuller, 1985).

Taking the first of these, the degree of involvement, different techniques can be distinguished on the extent to which employees (or their representatives) influence the final decision. This can range from employees simply being informed by management, through two-way communication, or discourse, consultation, codetermination, to some form of employee or joint control. Perhaps this is best illustrated by the idea of an 'escalator' of involvement, with information on the bottom step and control on the top. The notion of an escalator also fits well with the prescriptive suggestion that EI 'should' evolve organically, and that it is problematic to expect effective codetermination if employees have not previously been informed about issues. In diagrammatic form, the escalator looks like this:

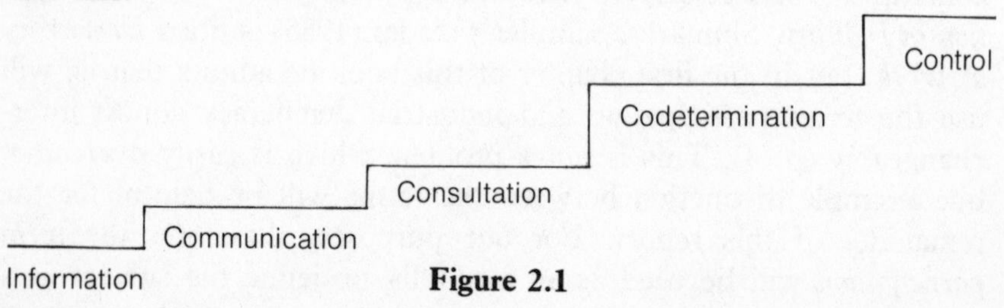

Figure 2.1

As we shall see below, virtually all the techniques of EI which are dealt with in this study tend to be towards the bottom end of the escalator, with few schemes coming within the edges of the co-determination step. For example, house journals and share ownership/profit sharing schemes are on the first step; team briefing covers the first and sometimes the second; suggestion schemes, quality circles and most forms of joint consultation are on the middle rung; some Works Councils and (in theory at least) employee share ownership plans may be on step four, as would be collective bargaining and employee directors, although it is doubtful whether any of these would satisfy Pateman's idealist notion of full participation; the final step is reserved for employee owned organizations, such as John Lewis partnership, or Scott Bader, and worker cooperatives.

Secondly, there is a distinction between various forms of EI, with the most common differentiation being direct, indirect, and financial. *Direct* EI is concerned with face-to-face (or written) contact between managers and their subordinates. It primarily involves the passage of information from managers to their staff, communication between the two parties, or some kind of upward flow of responses or ideas. The type of techniques which can be included within this category are team briefing, house journals, suggestion schemes, quality circles, and total quality management. The basic point about this form of involvement, however, is that employees are involved on a direct individual level, rather than through their representatives. Secondly, there is *indirect* EI, which covers the situation in which employees are involved in the process of management decision making via their representatives, who are typically elected by and from employee groups. Schemes would vary from joint consultation, which may operate at any level within the organization and indeed may link together managers and employee representatives from different establishments, through to company councils, collective bargaining, and employees on the board. Thirdly, there is *financial* EI, which relates to the economic participation of employees in the success (or failure) of their organization, and to link some proportion of their financial rewards to company, divisional, or departmental performance. Typically, this would include such schemes as profit sharing, share ownership, and a range of performance-related incentive payment systems. The degree of employee participation involved in such schemes varies quite widely. Thus employees (and/or their representatives) may be involved in setting performance targets, or they may be determined unilaterally by management.

Similarly with the scale of payments and their variation. Share ownership confers voting and attendance rights at Annual General Meetings, though typically employee shares are a small proportion of the total. More specific definitions of particular techniques/ schemes is provided in the glossary at the end of this chapter.

Thirdly, there is the level at which EI takes place, and this can be differentiated between task, section, departmental, establishment, division/region, corporate and (for situations where employers' associations play a major role in determining single-company arrangements) national as well. Clearly much depends upon the structure of the organization for this component but, apart from small single-site firms, this will usually involve four or more levels. Again, categorization depends to some extent upon the processes of involvement in particular workplaces, but broadly informal EI will be at task level, quality circles and team briefing will be predominantly at the section or departmental level – although there are some variations here. JCCs can operate at any level from department to corporate, and in some cases at as many as four different levels in the same organization. House journals tend to be produced at corporate or divisional level, although again there are sometimes newsletters which are written locally. Techniques for financial involvement, such as profit sharing and share ownership are almost always based at corporate level.

The final component of EI is the range of subject matter dealt with by the scheme. It is clearly important to be able to assess the types of issues covered by the scheme in addition to the degree of influence exerted. At one extreme, this refers to broad strategic decisions which affect the organization as a whole, such as financial or other commercial matters, whereas at the other the range may be more restricted, say to issues relating to items which are quite marginal to the running of the business – for example, the state of the car park or the canteen. In between these two extremes are issues of operational importance, such as those concerned with production or service decisions, slightly beyond the employee's own job description but nonetheless connected with it.

It is rather more difficult to place the various organizational arrangements for EI into any one of these three categories (strategic, operational, and task-related) given that so much depends upon the processes of involvement which accompany each scheme and the attitudes of the parties to these techniques. Taking joint consultation as an example, some JCCs are well-known for their discussion of strategic issues – albeit in very general terms – whereas others are criticized for their focus on trivial issues (Marchington, 1989, p. 384). Equally, for each EI technique, there is likely to be a mix of subject matter dealt with in any one interaction, say at a monthly JCC or a team brief, or in a quality circle. Even a house journal is likely to include items which relate to all three areas in the same issue.

Competing Paradigms of Participation

Because the subject of participation has attracted interest from a wide variety of disciplines, it is hardly surprising that its meaning is interpreted rather differently by scholars as well as practitioners. Four separate roots can be identified for the subject, and these appear to encapsulate the principal areas of interest in the subject. The four are satisfaction/Quality of Working Life (QWL), commitment/HRM, co-operation/industrial relations, and control/labour process, and they can be differentiated as follows:

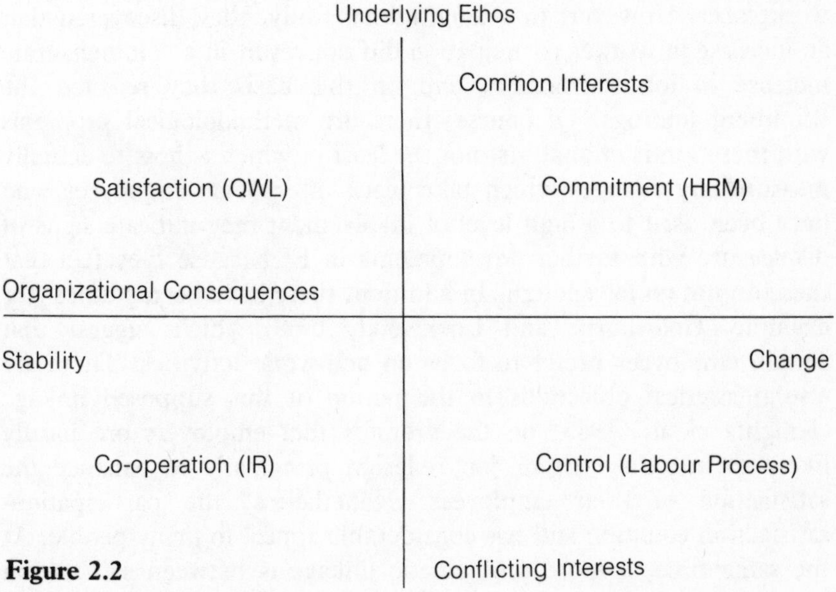

Underlying Ethos

Common Interests

Satisfaction (QWL)

Commitment (HRM)

Organizational Consequences

Stability

Change

Co-operation (IR)

Control (Labour Process)

Conflicting Interests

Figure 2.2

The first of these – satisfaction and Quality of Working Life experiments – has a long pedigree, particularly in the fields of industrial and organizational psychology, and it has become increasingly significant in the USA. This paradigm is based around the idea that involvement and satisfaction are related to each other, and that higher degrees of EI will lead to higher levels of employee satisfaction with various aspects of working life. As Blumberg (1968, p. 123) noted 'there is hardly a study in the entire literature which fails to demonstrate that satisfaction at work is enhanced or that other generally acknowledged beneficial consequences accrue from a genuine increase in workers' decision making power'. This review of the field studies included much of the research conducted by members of the human relations school, and it also incorporated work by management consultants. The idea in itself is intuitively attractive, and on one level it seems commonsensical to argue that employee satisfaction will be enhanced by greater EI. Indeed, the involvement = satisfaction link is one which is regularly made by managers.

However, there have been major criticisms of this viewpoint. Research by Wall and Lischeron (1977, pp. 146–7) found some support for the notion that there was a positive correlation between involvement and satisfaction in a variety of studies which they conducted with different groups of employees in quite disparate workplaces. However, in a longitudinal study, they discovered that an increase in worker participation did not result in a commensurate increase in job satisfaction, and on this basis they rejected the Blumberg findings. Of course, there are methodological problems with these kinds of analysis, not the least of which is how to actually measure any changes which take place. Moreover, employees who have been used to a high level of involvement may indicate signs of displeasure with further developments in EI because they feel that these do not go far enough. In addition, there have been studies (for example, Goldthorpe and Lockwood, 1968) which suggest that certain employees prefer to focus on non-work activities. There are also theoretical objections to the notion of this supposed linkage (Knights et al., 1985) on the grounds that employers are hardly likely to introduce EI or job redesign principally to enhance the satisfaction of their employees. Nonetheless, the participation-satisfaction equation still has considerable appeal to many people. At the same time, a more problematic linkage is between satisfaction and higher levels of job performance.

The second paradigm is where involvement is reckoned to lead to an increase in employee commitment to the organization, and this is central to the HRM (human resource management) literature. It is further assumed that commitment leads to more positive behaviour at work, including higher levels of performance. The HRM paradigm has its roots in some of the eulogies delivered by American consultants/academics such as Peters and Waterman (1982), who argue that managers are themselves the major barrier to high levels of commitment on the part of staff. People come to work motivated and interested but they are soon alienated by the web of rules and constraints which govern their working lives. If only management could find ways to release and tap employees' creativity, via EI, then their commitment to organizational goals would follow. This belief is also contained within the IPA/IPM Code of Practice (1990, p. 11), where EI is defined as 'a range of processes designed to engage the support, understanding, optimum contribution of all employees in an organization and their commitment to it'. It works upon the assumption that common interests are achievable in organizations, although most managements fail to capture the interest of their staff, partly because communications are ineffective but also because contributions are not welcomed. Accordingly, wide-ranging change programmes are introduced with the objective of creating and sustaining a common culture throughout the organization, one which in all parties become committed to corporate goals.

Once again, though, despite the widespread appeal of these ideas to many practitioners and academics, there are some doubts about whether there is any association between involvement and commitment. HRM operates according to values which are essentially unitarist and individualistic in focus, and EI is one major component of HRM (Guest, 1989, p. 43). Guest also suggests that proponents of HRM assume that 'EI will lead to greater organizational commitment which in turn will lead to enhanced motivation and performance' (1990, p. 10). However, on the basis of research from both the UK and the USA, he is dubious about the link between involvement and commitment, partly again because of the difficulties in measuring what is meant by commitment, and in assessing whether it is commitment to one's job, work or organization. Other studies (for example, Marchington, 1982, p. 66) also suggest that commitment is rarely given at anything more than a calculative level. Alternatively, Martin and Nichols (1987, p. 15) believe that commitment is sustained by three pillars – a sense of belonging to the employing organization, a sense of excitement about the job, and confidence in the leadership of management – of which the first two relate clearly to EI. They provide support for their model with case studies from a range of organizations, but many of these were written following only the briefest of contacts with the organizations concerned.

The third paradigm links involvement with collaboration/co-operation, and this has its roots in the field of industrial relations. It can operate at either a collective or an individual level, and here EI is seen as a device which will help to prevent or minimize conflict. Collective bargaining is the mechanism which is adopted by many trade unions and employers to regulate major elements of the employment relationship, and as such is a form of involvement which may produce greater order and stability at work. Similarly, some JCC machinery appears to have operated as a safety valve, as shop stewards articulate their discontent in meetings rather than via a withdrawal of labour (Marchington, 1989a). At an individual level, it is argued that involvement can reduce the likelihood of employees choosing to deploy negative sanctions against employers – such as sabotage, pilfering, or non-cooperation – and instead display co-operative behaviour at work. Involvement may also lead to greater co-operation with the process of change. Indeed, central to this whole paradigm is the notion of trust, and the fact that each party at work sees greater advantage in working with the others rather than working against them.

However, because collective bargaining is predicated on the assumption that there are underlying conflicts of interest between employers and employed in any organization, there are times when it is not possible to reach an agreement. Indeed, it is central to the ethos of bargaining that either party retains the right to employ sanctions against the other, and trade unions maintain their power only so long as they remain independent of employers. Accordingly it becomes a matter for empirical investigation in particular workplaces whether or not involvement through bargaining or extended consultation actually does lead to greater co-operation at work. Equally, some would argue that the opportunity to utilize negative sanctions sets bargaining apart from other methods of EI in which employees do not hold the latent power of potential veto over management decisions.

Finally, within the fourth paradigm, 'real' involvement is restricted to situations where there is some actual transfer of control from management to employees, and conventional decision making structures are challenged and redrawn. Much labour process analysis dismisses EI as an ideological sham, none more forcefully than Braverman (1974, p. 35) who regards employers' 'faddish' policies of participation as 'a glamorous liberality in allowing the worker to move from one fractional job to another, and have the illusion of making decisions by choosing among fixed and limited alternatives designed by a management which deliberately leaves insignificant matters open to choice'. Others view management in a less conspiratorial light, but the result is much the same; participation is 'pseudo', 'a ruse', 'a distraction', 'phantom'. Given that most – if not all – methods for involving employees fail to achieve a change to the status quo, to be effective, it is argued, involvement needs to provide employees with access to and control over strategic decisions.

There are also problems with this paradigm given its underlying assumptions about both the objectives of employers and the interests of employees. For the former, control over the labour process represents either *the* or at least *a* major objective for employers, and this argument is difficult to sustain for a whole variety of reasons. Similarly, the assumption that labour is actively and continuously engaged in a struggle with capital is highly unlikely, especially in the sectors where union organization is not well developed or where managers tend to operate with a degree of 'innocence' in formulating their employee relations practices. But, the equation of involvement = control is rather easier to measure than any of the others.

Glossary of Terms Used in the Book

- *attitude survey*: a questionnaire survey of employees on a one-off or regular basis, which is designed to discover their views about a variety of factors connected with work. It is generally distributed to a sample of employees.
- *collective bargaining*: negotiations leading to joint regulation of pay, hours, working conditions and other terms of employment between employer and employee groups. As well as being episodic, collective bargaining can also operate on a virtually continuous basis at workplace level, dealing with contingencies, the interpretation and application of

agreements, changes in working practices or technology, the effort-reward and authority relationship.

- *customer care programme*: an initiative designed to involve employees in improving relations at the interface between staff and the customer, and to encourage staff to treat customers in a positive way.
- *employee report*: a statement produced at least annually, in written form, especially for all employees, which provides information relating to a financial performance of the undertaking in an accounting period.
- *employee share ownership*: the involvement of employees in the financial success of the organization, by using part of the profits generated or earnings of employees to acquire shares for the employee in the company concerned, or discounted shares on privatization or public quotation.
- *horizontal job redesign*: the number and variety of operations which an individual performs at the same skill level in the organization, often referred to as job rotation.
- *house journal/newspaper*: a publication produced on a regular and continuing basis by the company for distribution free to staff and other interested parties, which contains information about the organization and its employees.
- *joint consultation*: a mechanism for managers and employee representatives to meet on a regular basis, in order to exchange views, to utilize members' knowledge and expertise, and to deal with matters of common interest which are not the subject of collective bargaining.
- *profit sharing*: where a cash bonus or payment is made to employees based upon the share price, profits or dividend announcement at the end of the financial year.
- *quality circle*: a small group of employees who meet voluntarily on a regular basis to identify, analyse and solve quality or work-related problems relevant to the organization.
- *suggestion scheme*: a formal procedure which enables employees to put forward ideas to management for improvements at work, and which provides for a system to reward acceptable suggestions which save money.
- *team briefing*: a regular, structured system to enable management to cascade throughout the organization news and developments which are thought to be relevant to particular groups of employees.
- *teamworking*: a form of work organization in which tasks are assigned to the group as a whole rather than to specific individuals or roles. In addition, the group assumes responsibility for making decisions relating to its work within defined boundaries.
- *total quality management*: a systematic process of management in which all employees are expected to see others, both internal and external to the organization, as customers for their services.
- *unit-wide bonus scheme*: a system whereby a proportion of an individual's

payment is related to the financial performance of the establishment, via a predetermined formula.

- *vertical role integration*: the degree to which the job holder controls the planning and execution of his/her job, or completes tasks at a higher skill level than previously undertaken.

3 Written and Audio-Visual Communications

Introduction

The last decade has seen an upsurge in the amount of material – especially of a written and audio-visual nature – which organizations are trying to communicate to their employees. Some of these have been operating for years, whereas others reflect the renewed interest in regarding employees as one of the most important resources an organization has in its quest for competitive advantage. Either way, as Townley (1989, p. 329) notes, it is now apparent that management 'is beginning to take the area of employee communications more seriously, with a growing awareness of the role a formal programme may play within the organization'. To some extent, this is in stark contrast with the more traditional view that employees are not to be trusted with information (especially of a financial nature) about their organizations for fear they would disclose it to any interested outside party.

There has been a number of stimuli for this increase in written and audio-visual communications from management to staff, and these tend to mirror the general reasons for the growth of employee involvement discussed in the previous chapter. Broadly, though, they take two different forms:

1 *attempts to reinforce the unitary conception of the organization*. Over the last few years, an increasing emphasis has been placed on the need to 'educate' employees about the financial and commercial position of their organization, and gain their commitment to corporate or business-unit goals. This is pursued not as an end in itself, but as a mechanism for helping the organization to attain/maintain competitiveness.
2 *responses to legislation in employee relations*. Since the 1970s, there has been a number of statutes which have placed extra responsibility on employers

to communicate with their staff, but for the purposes of this chapter, we will focus on Section 1 of the 1982 Employment Act – this will be dealt with in the next section.

Below, four different instruments for communicating written or audio-visual information to employees will be examined, namely statements in annual reports, employee reports, house journals/ newspapers, and videos. Although a number of these (videos in particular) are usually complemented by oral presentations, all four rely on the transmission of a standardized message to all employees. Consequently, no allowance can be made for individual variations in ability, interest or receptiveness, and as such each technique runs the risk of being seen as inappropriate for specific employee needs. On the other hand, it does mean that a single message is at least conveyed *from* management, if not necesarily *to* employees. Having examined these four instruments, we will then turn to a case study of an organization which uses all of these, before concluding with some general points about the impact of written and audio-visual material.

Statements in Annual Reports

There has never been anything to prevent employing organizations including statements within annual reports which relate specifically to employees and their particular interests, but it has been comparatively rare for this to happen. Nevertheless, some organizations have regularly made reference to employees in these documents for a number of years, although unfortunately this has often been little more than a ritual vote of thanks for services rendered during the previous period, using well-worn and oft-repeated terminology. A unitary conception of the enterprise is conveyed, with phrases such as 'working hard for the company, being loyal and dedicated to it, overcoming challenges faced by it, as part of the company' (Gowler and Legge, 1986, pp. 10–11). But, at least these organizations were proactive in being prepared to treat their employees as worthy of a mention in annual statements, whereas the vast majority appeared to regard their staff as almost invisible.

Legislation in the early 1980s, however, changed this, albeit at a level of superficiality. Section 1 of the 1982 Employment Act placed a requirement on organizations covered by the Companies Act which employed 250 or more people to include a statement in their annual report indicating what action, if any, had been taken over the previous year to 'introduce, maintain or develop employee involvement'. Four areas are specified in the Act: providing information systematically to employees on matters of concern to them, consulting with employees or their representatives so that their views can be taken into account on decisions likely to affect them, encouraging employee involvement financially in the performance of the organization, and achieving a common awareness among employees of the financial and economic performance of the organization. There is some degree of overlap between these given that the final area is goal-related whereas the others are more concerned with specific schemes for employee involvement; accordingly, the first three categories appear to be directed towards the achievement of the fourth.

Helpful though this legal adjustment might be, it is less than ideal for a number of reasons. First, large public sector and privately-owned organizations, and foreign–owned multinationals are excluded from this requirement, as are small firms which employ less than 250 people. Second, organizations are only obliged to report on what actions they have actually taken to introduce, maintain or develop EI, so if nothing has been done then a nil return can be filed. This is highly unlikely because of the third reason, namely that the hurdle to be jumped by the reporting obligation is extremely low, and it would seem virtually impossible for any organization not to have something to report about some aspect of EI. Fourthly, there is no requirement on the organization to provide a copy of its statement to employees or their representatives. Finally, there is no expectation that the insertion of a section on EI will have any impact on practice within these organizations. In sum, therefore, the legal pressure via Section 1 is virtually negligible.

Even before the legislation became operative, there were some doubts about its effectiveness. Wilding and Marchington, for example, conducted a survey of the top 200 companies in Britain, asking them for views about the legislation, their preparations for it, and their assessment of its impact. Most respondents felt that improvements in EI would come about irrespective of the legal changes, and that reporting via the annual report might even slow the process of change because 'it would encourage pious expressions of intent which will look good on the surface whereas the true reality will be hidden'. (1983, p. 33). Subsequent surveys by the Institute of Personnel Management (1988) have served to confirm this picture, illustrating a situation in which many statements do not change from one year to the next. Although the IPM did find some evidence that there were improvements in the number of headings under which companies reported that action was being taken, and it was common for the larger organizations to include a page or more in their annual statements about EI, there was an increasing trend towards the use of standard paragraphs. In addition, some organizations merely provided details of their EI policies rather than *practices* as required by the Act (1988, p. 5). A similar story is told by Mitchell et al. (1986) from their more detailed study of six Scottish organizations.

Perhaps this is to be expected however. It could be argued that the annual report may not be the most appropriate or effective vehicle for reporting on EI, given that so few employees will have sight of it – unless they happen to be shareholders. Moreover, just because a company reports that it is taking action to develop EI, this is no guarantee that anything is actually happening within the organization or that involvement practices are widespread across different sites. Equally, a bland report about some form of EI – for example team briefing or joint consultation – tells us little about the way in which it is operating in practice, and ignores the fact that the success of each technique is heavily dependent upon the commitment of the parties to it. Furthermore, directors are not renowned for their contact with or understanding of employee interests, as both Winkler (1974) and Fidler (1981) demonstrated a number of years ago, and their world is defined in such a way as to exclude 'ordinary workers'. Gowler and Legge's analysis of annual reports is also pertinent here, in that employees were often portrayed as costs or liabilities, depersonalized by reference to numbers or manpower (1986, p. 13).

On the other hand, it is difficult to square this relative lack of interest in employees in annual reports with more recent conceptions of human resource management – in which people are regarded as the organization's most important resource, the key to competitive advantage, and an untapped source of good ideas and suggestions. If people really are so important, perhaps this should be reflected in official documents irrespective of whether or not this is required by law; otherwise, it is tempting to regard comments that employees are the key resource as nothing more than shallow and misleading rhetoric. It also reminds us that people-issues are still inevitably subordinated to the logic of accountancy (Armstrong, 1989). But there are other reasons for making more positive and creative statements about EI in annual reports. Not only is it important for managements to be practising EI but it is also crucial that they are seen to do so. A proactive and better developed stance on EI might act as a valuable means of publicity for new recruits, especially graduates for whom the annual report is likely to be their first source of information about the organisation. Similarly, the knowledge that an employer is determined to build effective EI might be a useful source of information for customers, as we will see in relation to quality initiatives (such as BS 5750) in later chapters. Equally, a clear statement about EI in the annual report serves as a further articulation of senior management's commitment to the centrality of human resource issues within strategic decision making. In short, by enhancing the reputation of the employer so that recruitment is improved and there is a clear and consistent goal for managers to aim for, better prepared statements can add value to the organization. Of course, on their own and without any real EI, glowing statements in annual reports are likely to be counterproductive, so action is required to make it work.

Employee Reports

As we saw above, some people have doubts about the value of incorporating a statement on EI into the annual report to shareholders, largely because this is not seen as the most appropriate document in which to place a note of such action. An alternative, or a supplement in the case of companies covered by the Employment Act of 1982, is to produce a simplified yearly report specifically for employees, which would typically be sent to each individual employee, either at work or at home. This is known as an Employee Report, defined by Hussey and Marsh (1983, p. 70) as 'a statement produced at least annually, in written form, especially for all employees, which provides information relating to a financial period of the undertaking'.

The idea of Employee Reports became more fashionable during the latter part of the 1970s, with interest from both the personnel and the accounting bodies, stimulated to a large extent by discussions about the disclosure of information to trade unions. For example, The Accounting Standards Committee published a document entitled 'The Corporate Report' in 1975, which recommended that it was 'essential, if employees were to become involved and kept informed, that some part of the company's plans for the immediate future should be disseminated (to employees)' [quoted in Hussey and Marsh, 1983, p. 54]. Although the pressure to disclose information to trade unions dissipated after 1979, other reasons have come to the fore since then – especially relating to the search for employee identification and commitment – which have managed to keep employee reporting on the agenda.

All the surveys undertaken up until the early 1980s indicated that a sizeable number of firms issued Employee Reports, this being particularly marked in larger organizations. Three surveys from the late 1980s provide some evidence about the extensiveness of this method of reporting. The 1989 Vista Survey (p. 2) found that 35 per cent of companies which responded to their questionnaire used Employee Reports, a figure roughly substantiated by that undertaken by the CBI (p. 28) the same year. The results from the CBI study are particularly interesting given that their sample was largely made up of companies employing less than 400 people. An ACAS Survey in 1990 (p. 17) found that a slightly higher proportion (50 per cent) of companies either issued special Employee Reports, distributed copies of the Annual Report, or produced a supplement to their traditional forms of written communications. Again, size of organization is a key determinant of the propensity to produce written reports of company performance. Given the reported trend towards more communications between management and their staff during the 1980s, it would be expected that reporting is now a more common feature in UK companies, but the Vista Survey found through a series of repeat studies that there had actually been a *reduction* in the number of organizations issuing Employee Reports during the second half of the decade.

Why should organizations want to publish an Employee Report in the first place, given the fact that it may be costly and time-consuming, that employees may have little interest in its contents, and that companies may be concerned about disclosing confidential information to potential rivals? Several reasons have been put forward [see Hussey and Marsh, 1983, pp. 61–2 for a number of lists]. First, it may be seen as a device for helping employees to understand better the commercial position and future prospects of the organization, and by so doing persuade them of the 'logic' of management's plans and policies so that they will act 'responsibly'; in other words, an *educative* approach. Second, it may be used as a mechanism for increasing employee involvement within the company, so that employees are better qualified (through more information) to contribute to the achievement or corporate of sub-unit goals in a spirit of co-operation, a sort of *participative* approach. And thirdly, it can be viewed as a potential stimulus for higher productivity/motivation, as a way in which to improve working practices as an aid to *efficiency*.

Another way to look at the same question is to focus on what Hilton (1978, pp. 23–8) has termed the three specific *approaches* to the preparation of Employee Reports, and that managements need to decide which of these to follow. These are: the *shareholder approach* which is based on the belief that management is under an obligation to inform employees to the same extent as shareholders; the *demand approach* which rests on the principle that information should be given to employees if they desire it, provided this does not harm confidentiality, on the grounds that this will lead to more harmonious employee relations; finally, there is the *business planning* approach, in which the main purpose of the employee report is to provide a better understanding of the business because this is likely to stimulate adaptations in employee behaviour, which in turn will improve overall performance. The latter approach is the one which fits best with the theme of this book – strategic integration and employee commitment – in that it encourages senior managers to evaluate the relevance of specific forms of EI against other business criteria. At the same time, it needs to be recalled that an organization that is too hard-nosed, patronizing or selective in its approach to reporting may well end up with more problems. Like all the techniques dealt with in this chapter, it also rests upon the assumption that sharing information is more beneficial to organizational performance than are unnecessary restrictions on its dissemination. There are four stages in the business planning approach:

1 define the business objectives whose achievement may depend on employee behaviour.
2 define specific reasons why employees should want to co-operate in the achievement of these objectives.
3 define the factual information which must be presented to employees to make this happen.
4 develop a coherent structure for the Employee Report.

Given that this is a contingent approach to the design of Employee Reports, it is not appropriate to specify any model document, although Hilton does reproduce the contents and some of the material from an award-winning report at Staffordshire Potteries (1978, pp. 46–51). The report was commended for a number of features, not least its cover which was appealing to readers, and it was felt that the whole publication conveyed 'a sense of humour' throughout. Although the cover story and picture are often seen as crucial, arguably the contents are rather more important. Clearly, this will include presentation of the financial data, usually in graphical form such as a pie or bar chart. A number of organizations have chosen to present the figures in terms of their own products, for example as a beer pot or milk float. Some have become almost too keen for contemporary imagery, as in the case of McCorquadale's attempt to convey added value data via the form of a Rubik's cube in 1981, so that it becomes difficult to disentangle the precise information. Multi-divisional businesses (such as ICI) tend to present their reports in disaggregated form, with a page or two about each division, its products, its employees and its prospects. This can be done in a fairly factual way (as Ciba Geigy typically did during the 1980s) or it can print pictures of new technology/key people other than senior managers (as Courtaulds did in 1987). Some organizations choose to major on a particular issue in certain years, for example the role which the leading supermarkets have been taking in selling green products in the late 1980s.

The principal point to stress, however, is that the Employee Report should be consistent with the company's philosophy towards employment relations, and that it needs to be meaningful and believable to staff. No amount of glossy packaging can hide an inferior product. As Hussey and Marsh (1983, p. 113) suggest, 'an over-lavish publication may be regarded by the employee as a substitute for a valid policy on communications rather than an expression of such a policy. In some cases, employees may regard the exercise as little more than hypocritical.' To have any chance of reaching its readership, the report should contain information which is stated in terms and on a scale with which the employee is familiar, it should be organized around the financial interests of the employee in the business, and the wording/contents should appear sincere and honest to employees.

House Journals/Newspapers

By their very nature, Employee Reports tend to be produced by organizations once – or at most twice – each year, given that they are used to convey financial information to employees. House journals or company newspapers are published rather more frequently, but typically these would appear every one, two or three months depending upon the organization and its policies in this area. A house journal or company newspaper can be defined as a 'publication produced by an organization at regular predetermined intervals for distribution to staff or other interested parties'. This definition leads to a whole series of questions about the production of journals, which are again contingent upon the organization's circumstances and the preferences of its key decision-makers. The following ten questions are particularly pertinent, and we will return to a number of them later in the section:

- what are the objectives of the newspaper?
- how much money should be spent on producing the paper?
- who should be the editor(s) of the paper?
- what should be the mix of items included in the paper?
- how often should the paper be published?
- who should be the recipients of the paper?
- how should the paper be distributed?
- should the paper be focused on one site or the organization as a whole?
- how can opinions for and about the paper best be tapped?
- how can the impact of the paper be monitored?

House journals have a long history in some companies and, according to the Institute of Personnel Management, the longest-running journal still in production is that of the Norwich Union (IPM, 1989). The number of organizations publishing journals grew significantly during the late 1940s and early 1950s, in line with other developments in EI following the end of the war, and many of these continue to appear at the present time, albeit with several changes in regularity, mix of contents and style since then. As with some of the other EI techniques to be discussed in this book, it is difficult to be precise about the number of organizations which do publish journals since some of the survey data is now a little out-dated. Townley (1989, p. 331) reproduces the results from a number of studies undertaken in the 1970s and early 1980s, and the general observation from these is that the journals/newspapers have been on the increase over that period, a point substantiated by the recent IPM Factsheet. My own research on employee participation would also confirm this, especially amongst the larger employers who often have more than one journal depending upon the structure of the organization; for example, some employees of Ciba Geigy can receive up to three different types of journal produced for differing target audiences. It is highly unlikely that any large organization would not produce some type of journal at least twice per annum, and some are extending the number of journals with special supplements/separate issues. Indeed, the three most recent surveys would indicate that about half of all companies do produce a newspaper/journal for employees. The CBI (1989, p. 28) found that over one-third of small companies (employing less than 400 people) produced a paper, whilst nearly 90 per cent of larger organisations (2,000+) did so. The ACAS figures were broadly similar (1991, p. 17). Vista results suggest a slight increase during the latter part of the 1980s (p. 2). Foreign-owned companies are much more likely to publish papers than British employers.

Employers need to be clear about their reasons for publishing a journal, however, and there are usually several sorts of objectives which may be sought. Typically, these fall into three categories, the first of which are those designed to ensure that *information* about the organization, its product markets, long-term plans, and new developments is disseminated to employees (or at least confirmed in the paper) in sufficient detail for them to understand what is happening. One of the most common complaints by staff is that they find out about key developments via the local or national news media before they hear it from their own management, and a good newspaper can provide fuller stories about recent events or about the background to forthcoming announcements. A second objective is to provide a *forum* through which staff may be able to indicate their views about a wide range of matters relevant to the organization, either through letters to the editor or through specific columns for employee opinions, or even to create a mechanism for sales and purchases of various items. Clearly, it is important for the paper to be seen as a publication which is able and willing to represent different viewpoints if it is not to be discredited as a crude tool for increasing management control. It is not always easy to maintain this balance, especially in large, dispersed organizations. Finally, and to a large extent implicit in the previous two categories, papers should encourage employees to *identify* with the organization, to increase commitment to management objectives and actions, and to foster good relations at work. This is done largely by providing up-to-date accurate information that is presented in a way which is meaningful to employees. To be successful, this strategy for increasing commitment and integration needs to be managed with care and sensitivity, and has to correlate with corporate philosophy and management actions in the workplace.

Although most company newspapers are (theoretically) directed towards employees, an important target is also potential customers or future recruits which employers might wish to impress. This is even more apparent when the papers are produced by a Public Relations department or consultancy. In addition, some newspapers are more specifically aimed at other topics or audiences. For example, a number of organizations have started to produce special supplements about quality (for example, Kodak's *Quality Counts*) which are designed to heighten awareness about the importance of quality issues in the company and inform staff about new developments in the area. Others, such as Clayton Aniline (part of Ciba Geigy), have introduced a newspaper specifically for the local community which aims to improve relations with residents of the area in the vicinity of its chemical works. *Community Matters* was launched in 1987, and distributed to nearly 7,000 homes in the area as part of a joint community and company campaign to explain what the company was doing to improve safety and environmental protection, as well as support local charities and people. The newspaper was one part of a coherent strategy to generate closer links between the company and its neighbours, other parts of which included open days and regular meetings with community leaders.

As with all other mechanisms for developing EI, it is important to assess the impact of house journals on readers, and whether or not they actually influence behaviour at work. The few available studies which have been done (for example, Homer, 1987; Marchington and Parker, 1990) indicate that company newspapers have a minor positive impact on attitudes to work, and that most employees/other readers enjoy 'flicking through' the journal to find out what is happening in the organization. Employees are generally interested most in information relating to sports or social activities, and sometimes the obituaries column is the first page to be looked at. Rarely is the newspaper the first source of information about a new development and, given the rigidity associated with production due to copy deadlines as well as the more immediate value of other mechanisms (such as briefing) for passing on information, it is not appropriate that it should be. An alternative way to evaluate the importance of house journals is to ask readers whether or not they want to continue receiving the publication, and both the above surveys indicate that readers would not want their employers to abandon this form of EI (Homer, 1987, pp. 103–5). There are always bound to be problems ensuring that the information conveyed is relevant to readers and of interest to them, especially in a large, multi-site, geographically dispersed organization. Inevitable conflicts arise about the amount of news space given to other divisions or establishments, or to other people – in particular senior managers as opposed to shop-floor or office staff. But, provided that the objectives for the paper have been thought through, this problem is likely to be minimized, and indeed one solution might be to have several publications within the organization, each of which serves a different need.

A more serious problem, however, is the lack of management attention typically given to journals, and the fact that it is probably rare for organizations to have a set of clearly articulated objectives or a worthwhile budget for publishing the journal. The sophisticated approach adopted by the case study organization reported on below is still somewhat unusual, but it reflects the weight (in both management and financial terms) which is attached to formal, written communications in this company. On the other hand, there are many organizations which merely go through the ritual of producing a journal without considering how its impact might be improved. If it is worth the expense of publishing a regular paper, it seems strange not to have some idea of why this is being done!

Company Videos

In common with the other techniques so far discussed, there has also been an upsurge in the use of videos by employers during the last decade. Videos have been used for all kinds of purpose: (1) as part of an induction programme for new employees, in which information is conveyed about the company in general, its history and mission; (2) as part of the process for disseminating financial and other commercial information to employees on an annual or other regular basis; and (3) as a key part of specific change programmes, so as to give information about a new intitiative in areas such as communications, reward strategies, or a shift in company direction. For example, in the last few years, Kodak have produced videos to be shown to all staff about a new communications package and about a change in the philosophy behind the payment system, whereas Tesco have communicated via video about issues such as customer service and a programme for improving communications at work. As ever, it is difficult to be precise about the extent of video usage within employing organizations, but most large companies will have experimented with this technique on more than one occasion for the last few years. Indeed, a survey by Vista Communications (reported in IPM Factsheet Number 26, February 1990) discovered that training and personnel departments now commission a major share of all corporate videos for induction purposes, for promoting a corporate image, as well as for customer care exercises and the presentation of annual results. Vista found that 50 per cent of their respondents used videos on a regular basis (p. 2), whereas the CBI survey – not surprisingly given the high proportion of smaller companies in its sample – reported a lower usage at 29 per cent. Once again, though, larger organizations were much more likely to resort to videos.

There is a number of advantages of using videos if these are put together properly, and tie in with both HRM and organizational objectives. Most important among these is that videos provide for a consistent and unified message to be conveyed by management, and in so doing hopefully lessen the risk of competing versions of reality or Chinese whispers, as well as the speed and immediacy of the medium. Rather than rely on a long-winded process of cascading information down the hierarchy according to a structured timetable, the video enables the same material to reach many audiences at the same time. It also has the potential of bringing senior managers to life, allowing them to be seen by staff via the television screen, and making them seem less invisible and distant than might otherwise be the case. Used in conjunction with other techniques, videos can also be highly useful in that they can form the basis of a training session or provide for greater variety in the presentation of company results or a new development within the organization. Interestingly, the greater professionalism now exhibited by television companies in their presentation of events, and the more extensive reporting of statistics via bar charts or colour diagrams, now enhances the need to use videos to put across information because they are now expected, rather than being seen as the exception. The flexibility inherent in video technologies, principally the ability to stop a tape to check understanding, highlights their potential as a training or communications aid.

But, like all schemes for employee involvement, these are no more than *potential* advantages, and the success of videos depends to a large extent on the commitment of senior managers to the messages which are being communicated, and the ability of their more junior counterparts to ensure that the 'intended' messages are in fact received by staff. Neither of these can be taken for granted. The uniformity of the message, rather than being an advantage, can be viewed as a disadvantage if the video is shown to groups with widely differing needs and abilities. Determining the right level at which to pitch the video is always a problem, given that some employees may understand little of what is being put across whereas others may regard the video as an insult to their intelligence. Indeed, some of the customer service videos which have been produced seem to be directed at a level way below the grades of staff for which they are intended. Instead of encouraging employees to take greater care for customers, employees have resented the implication that they are currently uncaring or have pointed to the artificial environment in which the video has been shot and the unreal nature of the actors who are playing their own roles. Rather than heightening awareness of issues, the video may do little more than produce annoyance or hilarity in the staff who watch it. As we will see in chapter 5, attempts to 'manage' the feelings of employees are highly problematic.

Some organizations, rather than using actors to play parts or celebrities to feature in the video, prefer to use their own staff, most typically senior managers. Sometimes, this can work well, and a senior manager comes across in the way which is intended, appearing to viewers as honest, caring, professional, or whatever. But equally, the senior management team can appear confused, inarticulate, shifty or pompous, and the message is lost as people concentrate on the features of the person on screen or their mannerisms. The problem facing programme makers is how the message will be received, and the potential advantage which comes from a unified message can alternatively turn into a problem of rigidity if certain groups pick up a different feel from the video than was intended. As an example, a short clip featuring the chief executive giving his seal of approval to a new communications programme in the company can appear to staff like an advert from a second-hand car salesman. In another case, the omission of the Managing Director from a corporate video about future developments in the organization was interpreted as a sign that he lacked any commitment to the company, whereas this was done because he failed to present himself in a way which would have instilled confidence.

However professional the video may be, a considerable amount rests upon the managers who are responsible for using the programme in specific workplaces or departments. The import of the message can be influenced by the timing of the sessions set aside for the video presentation or by the location chosen (or available) for this. The actual – as opposed to the espoused – commitment of management can be seen in such seemingly minor decisions as where and when to show the video. Equally, the willingness of middle or junior managers to identify personally with the message contained in the video is too often taken for granted, as too are their abilities/skills to ensure that sessions are conducted to maximum effect. Indeed, one of the major problems facing any organization which is hoping to develop employee involvement, is the commitment of junior managers to notions of sharing information and ideas with their own staff, of 'empowering' employees, or of treating workers as the company's most valuable resource. To this can be added the fact that a large number of managers – and especially supervisors – have been promoted on the basis of their technical rather than their social skills, and the problem of ensuring a unified message is further compounded. In short, therefore, to be successful, senior managers need to ensure that plans are carefully conceived and implemented, and that the required building blocks (such as supervisory training) are in place before the programme commences. All the technical questions, such as whether the video should be produced in-house or by a consultant, are of little importance until these issues have been resolved.

Case Study: Involvement through Information-Passing

The first case study in the book is drawn from a company in the food retail sector, codenamed Hiclas. It is one of the market leaders in this competitive industry, and it is also acknowledged to be highly professional in its dealings with staff. Compared with other organizations, it is known to be at the forefront in terms of formal, written or audio-visual communications with employees. Additionally, in much of the literature emanating from senior management, high quality staff are seen as one of the principal reasons for this position of competitive advantage. Consequently, the case fits well with the philosophy of this book.

The trend in food retailing during the 1980s has been for the major multiples to increases their overall share at the expense of smaller shops so that the top six now have over 60 per cent of the market between them. New stores have also opened at a steady rate over the last decade, and Hiclas has about 300 outlets. The average size of these stores is on the increase as well, and a typical superstore now has about 300–400 employees, with a sales area of approximately 30,000 square feet. Hiclas employs approximately 70,000 people in its food supermarket sector, and a further 10,000 in other parts of the business. The company has turned in healthy profits during the past decade, with more than a 20 per cent increase each year since 1980. Nearly 7 per cent of these profits are distributed to staff through the company's profit sharing scheme.

Hiclas has a recognition agreement with the Union of Shop, Distributive, and Allied Workers (USDAW) and the Transport and General Workers' Union (TGWU), and a formal consultative system operates at area level once this has been triggered by a set number of staff (basically about 10 per cent) joining the union(s) in the stores covered by the arrangement. The consultation system does function in many areas, despite the fact that the combined union membership is only at 6 per cent overall, and the company's position in relation to the unions is primarily neutral, at least at store level. Management style has become more open during the course of the last decade, and now store managers are encouraged to involve staff in the business, especially by keeping them informed about new developments and aiming to find out their views and concerns at the earliest opportunity through the management chain. Incidentally, within each store, there are likely to be three layers of management between the store manager and sales staff, so the potential for communications blockages is not dissimilar from those faced in a medium-sized manufacturing establishment. Additionally, however, it is rather more difficult to arrange for a structured system of face-to-face briefings given the immediate demands of customer service, the high proportion of part-time workers, and the tight controls on staff numbers in a store. Consequently, in order to ensure that the majority of staff are kept in the picture, written communication plays a key part in the process.

The company uses all four of the techniques for EI discussed in this chapter, and we can now turn to an examination of these, commencing with directors' statements in the Annual Report. It needs to be recalled that the Annual Report is received by a large number of staff because they are part of the profit sharing scheme and share option scheme; in 1990, this was approximately 56,000 people. The Chairman has noted in several recent reports that the company received national recognition for the high performance of its staff, coming in the top few for the country as a whole, and first in the food retailing sector in the late 1980s. Within one of the recent Annual Reports, four pages are devoted to 'People at Hiclas', with a focus on education and training, communication and participation, and community involvement and sponsorship; this compares well with many organizations, which allocate no more than a few lines (often repeated from one year to the next) which concentrate on the statutory obligations under the 1982 Employment Act. Under communication and participation, the statement refers to the Hiclas Journal – which is seen as an essential element in the company's programme for ongoing communications – plus, in relation to financial information, the employee report and year-end video. Additionally, there is reference to the profit sharing and share option schemes. As we shall see below, both the house journal and the employee report have regularly won awards in recent years.

Up until 1989, Hiclas issued a special Employee Report, up to 24 pages long. It contained a spread of information, including the financial results, news clips, people and prospects, new products, store openings, and environmental and community issues. The whole report was full of photographs of employees, new stores and products, and famous celebrities who had been involved with the company. The financial information was presented in a traditional manner, in the fairly safe but understandable format of piles of coins repesenting sales, costs and investments. Particularly interesting was a page of comparisons with other companies in the food retail sector, in terms of market share and price competitiveness. The news clips pull together key events during the course of the year, for example on the purchase of a new company, food safety, or an environmental conference. The section on people concentrated on an adjustment to the profit sharing scheme, health education, and a series of training initiatives. Compared with most Employee Reports, this has far more information about the position of the company in the market, as well as being more extensive in its treatment of other developments. In common with other Hiclas material, it is colourful and easy to read, and it is hardly surprising that this document won awards in recent years.

Notwithstanding this, the company decided to change the format for 1990, and incorporate the employee report into the May issue of the Hiclas Journal, sub-titled a Company Results Special. This was done as a consequence of independent market research into the company's mechanisms for communicating information to staff, which suggested changes to the Hiclas Journal that made it compatible in design terms with the Employee Report. The Company Results now stretch over just six pages, but much of the material which was incorporated into the 'old' report is now included within the main body of the house journal. As well as a brief report on financial affairs, mostly in the form of diagrams, the sections on market share of the major companies and the summary of new store openings are still retained. Given that company performance and growth over the 1980s has been good, these two items present favourable information to staff; had there been major losses or a reduction in numbers employed – as in British Coal, for example – it is unlikely that such information would be included.

Hiclas produces a range of journals/magazines for its staff, depending upon their location, but all staff are catered for by the house journal, a paper which was first published over 40 years ago. This has won a string of awards since then from various bodies such as BAIE (Editing for Industry Awards). The journal is published 10 times per year, is A4 size, 28 pages long, and is full colour. The journal has recently been revamped (see below), both in style and content, and its print-run has been doubled to 45,000; in other words, there should be a personal copy for at least half the staff. The journals are distributed to each store via the Personnel Manager, and these are placed in a convenient position in the restaurant, often in dispensers. Although there is not a personal copy for everyone, staff are encouraged to take the journal home with them if they want. The Hiclas journal, as well as the other newspapers and reports, is edited from HQ by a team of three people reporting in to the Head of Public Relations, who themselves have a sizeable budget. The staffing and financial commitment demonstrates that the company takes the journal seriously, as too does the fact that the company actually has written objectives for the journal. These are:

1 to convey company information effectively and accurately.
2 to obtain feedback and response to that information.
3 to present a credible and objective view of life at Hiclas.
4 to further good employee relations.
5 to assist management in influencing attitudes towards change in a fast growing organization.

The independent surveys undertaken on the company's behalf during 1989 indicated that the journal was wanted on a regular basis, at least monthly, and that staff would prefer it to be more like a colour magazine. Most employees reckoned to 'flick through' the journal, and it was felt that its impact would be greater if every individual had their own copy to take home. A universal concern was that the journal was a 'propaganda' document for the company, designed to please the top management in the 'ivory tower', and that there were far too many pictures of 'men in suits'. A whole host of specific suggestions were made – in the group sessions which formed the basis for the study – about potential improvements to the journal, and this has now led to a revamped publication which takes into account a large proportion of these suggestions. The 'new' Hiclas journal is well presented, now having the feel of a Sunday colour supplement, and it contains a broad range of information (e.g. on store openings, letters, appointments, deaths, new product lines, and special items – e.g. a personnel manager who went round the world, a store which has won an award for employing a large percentage of disabled people, bottle recycling etc.). The company has also taken on board suggestions to liven up the letters page, ensure that the news items reflect stores around the country as a whole, and introduce cartoons, and a prize crossword (which incidentally requires some information from the previous journal).

Staff seem to value the journal as a means of finding out information about developments and major events in the company, in addition to hearing news about people with whom they may have worked in previous stores. My own study of employee opinion (interviews and questionnaires to 60 staff in two stores) reinforced the views of the Journal Editor, in that most staff reckoned to read the paper, if only to find out who had died in the previous month. New store openings attracted a good deal of attention, as did the letters page and the competitions. New product information was usually known about before the journal arrived, as were other developments, according to the staff. Indeed, despite the view from the independent survey that the journal was seen by many staff as a propaganda device, it contains little 'overt' information about company performance (except in the employee report issue) compared with other papers where much is made of TQM, cultural change or whatever. Responses to my questionnaire showed the journal to be ranked below the line management chain and departmental noticeboards in terms of where to get information, although more useful than staff meetings and the union. Given the precise objectives of the journal, especially in relation to staff attitudes however, its impact on employees appears to be slight.

The company makes a range of videos to be shown to staff, either as part of the induction programme or on specific issues at various times of the year. In addition, all staff should see an 'end of year' video, outlining company performance and dealing with a number of other items. For the most part, the videos are shown by a store instructor (trainer) who then develops the themes within them; occasionally, these sessions may be attended by members of management, but there is little in the way of explicit team building through this avenue. The three most recent sets of videos shown to staff have been on Customer Care, the End of Year Results, and Job Evaluation; the latter was part of a campaign to inform staff about a major exercise to re-evaluate jobs throughout the company. The customer care programme has come in two parts; the first video package aimed to get across ideas about the importance of the customer to everybody within the business, and this uses the concept of a circle with the customer at the centre and all staff radiating out from this point. The idea was to get staff to look at their own self-image, examine problems which they encounter both inside and out of work, and the ways in which they can overcome them. Much of the video features a young check-out operator who does not feel like going to work, but who eventually persuades herself to do so. The approach to customer care is not totally prescriptive, and staff are asked to consider how they would like to be served as well as their own preferred style for achieving company service standards. The follow-up campaign is much more prescriptive, and lays down more precise techniques for how to achieve high levels of customer service by following simple general rules. The video proceeds by showing two different and highly stylised ways in which to serve customers (bad and good), before reinforcing the latter in a series of interactions. Throughout the video, certain phrases are repeated:

> Customer care is the number one skill all Hiclas employees must have. Our future success will depend on how well *you* apply this skill. You know it makes sense.
> Remember it is not *what* you are doing that is the most important thing, it is what the customer *perceives* you are doing.
> Make sure that you say good morning etc., please, thankyou, use the customer's name if known, always apologize if something is wrong or there is a delay, take customers to a display, always show concern.

These messages are then further reinforced by the store instructor after the end of the video, and each employee is given a short booklet (folded A4, two sides) outlining the basics of the session. The message really is very straightforward, and over-simplified, but it seems to fit in with the general trend throughout the service sector at the moment. Unfortunately, a number of the training sessions at the two stores where I did my study ended up with staff laughing and joking, and trying to imitate the people on the film. The locations in which the filming took place caused some consternation as the speed at which the actors were working was felt to be extremely leisurely. The experienced staff who took part in the training sessions at the two stores resented the way in which the message was put across, and the patronizing and condescending nature of the presentation. Equally, many of the first line managers believed that the package had not been particularly successful, perhaps being unnecessary because so many of the staff felt that they already took a great deal of care for customers.

Each year, the company also shows an End of Year video soon after the results are announced, and all staff (including managers) see this. Again, the system is standardized with Store Managers using the video as the centrepiece of social event(s) with the managers. The company results are presented via the video, and then the Store Manager goes on to deal with the branch performance in a similar way – in terms of sales, profits, labour and service costs, controllable expenses. The Chairman plays a major part in the video, introducing the results and thanking staff for their efforts as ever. The video for 1989, for example, stressed how much Hiclas was ahead of the field in all areas (e.g. new stores, scanning, direct debit facilities, management structure, environmental), and then provided a series of more detailed descriptions of the work done in certain parts of the company (e.g. distribution, meat preparation, sponsoring of the Arts). In the few weeks after the management showing, staff see the video in the presence of the store instructor, with managers there on an *ad hoc* basis if time permits. Perhaps these sessions could have delivered more effectively by line managers, as part of a team-building strategy designed to increase employee commitment to the organization and the establishment.

Conclusions

Written and audio-visual communications from management to other employees has become a major feature of EI during the last decade, especially in larger organizations. These have taken a variety of forms – from Employee Reports to videos – and in many cases several different sets of techniques are used in the same organization. Although these are often for different purposes, it is quite possible that information about annual results will be conveyed by all four of the media analysed in this chapter. Other items of key importance to senior management may also be disseminated by several of these techniques – for example, a programme of organizational change may be the subject of a video campaign as well as special supplements to the company newspaper. In addition, as we shall see in subsequent chapters, wide-ranging quality initiatives (for example) may also be communicated via team briefing and informal management communications.

The key points to emerge from this chapter are:

- written and audio-visual communications are an essential part of an organization's EI practices, and can form the base for a more comprehensive policy.
- a clear statement in the Annual Report about EI practices can demonstrate to employees, potential recruits and customers that the organization is serious about its view that 'people are our most important resource'.
- an Employee Report needs to transmit strategic and other business information in a way which is accessible to readers, and is seen as an accurate interpretation of events.
- an effective house journal/company newspaper needs to have a proper budget for its operation, it should be well organized and presented, and its design and contents ought to be updated on a regular basis.
- videos must convey a realistic picture of the organization and its employees in order to be acceptable to staff.
- since all of these techniques cost money and take up time, each one needs to be carefully devised, implemented and monitored to ensure that they are consistent with organizational objectives.

In conclusion, it should be stressed that the techniques discussed in this chapter represent the least extensive form of EI, the bottom step on the 'escalator of involvement' which was outlined in the previous chapter. The principal purpose of all these written and audio-visual information-passing devices is 'educative', that is designed to persuade employees of what management sees as the efficacy and logic of its decisions and ideas, as well as its long-term vision in some cases. On their own, however, these techniques are fairly restricted, and most employers would wish to supplement them with other forms of EI. Of these, face-to-face communications (both formal schemes and informal arrangements) represent one of the most common forms of EI to be used in British industry. It is these to which we turn in the next chapter.

4 Face-to-Face Communications

Introduction

In most organizations, whatever other techniques are used for employee involvement, far and away the most common method for communicating information and ideas is face-to-face interaction between managers and their staff. Sometimes, this can take the form of regular and structured mechanisms for ensuring that staff are made aware of what is going on in the organization – such as via team briefing – whereas in other situations, communication of business or related matters takes place during daily contact between individuals, often in an *ad hoc* fashion. Indeed, whilst many would accept that this informal approach to communicating ideas to staff is potentially more beneficial than formalized arrangements, it is difficult to ensure that each and every employee actually receives sufficient information from their manager. Even if they do, there are doubts about the uniformity of the material which is conveyed, and a primary concern is that confusing (and sometimes highly counter-productive) messages may be received by employees. While acknowledging that informal communications are bound to remain important in the workplace, many organizations have sought to supplement (and in some cases, supplant) this haphazard method of communicating with more formal and regularized systems. As we shall see below, the 1980s were characterized by a growth in schemes such as team briefing, so a critical discussion of this technique will form a major part of the chapter. Consideration will also be given to more informal, day-to-day, one-to-one – and additionally, mass – information-passing exercises, although it is much harder to write about these sorts of arrangements because they tend to be implicit in management activity.

Before moving on to deal with the substance of face-to-face communications, we need to explain why such techniques have been on the increase during the last decade, and look likely to continue becoming yet more extensive in British industry. Aside from the specific reasons attached to the growth of team briefing, there are a number of more general reasons which help to account for the popularity of these methods in recent years. Two in particular are worthy of mention (Townley, 1989, pp. 341–5):

1 *attempts by employers to 'educate' their staff*. Since the 1970s, employers have become increasingly attracted to the idea of making their employees more aware of the business and commercial environment in which the organization operates. The reasons for this have varied depending upon the time; in the 1970s, management sought to make staff more aware of the level and meaning of company profitability in the hope of encouraging more 'informed' or 'realistic' collective bargaining with powerful trade unions. In the early 1980s, a number of comprehensive communications exercises emerged out of a perceived need to inform employees of future developments, and especially those designed to cope with recession via rationalization and redundancy. In the latter part of the 1980s, attention turned to messages designed to reinforce employee awareness of the continuing importance of further improvements in competitiveness within international markets. Sometimes, all three are combined, and managements differ in the primacy accorded to separate parts of the educative message depending upon specific circumstances. In all cases, however, the principal purpose behind a drive to increase face-to-face communications has been the idea of 'education'. Of course, it should be recalled that such information-passing exercises may be seen by employees as controversial, as anything but neutral attempts to communicate with staff.
2 *strategies designed to increase employee commitment*. In a sense, this develops out of the previous reason for increasing communications, because it is suggested that employees who have been 'educated into the realities' of organizational life are then more likely to show greater commitment to the aims and objectives of the employer for whom they work. Given increased product market competition during the last decade in most sectors, a large number of senior managers now argue that their employees are a major key to competitive advantage, whether this is in the form of better customer service, higher quality products, or improved productivity. In many cases, it has become commonplace to suggest that these goals can be more effectively achieved by committed employees who are prepared to offer more than their contract of employment actually requires of them. Consequently, managers who are willing to adopt a more open approach to the staff working for them might be able to engender a greater sense of employee commitment to the organization.

This sets the scene for the remainder of the chapter in which we will examine team briefing in some detail before moving on to consider other methods of face-to-face communication. In addition to informal, one-to-one interactions, attention will also focus on the role which managers can play in speaking to mass meetings of employees. In contrast to the previous chapter, in which one of the potential drawbacks of written or audio-visual communications was their inherent rigidity, the concern here is more with the opportunity which arises for messages to be altered – either by design or inadvertently – by managers in the process of conveying information to their staff. Finally, we will pull this material together via a case study and conclude with some general points about face-to-face communications.

Team Briefing in Theory

Team briefing is a system of communication operated by line management, based upon the principle of cascading information down the line. Its objective is to make sure that all employees know and understand what they and others in the organization are doing and why. It hinges around the principle of leaders getting together with their teams on a regular basis in a small group in order to put across information relevant to their work. Although there is provision for information from the top, the major priority is local or departmental matters, and it is the leader's job to ensure that this occupies most of the meeting. There is nothing essentially new about the ideas behind briefing, because these rest upon the sound management principle that good communications are an essential part of organizational effectiveness. What is perhaps more novel is the more structured and formalized approach which has been developed over the last decade or so under the auspices of the Industrial Society, the major proponent and installer of team briefing in the UK. We also need to be aware that some form of team briefing is probably practised in a great many organizations, either under the guise of a different name (e.g. Communication Groups in Tesco) or with a different format (e.g. The Quarterly Review in parts of Ciba Geigy, or Key Communicators in Kodak).

Most publications suggest that team briefing (or something similar) has become more extensive since the late 1970s, at which time there was little mention of the technique aside from the development of briefing groups at Scottish and Newcastle (Benson, 1979, pp. 80–95). During the 1980s, a variety of surveys indicated a growth in their usage; Batstone (1984, p. 268) reported that there had been a sharp increase during the early 1980s in the extensiveness of briefing groups in large manufacturing plants, whilst Millward and Stevens (1986, p. 310) found that this sort of techniques was becoming more common across all sections of industry, including the public sector. Edwards' survey of factory managers (1987, pp. 139–40) found that terms such as 'consultation, communication and involvement loom large in the description of personnel policy' at their establishments, and sufficient examples were provided to convince him that this was a reflection of practical attempts to develop EI rather than mere rhetoric. My own case study work (see, for example, Marchington and Armstrong, 1985) also illustrates the degree to which employers were moving towards more extensive communications policies with individual employees (rather than relying solely on trade union channels) during the first half of the 1980s.

Four further surveys in the late 1980s/early 1990s show that the interest in team briefing or similar techniques has not yet waned. The first, by the Industrial Society and MORI, was based upon interviews with over 1,000 adults, each of whom was in full- or part-time employment during the summer of 1988. Only a small part of the survey related to communications. Over one-third of the sample reported that the organization for which they worked used team briefing/briefing groups at their place of work, and a similar proportion noted the existence of department or group meetings – which probably covers similar ground. Given the nature of the sample, this is a high figure. Even more interesting were the proportions who regarded briefing as the most preferred method of receiving information, and indeed this was higher than for any other technique (Webb, 1989, pp. 42–3). The second survey, by Vista Communications (1989), shows that team briefing is used by approximately 80 per cent of their sample, and that it is the third most extensive method of communicating with employees (just behind notice boards and internal memos). Well over half the sample reckoned to hold briefings on a regular basis at least once a month, whilst about 20 per cent held them whenever management felt they were needed. The CBI Survey of 1989 found that 62 per cent of organizations admitted to using briefing, although this percentage increased considerably to 87 per cent at establishments employing more than 2,000 people. In these larger companies, briefing – along with a variety of written techniques – is the most extensive mechanism used for communicating with employees. However, this figure may well be inflated, as answers to a subsequent question about whether or not the organization operated a formal 'team briefing' structure brought the figure down to just 36 per cent of all responses. Again, given the high proportion of small companies in the sample, this is still a sizeable proportion. Respondents were split as to the effectiveness of team briefing, although rather more felt that the system was effective or highly effective (41 per cent) than those who regarded it as ineffective (6 per cent) or in need of improvement (23 per cent). The rest (30 per cent) reckoned it was adequate (CBI, 1990, p. 28). Finally, the recent ACAS Survey found that 55 per cent of organizations which were questioned used some form of briefing system.

Having shown that team briefing is in regular usage throughout industry, we can now move on to examine how it operates and what employers may expect to gain from its implementation. Team briefing which follows the Industrial Society model has several key principles, which are:

- the central message should be derived from issues dealt with at a senior management or board meeting.
- there should be no more than four levels in the cascade system between senior management and the office or shop-floor.
- at each level in the cascade, the central message should contribute no more than 30 per cent of the total message.
- teams should be based around a common production or service area, rather than an occupation.
- the leader should be the manager or supervisor of the section concerned.
- leaders must be trained in the principles and skills of how to brief.
- the team should comprise between four and 15 people.
- meetings should be held at least monthly, and on a regular, prearranged basis.
- the aim should be to brief all employees within 48 hours.
- the meeting should not last more than 30 minutes.
- general discussion should be discouraged at the team briefing.
- time should be left for questions about the brief at the end of the input from the leader.

In an Industrial Society booklet, Grummitt (1983, pp. 4–7) suggests that there are six principal benefits which can be derived from team briefing:

1 *it reinforces line management*, because (it is suggested) the provision of team meetings helps to ensure that the manager is seen as a reliable

source of information. Moreover, it clearly differentiates the supervisor/manager from the group, also reminding the former that they are accountable for the performance of their staff.

2 *it increases commitment*, not only for the task but also to the organization/establishment as a whole, because talking to people gives them an idea about how the 'team' is doing, and consequently provides an objective for which to aim. It is argued that 'even if people do not agree with something, they can accept it if they understand the reason for it.'

3 *it prevents misunderstandings* which can be costly, time consuming and even embarrassing, by ensuring that employees receive information from the right person at the correct time. There is often an assumption that people know what is happening, but it is probably safer to rely on the old adage that 'to reinform the informed is better than to leave the uninformed uninformed.'

4 *it helps people to accept change*. Most people dislike change, and giving them the longest possible time to understand why it is required will help them to understand, if not necessarily agree with, the changes proposed. It should also help to provide the climate for a smoother introduction of any adjustments within the workplace.

5 *it helps control the grapevine* by increasing the likelihood that information finding its way onto the office or shop floor is that which management wishes to arrive there. The Industrial Society booklet states that the grapevine is 'destructive and can strangle morale unless it is controlled . . . if people cannot be held accountable, any amount of "slanting" can take place en route. The "slanting" is nearly always to the disadvantage of management' (Grummitt, 1983, p. 6).

6 *it improves upward communication* because team briefing provides a base of information on which individuals can build and start to offer constructive ideas for their work. However, briefing is not seen as an appropriate forum for consultation or problem-solving because mixing the two can confuse the issue.

Team Briefing in Operation

This section is concerned with how briefing actually operates in practice and the extent to which reality conforms with the prescriptions outlined above. As one might expect, there are a number of ways in which briefing practice deviates markedly from the principles laid down by The Industrial Society, some of which cast doubt upon the value of the whole system whereas others might be better seen as appropriate modifications to suit local practice. We will discuss these under three headings, some of which are similar to those considered by Thomson (1983), before offering some conclusions about briefing in practice. Some of the examples which are used in this and the next section are drawn from Marchington et al. (1989, pp. 25–9).

1 *Timing*. There are two typical problems which have been experienced with the timing of brief. The first of these is likely to be common in organizations which operate in irregular (either unpredictable or seasonal) product market circumstances, and where production or staffing levels are consequently highly variable over the course of a day, week, month or year. Setting aside a specific time each month may prove extremely difficult in this sort of situation, and indeed may run counter to the imperatives of production or customer service. For example, in a food manufacturing firm where team briefing had been introduced, the system had run into severe problems at certain times of the year because of the highly seasonal nature of demand and the effect which this had upon production schedules. While there appeared plenty of time for briefing during the slack periods, in the run-up to Christmas these were often overlooked because of 'more pressing' priorities; team briefing either lapsed altogether during this period or maintained a somewhat sketchy and haphazard presence. To have stopped production in order to brief employees about the need to work extra hard would have appeared nonsensical. Alternatively, the failure to hold briefs during this period only caused employees to question the depth of management's commitment to provide regular and comprehensive information. Similar though more short-term problems also disrupted the briefing system at a supermarket as well, and it was not uncommon for some groups to remain unbriefed for months on end because the exact timing of meetings depended on business constraints. The second problem with timing is trying to maintain the organization's commitment to briefing all employees within 48 hours of the initial message; this is bound to be a problem with organizations where employees are geographically dispersed or in those where working patterns mean that some employees are not in for several days at a time. This was experienced by the NHS district we examined, and was especially severe for those staff who were employed in the community. In both types of situation, however, the problems with the system merely caused staff to question management's commitment to briefing at all.

2 *Content*. The Industrial Society suggests that the type of information to be communicated at briefings should be weighted 70:30 towards local (that is, departmentally-oriented) material rather than comprising predominantly central directives. Moreover, briefers are held responsible for presenting material in a manner which makes it relevant to the group in question. The major problems which seem to be encountered in this area are in finding sufficient material for the brief, either for the core or for those which form the local supplement and commentary. On the former, it is generally easier to compile a brief if there are regular updates on orders or sales, on the progress of building work for a new plant, or on deals to secure new markets. Writing the core brief did not appear to be a problem in any of the organizations studied by Marchington et al., since the process was triggered by a regular management (or in the case of the NHS district, authority) meeting to review performance. This is not always the case of course, and one water company – just before privatization – produced a very short core brief due to fears about commercial sensitivity, with the net result that employees could recall only one piece of information from this series of meetings – that senior management had met over breakfast. Since briefing had only recently been introduced, this led employees to question the commitment of senior management to its success, and ask who paid for the breakfast. Subsequent to privatization, normal service has been resumed, but this has not been without some cost to the morale of more junior managers. A shortage of material for local briefs is often more of a problem, not because there is nothing meaningful to say, but due to the commitment and capability of supervisors. In the NHS district, there were complaints about the lack of locally-derived material in the team briefs compared with those which formed the 'core', both in terms of numbers of items and their relevance. In addition, the briefers often made comments on the core which succeeded in diminishing its impact on the audience, either by using a poor example in order to convey a general message or by querying the basis upon which the message was built. The commitment of briefers to the system clearly has a major effect upon the type of material conveyed as well as the manner in which it is put across.

3 *Actors*. a third key feature of team briefing is that all employees should receive the message contained in the brief, via a face-to-face interaction, usually delivered by their immediate supervisor. At each of the organizations studied by Marchington et al., it was intended

that the immediate supervisor should be the briefer. This did not always happen, for example in the case where a briefer failed to turn up for the meeting, did not delegate the task to anyone else, and even failed to tell the team that the meeting would not take place. Perhaps more problematic for the organization is the briefer who always turns up, but fails to present the message in an effective way, either due to inadequate communication or presentational skills or because of a lack of commitment to the brief itself. There are many examples where the briefer merely reports on the core message in terms such as 'this month, I've been told to tell you . . .', or just leaves the core brief for employees to read at their leisure. One of the major problems has been that employers have failed to ensure that their briefers are trained sufficiently in interpersonal skills or have been convinced of the need for briefing in any event. Alternatively, employees may be suspicious of a brief delivered by a supervisor who has recently been trained up to deliver a 'slick' performance and which masks his/her natural style. As we shall see in the case study outlined later in this chapter, some organizations choose to operate the system through middle or senior managers – rather than supervisors – and this can be turned to advantage with some ingenuity from management.

The other issue is whether employees are required to go to all sessions, or if attendance is voluntary. Both present problems; for those who are conscripted, it is unlikely that commitment to the sessions or the company will be high, and such employees can act as a disruptive influence on the proceedings. In each of the organizations studied, quite a number of those interviewed regarded the briefings as little more than an ideal opportunity for 'a smoke and a sit down', regarding it favourably in comparison with having to work on their normal tasks. Alternatively, however, if people do not attend the briefings, it is very unlikely that they will receive the message from management in the way which was intended. Moreover, non-attendance means that any attempts at team building are severely limited. In the superstore we studied, it was recognized that briefing would be problematic during working hours, especially for part-time staff who were employed at precisely the times they were needed. Accordingly, for these groups, the company agreed to pay for an extra half-hour per month in order to ensure that briefings took place without conflicting demands on employees' time. For most people, this worked well, but some staff were effectively disenfranchised because they had alternative commitments outside of their contracted working hours. Other staff never attended briefings because they were held on their day-off each month. These people were expected to find out the key points of the brief from colleagues (with the associated problem of the grapevine) or they were dependent on their supervisor remembering to talk to them informally (with the associated drawback that this may be squeezed out by other events).

This discussion of team briefing in practice raises two further questions. First, whether or not team briefing (or any regular, structured system for communicating information down the hierarchy) is appropriate for all situations? Given the examples which have been highlighted above, it would seem that the decision to use briefing could well be contingent upon organizational circumstances. Extending this, it could be argued that certain contexts offer rather barren ground for reaping the benefits of briefing; for example, when production schedules or market demand is highly variable, when employees are dispersed around a wide geographical area, when patterns of working time make it difficult to convey the message over a short period, when there is little new to say in the organization, or when supervisors lack commitment to briefing or the goals of the employer. The danger with this response is that it provides management with a reason to legitimize their failure to communicate with staff. Moreover, employees who work away from the head office or factory environment might be precisely those people with whom managers most need to communicate in order to overcome their sense of isolation. This is even more important if they are a key focus of contact with customers.

The second question allows for a more positive response. Assuming that the organization decides to proceed with this sort of communications initiative, what action will management need to take in order to increase the likelihood of the system proving successful? Accordingly, the company which operates in a variable product market situation could make it clear to employees that briefing will only be the central element in communications at certain times of the year, while at others it will be replaced by alternative methods. Briefing, however, may well help to facilitate the achievement of higher production targets later in the year because of the team building which has taken place during its operation. Equally, employers need to plan carefully in advance when considering the regularity of briefing so as to ensure that there is always sufficient material to maintain the system. Briefings to dispersed groups of employees may be combined with other activities which make a day in head office more valuable. Finally, employers have to ensure that the briefers are fully committed to the principle of briefing and have sufficient presentational skills before introducing the programme in the first place. If necessary, briefing can be undertaken by more senior managers, and supervisors can learn from this. Alternatively, the organization will need to spend considerable time training supervisors prior to implementation. Rather than rush into briefing because it is fashionable, as some employers undoubtedly did, a more thorough appraisal of the benefits and drawbacks before its introduction should help to facilitate a more effective operation.

Team Briefing in Context

Unlike the material in the previous section, which was designed to evaluate detailed aspects of the briefing system, the purpose in this section is to focus on issues of broader principle. This will be organized into three parts, commencing with a review of some of the grander claims made by its proponents about the benefits of team briefing.

Reality or rhetoric?

Some of the principal benefits which are supposed to flow from a good briefing system were outlined above, but there have to be doubts about the extent to which these views have been derived from independent and/or detailed research. Several of the reports on briefing have been written by managers who work for the company in question, whereas others have relied heavily on managerial interpretations alone, often on the basis of just one visit to a site (see, for example, the reports in Martin and Nicholls, 1987, pp. 35–46). It is unlikely that such research can be sensitive to any of the deeper issues accompanying the briefing system. Equally, there is a danger, as has occurred in other areas of employee relations in recent years (e.g. with the debate about flexibility), that rhetoric may run ahead of reality, and that typicality may be assumed on the basis of unestablished claims.

While it may seem reasonable to assume that team briefing *can* reinforce management as the 'natural' leader within the workplace, this claim is also highly dependent on managers briefing with commitment and ability, as well as on the support of senior management for the system as a whole. In each of the cases analysed by Marchington et al., there were examples whereby managers or supervisors did not take the system seriously, and showed little enthusiasm for the process. Indeed, in the NHS case, given the initial scepticism and apathy of the managers themselves, it was highly improbable that briefing would ever reinforce the management chain. Similarly, reinforcement can only occur if the briefers are able to command the respect of those they brief, and that cannot be taken for granted; indeed, some supervisors may well lose status by virtue of poorly-handled attempts at briefing. Equally, there must be doubts about the claim that team briefing increases worker commitment, and again the theoretical foundations for this view rest upon shaky foundations. The argument relies upon the notion that informing employees of current activity and future plans necessarily produces a greater commitment to the organization; that is, it leads to a behavioural change. Research by Ostell et al. (1980) casts some doubt upon this; they found from detailed and multi-method research that a communications exercise in a chemical company – incidentally, one well-known for its long history of employee involvement – had little effect on the workers there. Only a third of the employees who took part in briefings could recall much of the material several weeks later, and no more than a few could remember any of the general economic factors relevant to the plant. The authors conclude that the exercise had little success in motivating workers, and in fact might have increased insecurity amongst the group. Similar points could be made about the other claims; for example, it is difficult to believe that employees about to be made redundant will accept company plan just because they are aware of the reasons for such a decision. Yet another constraint in assessing the impact of briefing (or any other initiative for that matter), is how to establish a benchmark against which to evaluate the degree of change which has occurred. Part of the problem is choosing an appropriate point at which to start measuring, and whether this should be at the time briefing is actually implemented, or when it is first mooted, or at a set time prior to its introduction. Additionally, there are difficulties in establishing whether changes are due to this technique, or others, or indeed factors which occur outside of the workplace. Indeed, it could be argued that team briefing has the greatest chance of success in those situations where it is least needed by management – that is, in situations where high trust and commitment already exist – and the least chance of success in those where it is needed most.

Undermining the unions?

Some commentators feel that schemes such as team briefing are expressly designed in order to by-pass workplace trade union organization, and in so doing reduce its role within the organization. There have been some examples where it appears as if this was at least one motive behind management's decision to implement new communications plans, and that employers were keen to wrest back control from shop stewards in the workplace. Additionally, the evolution of team briefing may also coincide with a reduction in union influence within a workplace, although this does not confirm that weakening the unions was necessarily an explicit (or even implicit) objective of management in introducing the scheme. At two of the organizations studied by Marchington et al., trade unionism became less central to employee relations activity after briefing had been introduced, but it seems unlikely that this was as a direct result of the briefings themselves; since the implementation of briefing coincided with a number of other initiatives – such as a three-year, no-strike deal at the food factory – it would be unwise to credit briefing with such a key role. In the NHS, briefing itself had made only minor inroads, so its impact on trade union organization was also minimal. Clearly, it is important to recognize that the interrelationship between briefing and workplace trade union organization is highly complex, dependent on a range of factors which vary between organizations; for a fuller discussion of this, see Marchington and Parker (1990).

Evolution

A formally conceived, team briefing is intended as a one-way information dissemination device, with room for questions which clarify or amplify the brief itself, but not for discussion of other issues which concern the group. Organizations are advised to set up a monitoring system so as to ensure that the scheme is working, as well as respond to questions raised during the briefs. Consequently, upward communications are seen as no more than responses to the management message rather than acting as a channel for conveying the groups' grievances or anxieties. There is a good deal of evidence, however, that briefing does develop beyond this limited role in practice, and in the supermarket it did operate as a two-way communications device, much to the satisfaction of all concerned. Shop-floor staff regarded this as particularly beneficial because it gave them an opportunity to raise grievances directly with their immediate boss in a formal arena, and this enhanced the possibility that they would receive a prompt reply. It also cut out a stage in the grievance process, which further reduced the potential influence which the stewards could wield. Managers, too, felt that it provided a quicker and highly effective route for resolving problems, as well as an opportunity to talk with staff away from the immediate pressures of the job. More senior managers were aware that deviations of this kind from the formal model did occur, and saw no reason to stop them developing. Indeed, by progressing from a system which rested upon the downward communication of information to one which allowed for a more effective two-way dialogue, this evolution could lead to team briefing fulfilling a more participative role within the organization. In a sense, therefore, some forms of team briefing could become more of two-way communications device, possibly moving up one step on the 'escalator of involvement'.

Other Face-to-Face Communications Devices

Valuable though structured communications devices are, they only provide for a direct link between shop-floor or office employees and their immediate supervisor or local manager. Whilst this is clearly crucial for a whole variety of reasons, some chief executives have felt that they or the most appropriate senior manager at site level, should also attempt to establish contact with the more junior people who work for their organization. This finds expression in a variety of ways, and is reflected in a range of different terminology; for example, MBWA – 'Management by Walking About', GOYA – 'Get Off Your Ass', 'Walkabouts', to name a few. In the *Excellence*-type literature, this sort of practice features quite forcefully, in particular in Goldsmith and Clutterbuck's (1985) chapters on leadership and involvement. There, a number of references are made to executives in large companies who make a point of establishing contact with their staff from a range of units and different levels in the hierarchy. For example, they report on the action taken by the Group Managing Director of Bulmer's who aims to spend a couple of days each year out on the delivery trucks, and on Sir John Sainsbury who visits at least 100 supermarkets each year and is well known for his detailed knowledge of store layout and design. This style of management is also encouraged in his managers, and much of the job of a regional manager is spent visiting stores without warning, checking on progress and talking with staff. Store managers (who employ 300–400 staff) also spend quite a lot of time each day on the shop floor – talking, overseeing, solving problems, being 'visible' to their employees, and even undertaking routine jobs on occasion to an extent which is rarely equalled by the counterparts in manufacturing or the public sector. Indeed, in some companies, despite exhortations from the top that senior managers ought to spend more time on the shop-floor, this is something which is often overlooked or relegated due to what are seen as more pressing, important, and scheduled engagements. Presumably, if managers are serious enough about this aspect of their work, time will be scheduled for this in just the same way as any other activity. More often, perhaps, its relegation indicates their actual – as opposed to their espoused – commitment to meeting with the shop-floor. But, some senior managers in the manufacturing sector do find the time for this, and several Divisional Managing Directors within parts of Ciba Geigy make a point of visiting separate departments/manufacturing units on night shift so as to introduce themselves to the operators. Indeed, one newly-appointed Managing Director spent a couple of hours on Christmas Eve with process workers soon after he took over because he was concerned that they were missing out on communications.

Of course, visits by senior managers are not always interpreted in such a positive way, and employees or supervisors/middle managers can view these with suspicion. In workplaces with a history of low trust or adversarial employee relations, the sight of senior managers on the shop floor or in the office can be regarded as 'spying missions' or an attempt to unearth some problem which will be rectified later. Additionally, in some retailing organizations, one of the duties of regional managers is to ensure consistent and high-quality delivery of service by making regular visits to all the stores in the region. In order to prevent the likelihood of staff 'preparing' for a visit and getting everything in order, regional managers tend to turn up at stores without advance warning; this can be seen in a very negative light. Alternatively, if senior managers are encouraged to meet selected members of staff, they are likely to pick up potentially distorted pictures of employee relations and morale. In some cases, this can cause them to disbelieve the results of formal attitude surveys because they contradict previously-held impressions gained from their own interactions with staff.

Face-to-face contact need not only occur via walkabouts during working time, but can also be generated informally or formally over lunches or other mealtimes. The former can be facilitated by common canteens brought about by moves toward greater harmonization of terms and conditions, and some senior establishment-based managers have been keen to use this time to talk with different individuals each day. Other organizations have started up series of meetings for a variety of purposes; for example, Goldsmith and Clutterbuck (1985) report that STC's chief executive has long practised informal briefing lunches with representative groups of about 12 employees at a time when a wide range of matters are discussed. Other organizations quoted by them arrange lunches for groups of managers. From my own research, some firms have set up lunches for staff to meet with the general manager as a reward for winning an employee-of-the-month competition, although this sometimes causes more anxiety on the part of the employee than it does a feeling of recognition. Once again, though, the idea is that commitment may be enhanced by senior managers meeting with their more junior staff.

Finally, in a somewhat more formalized though more *ad hoc* way, some organizations have set up conferences or mass meetings for senior managers to communicate with staff about a key issue or event which is confronting the company. Sometimes, as we shall see in the case study, the Managing Director can address the whole workforce about a particular problem or plan affecting everyone at the site. As the ACAS Advisory Booklet *Workplace Communications* (1982) notes, these meetings are 'good for presenting the company's performance or long-term objectives; they require careful preparation but allow only limited opportunities for employee response. They should be used sparingly and *need to be followed up in other ways*' (p. 17; my emphasis). There are dangers with this sort of approach, especially if the mass meeting has not been well prepared or the audience reacts negatively and with hostility to management proposals. Alternatively, these sessions can be counterproductive if they are seen as ritualistic, lacking in energy and substance.

How extensive are these arrangements for senior managers to communicate face-to-face with their staff, and are the above cases merely isolated examples of this approach? Unfortunately, the fieldwork undertaken earlier in the decade did not ask specific questions about this, but the recent surveys have. For instance, a new question on management walkabouts was introduced into the Vista survey of 1989, and the responses indicate that 59 per cent of the organizations who replied to the questionnaire stated that this was now practised in their organization; walkabouts were ranked seventh (out of 14) in this study in terms of extensiveness, roughly equal with the use of management conferences but rather less common than briefing. The perceived effectiveness of walkabouts was also fairly average. The CBI survey (1989) also found that walkabouts figured prominently in 'action taken over the last three years' which contributes to employee involvement (65 per cent of the firms reckoned that this was now done) and that such exercises were seen as relatively effective as well. Additionally, about half the respondents also indicated that their chief executive now addressed employees, although it is not possible to determine from the results whether this is a regular occurrence, or whether or not these addresses are restricted solely to managers.

There are a number of reasons why employers might have chosen to introduce techniques such as these over the last few years. First, as a sign that senior management is actually committed to the idea of involving employees in – or at least informing them about – the affairs of the organization. It is felt that Chief Executives should show commitment from the top by 'walking the job' and ensuring that the rest of the management team do the same'. There is some indication that employees resent managers who are seen as faceless and remote, so anything which helps to break down these sorts of barriers might be beneficial to the organization. Secondly, and associated with this, communications may be improved by such a process, either through the transmission of a uniform message from senior management, or by creating a feeling among employees that their views are being sought by management; it may help to 'open up' the hierarchy. Finally, walkabouts or acting as a drivers' mate can also help to 'educate' senior managers about the nature of shop floor work, give them an opportunity to meet customers and talk with individual employees first hand, rather than just through the management chain. Each of these advantages can help to reinforce the belief that management takes seriously the view that 'employees are the company's most valuable asset'.

But, caution also needs to be exercised with these practices. A considerable amount rests upon the ability and commitment of senior managers to make mass meetings and walkabouts actually work to the firm's advantage. Many managers probably feel uncomfortable speaking to large gatherings of shop-floor employees, in which case there is little point in proceding with this sort of event. Some individuals find it very difficult to talk informally with staff, and may end up creating greater feelings of remoteness than overcoming this. It is also important for senior managers, on their walkabouts, not to undermine the position of line management by agreeing to changes or putting alternative interpretations on events which create further industrial relations problems for the department concerned. A final issue relates to the need to maintain the impetus for face-to-face contact once this has been established; a one-off exercise aimed at achieving closer relations is likely to be regarded in a poorer light by staff than no attempt whatsoever.

Case Study: Involvement through Communication

The case study in this chapter is drawn from one division (Ichem) of a foreign-owned company in the chemical industry, codenamed Multichem. The company publishes a corporate philosophy statement, a copy of which goes to all employees, in which the key contribution of staff is recognized and the policy towards EI is outlined. The division on which the case study is based, is perhaps further down the road to HRM than most in the UK, although this terminology is not employed in the company. In addition, Ichem practises all of the techniques which have been the focus of this chapter, even though the approach to briefing used in this division is somewhat at odds with that promulgated by the Industrial Society. Nevertheless, management operates firmly within the spirit of HRM and EI advocated in this book.

The division is situated on a large industrial estate near Manchester, and chemicals have been manufactured on the site since the late 1930s. Now, two sets of products are manufactured on site, and most of these are sold overseas to the industrial rather than the domestic market. Ichem is one of a handful of international companies which compete in this market. The products enjoy a good reputation with customers, and the company sells on the basis of reliability as opposed to low prices. Overall, the product market environment looks highly favourable and, whilst the market is competitive, it provides management with some room for manoeuvre in handling employee relations. The division employs about 580 people, and this number was halved as part of the company's 'reconstruction to profit' programme in the early 1980s. The cutbacks took place on a pro rata basis across the workforce as a whole, via voluntary severance and retirements, and the exercise was completed without any industrial action even though the site had experienced a spate of strikes during the 1970s. There are three separate manufacturing plants on site, each of which uses relatively high levels of computer technology to control the process which runs on a continuous basis. At any one time, therefore, only a small proportion of the process workers are on site. All process workers operate with a fair degree of functional flexibility, especially between tasks on the same plant, and there are agreements which allow for partial flexibility amongst the craft workers.

Employee relations at Ichem underwent a massive adjustment in 1980, as a consequence of the reconstruction programme. A New Deal was signed between the unions and management which led to sizeable increases in pay, an agreement on job security, and a series of measures designed to harmonize conditions between white and blue collar staff – such as common canteens, equal sickness benefits, the abolition of clocking off for manual workers, and a commitment to greater flexibility and openness. Management style at the site mirrors closely the corporate principles, and it can best be described as open and progressive. Overall, the employee relations style is based on a notion which puts primacy upon the reduction of direct supervisory control over employees and it encourages employees to accept responsibility and use discretion in their work. At the same time, Ichem recognizes several trade unions for bargaining purposes, all employees are encouraged to join the appropriate union, a check-off system is in operation, and stewards meet regularly with management via a JSSC. The convenor, however, is no longer full-time on union duties, although he was for a period leading up to and during the negotiation of the New Deal.

At Ichem, the principal formal means for developing EI is the Quarterly Review, and this exists alongside an open management style and attempts to provide process operators with a degree of control over the operation of their own plant. Communications meetings do occur in some areas, but this is at the discretion of the supervisor concerned, and it is not subject to formal monitoring by the personnel department. Indeed, the major emphasis at Ichem is on the necessity for systems to evolve within their own context, and an abhorrence of 'imported' techniques or expensive contracts with management consultants. The Quarterly Review was introduced as part of the New Deal, and consists of a series of meetings every three months, starting with the Managing Director and finishing with the shop floor. The Managing Director himself was the driving force behind this approach which he sees as the embodiment of his commitment to open management and increased employee awareness about the state of the business. The purpose of the meetings is to transmit information to all employees about the performance of the division, and about future prospects.

Every quarter, as part of the formal monitoring process, all managers are required to write progress reports on their departments. These are then sent to the personnel department for compilation into a single script which goes to the Managing Director for his approval. In line with a published schedule, every three months the Managing Director makes two detailed presentations on the same day, both with exactly the same material – according to the personnel department; in the morning, he speaks to senior managers and in the afternoon to the employee representatives, with both sessions lasting up to two hours. All participants are also provided with a script of the presentation, apart from the confidential material which is retained. During the following week, all the senior managers brief the staff for about one hour, this being organized to coincide with shift and production requirements; once again, a summary sheet is distributed to all employees for reinforcement. Questions are encouraged, and each quarter all these are noted and compiled by a senior manager before being shown to the Managing Director; typically, this would total some 70 or 80 questions. Those which can not be answered immediately are put on an action list for reply as soon as possible. Though there are some similarities between this system and team briefing – namely in the regular dissemination of information from the top to the bottom of the hierarchy – there are also some fundamental differences. Individuals are not usually briefed by their immediate boss, and indeed a recent initiative has been to encourage presentations from senior managers from other departments (line or staff) precisely because it can lead to a wider awareness of business matters. Other differences relate to the length of the presentations, their regularity, the handouts, and the number of levels involved in the cascade down the management chain.

The content of a Quarterly Review typically has the following components:

- sales relative to plan and to previous year, broken down into individual businesses within the site, and between home and overseas markets. Costs of inputs. Raw materials targets for the next quarter. Major customers.
- new technology, new building work, and product development.
- logistics, warehouse and transport.
- safety issues such as recent records, and awards from the British Safely Council, Rospa, Chemical Industries Association. Environmental protection.
- quality assurance.
- public relations.
- medical issues, such as health and anti-smoking campaigns, blood screening, breast examination facilities.
- personnel statistics, leavers and starters, training programmes.
- added value as a percentage of turnover, and in relation to the price of raw materials and revenue costs.
- outlook for the forthcoming year.

In several recent Quarterly Reviews, two messages have been central to the meetings, both of which reflect more deep-rooted concerns within the company. Firstly, the notion of quality has pervaded all aspects of the presentations, with an emphasis on 'efficient service to the customer'. Secondly, the Reviews stressed the importance of 'teamworking' and 'people management', issue which again were central to the training initiative throughout Ichem. Following a review of the format for the system, senior management have also made it 'snappier' and have increased their use of visual aids in the presentations. Initial responses seemed favourable to this shift in direction as well.

The stewards appeared to value this forum, largely because they receive detailed information direct from the Managing Director, and they are able to ask him questions about this if necessary. One of the senior stewards felt that management was 'very open, they don't try to hide anything from us, and there is plenty of opportunity for us ask questions. The Managing Director seems a very genuine bloke'. However, the stewards were also fully aware that the information which they received served to reinforce management's interpretations of events, tending to support decisions which had already been made or were about to be taken; 'they tell us that the competitors are at the door when they want to keep costs down', said another of the senior stewards, but equally 'the information which we get is pretty useful for the wage negotiations'. The managers also found it a useful way in which to ensure regular communications with staff, and also to expose people in their own departments to thinking from other functions within management.

The manual workers who were interviewed seemed to value the Quarterly Review as well, and they even made suggestions on how to improve the meetings. They were all keen to receive confidential information from senior management since this was felt to illustrate their (management) interest in the workers and encourage them to be part of the firm, as one of the craftsmen put it. Another commented that 'some of the information is bordering on the release of commercial secrets. But the lads are responsible, conscious of the company's position and their own future'. Most of them felt the presentations could be made more interesting and appropriate for the staff, especially in relation to performance figures, and one expressed an interest in where the company's products ended up, that is their ultimate use.

In addition to the Quarterly Review, the Managing Director also practises EI through other means, and he is particularly renowned for his walkabouts as well as his 'open' style. At least one morning per week is scheduled in his diary for walkabouts, when he just drops in on individuals, whether these be in the offices or out on the plants. This is partly to find out what is happening around the site, but also it acts as a way of reminding employees of his existence, making himself more accessible to them. Similarly, he always tries to eat in the canteen, and again makes a point of sitting with different people each day. Although both of these practices might be regarded as little more than old-fashioned human relations, or alternatively as an intrusion on individual space, his style is such that employees do not appear to feel threatened by his presence. He has been Managing Director at the site for over ten years, having had the task of leading the 'Reconstruction to Profit' programme in the early 1980s. Part of this included mass presentations to the workforce as a whole in order to explain the reasons for and consequences of the turnaround at the division. Although the message he conveyed to staff at that time was gloomy because it involved job losses, employees who remained at the company believed that they could trust his integrity and accepted his commitment to the future of the division. Indeed, so as to illustrate that the process of job reduction was to be spread across Ichem as a whole, half the Board was sacked on the day of the mass meetings with staff. Several years on, what appeared most striking during my research in this part of Multichem was the positive employee attitudes to the company. Perhaps, this position was originally born out of relief at continued employment after the turn-around project, but it is reinforced by the buoyant product market circumstances which were maintained during the latter part of the 1980s.

Conclusions

In attitude surveys, one of the most common complaints to be levelled against management by employees is a lack of adequate communications. Employees often feel that they are kept in the dark about changes affecting the organization and/or that managers are not really committed to ensuring that they are informed on a regular and continuing basis. Concerns about issues such as this have been one reason why there has been a growth in regular briefing sessions in employing organizations within the UK over the last decade. Unfortunately, many schemes have been implemented without sufficient thought being given to the way in which briefing can be organized or its implications for existing patterns of employee relations.

Communication schemes can fail for a whole variety of reasons – irregularity, lack of relevant information, inadequate training, poor management-union relations, conflicts with production schedules etc. It is important for employers to ensure that their systems for greater formal communications are in line with the predominant organizational culture. Given the right conditions and a commitment by senior management to make formal communications systems work effectively, techniques such as team briefing can represent a valuable component of an organization's EI programme.

The key points to emerge from chapter 4 are:

- regular, structured, face-to-face communications techniques are crucial in any organization as a mechanism for maintaining contact with staff, especially as a supplement to written media and forms of representative participation.
- team briefing needs to be planned and implemented with care if it is to stand any chance of success – this relates particularly to the timing and content of briefs, the training of briefers, and of course the commitment of senior management to the briefing process.
- if a decision is taken to introduce a briefing system, the system needs to

be sustained and managed rather than being allowed to meander and (possibly) die.

- team briefing should be allowed to evolve into a two-way communication device as employees become more familiar with issues affecting the establishment/organization, and more confident about putting forward their own views.
- other forms of face-to-face contact between senior managers and employees – such as walkabouts and mass meetings – should be handled with care to ensure that they are not counterproductive and result in confusing messages being received by staff.
- none of the techniques discussed in this chapter should be viewed as a substitute for continuous, informal, face-to-face contact between supervisors and their teams.

Despite their importance, face-to-face communications from managers to employees are little more than the first step towards the creation of a more comprehensive approach to employee involvement. If employers are serious about their commitment to 'resourceful humans', greater information disclosure can help to prepare the ground for more extensive forms of EI, usually of a direct nature. In the next two chapters, the emphasis in the book shifts to an analysis of schemes designed to enhance the contribution of staff towards improved departmental or corporate performance. We commence this discussion with a consideration of problem-solving techniques, before moving on to task-based participation in chapter 6.

5 Involvement in Problem-Solving

Introduction

The previous two chapters have concentrated on employee involvement schemes which are designed to improve the flow of information down the hierarchy from managers to their staff, with the objective of enhancing employee awareness of business pressures and (hopefully) increasing their commitment to the achievement of organizational goals. In this chapter, the emphasis shifts to the provision of ideas up the hierarchy and to the possibility of contributions from employees which can help to improve the substance of decision making, as well as its legitimacy. Much of the chapter will focus on quality and continuous improvement, whether this be via suggestions from specific individuals or through the efforts of a team of people. More precisely, four different techniques will be examined, each of which has implications for EI. These are suggestion schemes, quality circles, total quality management (TQM), and customer care. Although elements of all of these may well be employed within the same organization at the same time, there is also a chronological rationale for treating the schemes in this order; suggestion schemes have the longest history, although often this form of EI has been marginal to mainstream employee relations; quality circles have a much shorter pedigree with the first reported cases towards the end of the 1970s; both TQM and customer care programmes only really became better known towards the end of the 1980s. This sequencing helps to explain the mix of EI techniques such as suggestion schemes, quality circles and TQM in the same organization, as does the fact that quality circles often form one aspect of a total quality management, customer care or other organizational change programme. In Japan, for example, it is not uncommon to find all of these operating together in the same workplace.

Although there are slightly different reasons why employers adopt specific schemes, a number of broad management objectives can be proposed for these various forms of problem-solving technique. These are:

1 attempts to improve decision making and (ultimately) organizational performance by seeking contributions from a wider range of people than would typically be canvassed. This can relate to improvements in the areas of product quality, working methods, health and safety, customer relations, and costs of manufacture or service; that is, those 'task-related' areas where employees are thought to possess specific skills which might lead to better quality decision making.
2 attempts to improve employee commitment to the organization and to the tasks on which they are employed which, it is argued, will be enhanced by the opportunity to contribute more fully to the resolution of problems. Greater involvement in the process of decision making, especially if this is seen to lead to the adoption of one's own suggestions, is likely to increase the individual's commitment to the ultimate solution. This may also have a spin-off in that other decisions, made with or without employee involvement, may be legitimized if employees feel that management is fair and to be trusted.
3 as part of a philosophical commitment to the involvement of employees in problem-solving, because this is seen as a just and proper way in which to make decisions. EI can therefore be seen as recognition of employees' rights to become more fully involved in work. This is likely to be limited to a small number of employing organizations, such as co-operatives, some charities or voluntary bodies, and those where the founder has a religious or deeply-held commitment to wider involvement – for example, Scott Bader.

The types of scheme to be discussed here – and especially quality circles – have been subject to widely different assessments of their potential. For some enthusiasts, quality circles are seen as one embodiment of management's realization that employees represent a valuable source of untapped expertise and knowledge, and that they are therefore to be welcomed both on efficiency and democratic grounds. In contrast, for others who are more dubious of their contribution, quality circles are seen as an exercise in 'pseudo-participation', a device initiated by management to strengthen their control by appropriating employee ideas under the guise of greater workplace democracy. In addition, from this perspective, most of the techniques discussed in this chapter would be viewed as a potential threat to trade union organisation.

Suggestion Schemes

According to Industrial Relations Review and Report (1989, p. 6), a suggestion scheme is 'a formal definite procedure, established by management, to enable eligible employees to voluntarily communicate their ideas; to provide machinery to investigate and appraise those ideas, and to reward employees whose ideas are acceptable for implementation.' This definition therefore excludes informal arrangements, especially those in small firms, whereby employees offer suggestions for improvements as and when appropriate. Equally, it does not cover the provision of ideas for improvements which are related to an individual's own job, and indeed this is also excluded from the formal schemes.

Suggestion schemes have a long history in many organizations, often going back over forty years. More recent estimates show an increase in coverage, although as ever it should be borne in mind that the sampling frames used in the various surveys do not allow strict comparability. For example, the 1984 WIRS survey (Millward and Stevens, 1986) found that about one-quarter of all establishments with 25 or more employees had some formal suggestion scheme. The surveys by the CBI (conducted in 1989) and ACAS (done in 1990) show that approximately 35 per cent of all establishments operate such schemes. As would be expected, these are more common in larger establishments, although the ACAS survey found no difference in extensiveness between manufacturing and service organizations (1991, p. 16). Townley notes that schemes are a common feature of North American companies (1989, p. 335) and various studies have suggested that they are much more extensive in Japan (for example, see Martin and Nichols, 1987, p. 21). Organizations can register their schemes with UKASS (The United Kingdom Association of Suggestions Schemes), but only 500 or so are on their books. Given the survey results reported above, schemes are therefore rather more extensive than this figure would suggest.

There are three major advantages of suggestion schemes according to the IPM (1988). First, they can lead to improvements in quality, reductions in wastage, increases in productivity, and of course cost savings. Specific organizations report massive cost savings through such schemes; for example, Lucas reckons to save over £1 m per annum in first year savings alone, and IBM over £0.5 m. Individual suggestions can also account for significant cost reductions, as Rover found with an idea to improve the attachment of door casings (£380,000 per annum). Overall, Townley (1989, p. 336) notes that estimates for savings from suggestions schemes as a whole come to over £8 m each year. The second advantage relates to improvements in the climate of employee relations in an organization and to an increase in two-way communications because employees feel that management is prepared to ask for their views. This clearly fits well with the idea that staff are a valuable resource whose creative potential needs to be tapped, as well as the notion that high trust is an essential aspect of good employee relations. Obviously, it is extremely difficult to quantify the benefits from this particular area. Third, some organisations feel that the existence of a thriving suggestion scheme can have positive public relations advantages, both in making customers aware of the organization and in attracting high quality employees to apply for jobs. Again, as with other forms of EI, an active and well respected scheme can contribute to the image of a good employer. Of course, as we shall see below, each of these potential advantages can be damaging if the system does not function well.

In designing a suggestion scheme, various technical questions need to be addressed, and it is not appropriate to prescribe a model to follow at all times. Four points seem particularly relevant:

1 employers need to determine the most appropriate method for *collecting* the suggestions and, associated with this, the best way to publicise the scheme so as to encourage a good flow of 'serious' ideas. The traditional method of placing a box in the workplace appears to be less attractive nowadays, and increasingly organizations are turning to postal systems.
2 there needs to be some consideration of how to *evaluate* ideas, and especially the composition of the suggestions committee. Some organizations restrict membership to senior managers or technical experts, whereas others – mindful of ensuring the legitimacy of schemes – also include employee representatives/shop stewards on their panels.
3 the system for *rewarding* suggestions needs to be clearly thought through so that it provides the right messages to employees. Generally, there will be an upper limit for the scheme (say of £5,000), and a sliding scale is usually in operation to link the reward to the level of the saving to the organization. Increasingly, employers are now offering a token award for any serious suggestion (perhaps £5 or £10) merely to encourage the

submission of ideas on a regular and continuing basis. Sometimes, the cash payment is replaced by a gift instead.

4 finally, the system needs to be regularly *monitored* in order to assess its applicability and importance. Quantitative assessments can be made on the number of suggestions per 100 employees; for example, according to IRRR Lucas has a participation rate of about 20 per cent, and approximately half of these resulted in a payment to the individual concerned. Of course, it should also be recalled that some individuals will submit more than one suggestion each year (Gorfin, 1969), so the actual proportion of staff who are actively involved in the scheme is probably lower than one-fifth.

Although suggestion schemes generally tend to be fairly marginal to the mainstream of employee involvement, their operation nevertheless has possible implications for other aspects of work relations. Three are worthy of highlight. First, the schemes may create bad feelings – as well as good – on the part of employees, for a whole variety of reasons. Individuals may feel that their idea merits a higher reward, or indeed one at all, than the committee is prepared to offer. Relatedly, employees may be resentful of the size of their own reward compared with the ultimate savings to the organization, and question whether or not it is worth submitting an idea in the first place. Moreover, regular suggestion-givers may find that their enthusiasm induces hostility from amongst fellow workers, although Gorfin's research from the late 1960s does not indicate that this is a problem (1969, p. 378). Secondly, as with many other aspects of EI such as quality circles, seeking ideas from staff may cause tensions for supervisors and more junior managers, especially if the latter have doubts about their role in more 'open' systems of regulation. This is likely to be particularly pronounced if supervisors feel that their technical expertise is threatened by suggestions from people in their own section. Indeed, two of the major reasons cited by Gorfin (1969, p. 370) for the failure of schemes were 'supervisory resistance' and 'management indifference'. Finally, there is a potential contradiction between the idea that employees should be rewarded for good suggestions and the notion that – with quality circles, TQM, and customer care – staff should be automatically searching for continuous improvement as part of their job. Under many of these programmes, the reward is supposedly psychological in character (that is, offering ideas is a reward in itself), or it relates to improved organizational/establishment performance as a whole. As yet, this has not been the focus of a research study, but interestingly enough, suggestion schemes do appear to operate in conjunction with all of these other techniques in some organizations.

Quality Circles

The second sort of technique to be examined in this chapter is the quality circle. There have been numerous definitions of these (see, for example, Collard and Dale, 1989), but essentially quality circles consist of small groups of employees who meet voluntarily on a regular basis to identify, analyse and solve quality and work-related problems. Membership of the circle typically comprises between four and a dozen people – from the same or associated work areas – who meet under the guidance of a group leader. Usually, it is supervisors who act as group leaders, although this need not be the case, and it is the leader's job to help develop the group into an effective team. They are aided by facilitators who train members, provide a source of information and encouragement, and act as a liaison between the circle and the remainder of the organization. In some organizations, such as parts of Ciba-Geigy, the facilitator's role has been strengthened into that of a 'godfather', a senior manager who is responsible for ensuring that the circles are able to acquire sufficient resources to allow the completion of tasks and sufficient authority to help put ideas into practice. In addition, the circles are initiated and driven by a steering committee which acts across the establishment or organization as a whole.

As with the other problem-solving bodies discussed in this chapter, there are two distinct sets of senior management objectives behind the implementation of quality circles. Firstly, they are introduced in order to improve quality and service, increase productivity and reduce costs, basically aims which relate to enhanced organizational performance. Secondly, they have as a further motive improvements in employee morale and commitment, and perhaps rather ambitiously the achievement of a better industrial relations climate in the organization. Many of the studies on quality circle implementation confirm that the former is a slightly more important objective than the latter (see, for example, F. Hill, 1986; Bradley and Hill, 1987; CBI, 1989), although Collard and Dale (1989, p. 358) suggest that enhanced employee development and satisfaction ranks higher than improved quality or service. In any event, the two objectives are closely related and likely to be included in any rationale for the introduction of quality circles.

Quality circles were first practised on any significant scale in Japan, although it should be recalled that the first proponents of the idea were American consultants who found Japanese managers willing to listen to their views. There are now estimated to be over one million circles in Japan, with over ten million workers participating in them. Developments in the USA and Europe occurred at a rather later date, and the coverage is nowhere near as comprehensive here. In the UK, the first recorded example of quality circles was in 1978 at Rolls-Royce in Derby, with the company using principles developed by Lockheed in the USA rather than from Japan. Estimates of coverage vary considerably, but all parties seem to agree that circles have become more extensive since the late 1970s, with perhaps a slower rate of growth during the last few years. For example, Collard and Dale (1989, pp. 356–7) reckon that there were about 100 organizations with circles in 1981, a figure which had risen dramatically to 400 by 1985. Robson (1984, p. vii) estimated that there were between 500 and 750 organizations with quality circles in the mid-1980s. In terms of coverage of course, this still means that circle programmes were only in operation in a small minority of organizations at this time; as Batstone (1984, p. 266) notes, less than one-fifth of the manufacturing establishments he surveyed had any quality circles by 1983, although this had shown a considerable increase since the late 1970s. Although there is evidence of circles in all sectors of the economy, Marginson et al. (1988, pp. 110–11) suggest that quality circles have been more likely to develop in manufacturing than in services, and interestingly there is greater likelihood of circles in unionised concerns as well.

Two more recent surveys suggest that quality circles now operate in about a quarter of organizations. In 1989, the CBI's survey of member companies (which, it will be recalled, had a high proportion of smaller firms in the sample) indicated that 24 per cent used quality circles, about one-third of which had been in operation for three or more years (1989, p. 29). In 1990, ACAS conducted a survey of the organizations which used its services, and found that circles existed in 27 per cent of these; the sample was overconcentrated on manufacturing, so it is likely that across the whole economy the figure is rather less than this. It also found that foreign-owned firms were twice as likely to have circles than their UK counterparts (1991, p. 14). However, one feature which emerges from these and other studies is the susceptibility of quality circles to long-term demise, and this is a point to which we will return below.

Even where organizations claim to be using quality circles, this does not imply that all employees, or even a majority of them, will take part in circle activities. Black and Ackers (1988, p. 13) found in their study of Brown's Woven Carpets that only about 6 per cent of the workforce were actually members of the 23 quality circles which operated in the company, and certain groups of employees (including the highly unionate weavers) were not prepared to 'buy-in' to the concept; interestingly, management was particularly keen to extend circles in an effort to improve industrical relations in this department. More recent studies at the company indicate that the weavers still remain outside the circle programme, and that this still covers less than 10 per cent of the workforce. Hill (1991) also reports on a longitudinal study of circles in several companies throughout the 1980s. In many cases, the participation rate was between 2 per cent and 10 per cent of those eligible to join, and even at the highpoint, this never exceeded a quarter of the workforce. He notes (pp. 7–8) that 'the majority of employees were at least indifferent while certain groups remained actively opposed, even in the companies with viable programmes.'

According to Brossard (1990, p. 11), there have been three distinct phases of research into quality circles. The first wave took a highly positive and somewhat prescriptive line about their potential benefits for organizations and employees alike, and reported on successes at various companies in the UK and the USA – such as at British Telecom, May and Baker, Blackwell's, Wedgwood, Mullard, and Jaguar Cars. The second phase of publications shifted the emphasis from the perceived benefits to that of sustainability, that is how circles could be maintained once the initial surge of enthusiasm had evaporated; not surprisingly, it also focused on the reasons for terminations, and attempted to apply contingency perspectives to this analysis. The latest phase, according to Brossard, is directed at members and non-members of quality circles, the reasons why people join in the first place, and an evaluation of the longer-term impact of quality circles on the organisation. As with much management research, it is only when schemes have been operating for a number of years that more critical in-depth studies begin to emerge, and the initial euphoria which surrounds the schemes starts to dissipate. The remainder for this section will therefore concentrate on the problems and shortcomings identified by research into quality circles; this will be organized into four categories.

First, is the impact of circles upon employees, either as members or not. Here the evidence is mixed. Several studies undertaken in the USA suggest that participation in a quality circle does have an impact on attitudes and performance, expressed by lower rates of absenteeism and tardiness, as well as by higher rates of productivity. Each of these studies compared these factors both over time and between groups of members and non-members, so as to minimize the methodological problems associated with this sort of research (Griffin, 1988). The 1989 Industrial Society survey found that employees who feel that they are allowed to solve problems at work were twice as likely to view their employer in a positive light than those who were denied the same opportunities (Webb, 1989, p. 23). However, there are also indications from the same research that the 'improvement' effect might be limited in its impact over time. There are also suggestions that the introduction of circles might exacerbate difference between members and non-members; the former start to view themselves as better than the 'outsiders', with the latter regarding the circle members as victims of 'pseudo-participation', of brainwashing by management (Bradley and Hill, 1983, p. 303; Marchington and Parker, 1990, p. 199). Moreover, Wilson (1989, p. 32) argues that two of the assumptions which underpin circle participation are questionable; firstly, that employees want to contribute their ideas so as to improve performance. On the basis of interviews with a number of workers in a motor components factory well-known for its quality circle programme, she finds little support for this notion, suggesting instead that employees are negative towards their jobs and employer due to their awareness of inequalities in the employment relationship. Secondly, she questions why employees should want to contribute ideas to the employer when there is no obvious gain for so doing. This need not be in the form of cash, as Brossard (1990, p. 14) indicates from his studies in the USA, and employees can be committed to quality improvement if this can be seen to increase the chances of continuity of employment in a competitive market.

There is some union hostility to the circle concept, with leaders fearing that they will be used to marginalize workplace union organization or that employees will start to identify with the employer rather than the union (see, for example, F. Hill, 1986, p. 28). The problems which Ford experienced when first trying to introduce quality circles into British factories in the early 1980s were principally due to union conerns about the motives behind and implications of a circle programme. Indeed, in order to overcome this anxiety, Ford and other employers have chosen different titles for subsequent initiatives in this area; for example, problem-solving circles, manufacturing cells, zone improvement groups, and Employee Involvement. At the same time, case studies suggest that unions are less antagonistic in many workplaces, and as Bradley and Hill (1983, p. 302) note, 'there is little evidence in the attitude data that circles sap the system of members' overall commitment to the unions . . . indeed, quality circles could enhance shop-floor power.' This is supported by the evidence from F. Hill (1986, p. 28) and Collard and Dale (1989, pp. 370–1), who note typically supportive attitudes from union representatives towards the idea of circles and their operation, especially in workplaces where the schemes have continued in existence. Involving union representatives in the process of introducing the programme, as well as in its running, has no doubt assisted here, as too have guarantees that circles will not lead to job cuts. Moreover, according to Collard and Dale, few circle failures, either of the programme as a whole or of individual circles, can be put down to union opposition. Black and Ackers (1988, p. 13), however, are more cautious, suggesting that union hostility and indifference have been important factors in limiting the development of circles, especially in a climate where union representatives are suspicious of all managerial actions designed to increase productivity. F. Hill's comparison of schemes which have been terminated versus those which continue in operation also suggests that unions are much more likely to be hostile to the circle concept in the former than they are in the latter (p. 28). In situations where circles are an integral part of union-based EI schemes, unions may have little to fear from their introduction. Conversely, where quality circles are implemented in an attempt to reform industrial relations in a climate of mistrust, the end-result is likely to depend more upon the relative balance of power in the workplace.

The third category to be dealt with is that of management itself, and each of the studies agrees that this is a major problem for circle continuity and success. Collard and Dale (1989, p. 371) summarize the evidence as follows: 'managers are the major obstacles to quality circles . . . many circle programmes and individual circles fail because of a lack of management support, the poor response to circle initiatives from management, a closed management style, and a lack of management recognition given to circle activities.' There appear to be two related sets of problems. Firstly, quality circles may be imposed on middle managers and supervisors without taking their views into account, and these more junior managers are more likely to view participation as akin to 'soft' management, as pandering to the workforce. Management insecurity is therefore highlighted, and there are doubts about prerogatives over labour in a more 'open' organization (see, for example, Bradley and Hill, 1987, p. 72). However, there is also a second reason for the low level of support for circles from middle managers and supervisors, and this relates more to an increased drain on already stretched resources than to negative attitudes *per se*. Bradley and Hill (1987, pp. 75–6) discovered that the UK managers they interviewed were much more hostile to quality circles than their US counterparts; it was felt that the QC initiative added to their workloads for comparatively small returns, and (because appraisals did not include performance of the circle, unlike those of the US managers) there was little personal advantage in making a success of circles. Indeed, it is suggested that 'there were positive disincentives'. Others go further and put forward the view that 'managers may actually have a vested interest in quality circle failure' (Wilson, 1989, p. 32) and that 'middle managers may have the power to "kill-off" a QC programme prematurely – perhaps by cancelling meetings, not releasing key personnel to participate in QC activities, failing to provide specialized information, or pre-empting circle proposals' (F. Hill, 1986, p. 30).

The final problem area is that of sustainability, and this has led to a research focus on quality circle failure. Collard and Dale (1989, p. 368) note that there are three sorts of failure; when an individual circle stops operating, and this is the most common type; when the programme as a whole is suspended; and (least common) when the programme is never implemented despite its serious consideration. Of those circles which do start, most analysts feel that there is a restricted life span before problems become a major concern. This can be anything from 18 months to 3 years, and in the cases studied by Bradley and Hill only one-fifth of the circles were still in operation three years after the inception of the programme (1987, p. 73). Once the honeymoon effect has worn off, apathy starts to creep in as members search for new projects and become disillusioned because ideas have not been implemented, thus making the circles vulnerable to problems. Griffin's study of quality circles in the USA shows vividly how unease with programmes gradually increased as time went on; for the first three years, the attitudes of those involved in circles remained positive, but soon after deterioration set in. He notes (1988, p. 352) that employees felt 'the company had started to take them for granted. They felt their efforts were no longer appreciated as much (and) that management was simply becoming less interested in their recommendations.' The plant managers at these sites agreed that the circles were declining in effectiveness, although he felt that the lack of interest stemmed from the workforce rather than managers. In all cases, the same pattern occurred whereby impressive initial results are followed by decline anywhere from one to three years after inception. For Hill (1991, p. 13), the dominant impression is one of 'fragility. Every programme needed constant stimulus to keep it alive . . . every company experienced a continued ebb and flow as circles went into suspension or collapsed and others started. The continued flux meant that companies were never certain how many circles were in operation at any moment.'

This has led some people to suggest that quality circles are merely a transitional mechanism, that we should not be surprised by their failure after a number of years. For Lawler and Mohrman (1985, p. 71), circles can evolve into more participative approaches, or decline altogether. They even suggest that if employers have not already implemented circles, they may want to avoid them altogether 'because the transition is so difficult to make'. Hill (1991, p. 15) argues that quality circles are bound to fail because of the way they were introduced into British and US organizations, generally as an additional grafted-on technique, and without much evidence of management training. He notes: 'it seems that oganizations outside Japan borrowed the part of a total system that was both the most visible and apparently the easiest to implement, without an understanding of the whole.' Total quality management (TQM) might stand a better chance of success, and it is to this that we now turn.

Total Quality Management

In a number of the companies investigated by S. Hill (1991), quality circles were either replaced by TQM and quality improvement teams, or they merely became incorporated into the broader organization-wide TQM programme. Other studies also report similar developments. That this should happen is not altogether surprising given that TQM is more attuned to Japanese developments and presents a more integrated approach to management compared with 'grafted-on' quality circles which had been implemented in some situations as a quick fix solution to organizational problems. Certainly, TQM has become the fashionable management technique of the early 1990s, and there is some discussion as to whether it will prove more resilient than its predecessors in the field. Of course, TQM is not primarily an EI technique, but its successful operation requires employees to become involved in the process of decision making at departmental or sectional level, and it is thus highly relevant for this chapter.

The British Quality Association (BQA) has put forward three alternative definitions of TQM. The first focuses on the so-called 'soft', qualitative characteristics, found elsewhere in the work of US consultants such as Tom Peters: customer orientation, culture of excellence, removal of performance barriers, teamwork, training, employee participation, competitive edge. From this perspective, TQM is seen as consistent with open management styles, delegated responsibility and increased autonomy to staff. The second definition places emphasis on the production aspects such as systematic measurement and control of work, setting standards of performance, using statistical procedures to assess quality; this is the 'hard' production or operations management type view, which arguably leads to less discretion for employees. The third definition comprises three features: an obsession with quality, the need for a scientific approach, and all in one term, thus borrowing from both the above definitions albeit in a unitarist fashion.

The leading UK proponents of TQM come from the operations management field, and thus offer variants of the 'hard' or 'mixed' approach. For example, Oakland (1989, pp. 2–3) sees it as 'a way of managing to improve the effectiveness, flexibility and competitiveness of the business as a whole', meeting customer requirements both external and internal to the organization. TQM is conceptualized in the form of a triangle – with the three points representing 'management commitment', 'statistical process control' and 'teamworking' – and a chain, indicating the interdependence of customer-supplier links throughout the organization. The concept of quality chains is central to Oakland's view of TQM. His concern is that the chain can be broken at any point by one person or piece of equipment not meeting the requirements of the customer (internal or external). Unfortunately, he suggests, this failure usually finds its way to the interface with external customers. Collard (1989, pp. 3–4) regards TQM as

> a systematic way of guaranteeing that all activities within an organization happen the way they have been planned. It is a management discipline concerned with preventing problems from occurring by creating the attitude and controls that make prevention possible. It is also about efficiency, productivity and long-term success.

Dale and Plunkett (1990, pp. 5–6) relate TQM more closely to employee relations, when they suggest that 'it is necessary to change behaviour and attitudes throughout the organization. Key features of TQM are employee involvement and development and a teamwork approach to dealing with improvement activities.' Although there is a recognition of the role which needs to be played by employees in making TQM operate effectively, the principal focus remains on the statistical and operational characteristics of the system.

Much of the debate and practice remains heavily influenced by the American and Japanese gurus in the field, although each of these places a different emphasis on the people-management aspects of the system (Dale and Plunkett, 1990, pp. 7–11). For Crosby (1984), whose theme is 'quality is free', and Juran (1989) (quality equals fitness for use), the role of employees in continuous improvement is minimal, limited to reporting problems to management or quality professionals. In a similar vein, Taguchi (1986) argues that quality is achieved by minimizing variance, and again, the predominant emphasis is on the 'hard' aspects of TQM. Although Deming (1986) is also keen on the use of statistical quality techniques, he also believes that employees should be trained to spot defects, improve quality, and be offered rewarding and challenging jobs. Feigenbaum (1983) goes further, suggesting that workers need a good understanding of what management is trying to do: 'improvement can only be achieved by everyone's participation.'

The TQM concept, therefore, comprises both production-oriented and employee relations-oriented elements, and this highlights the tensions between, on the one hand, following clearly laid-down instructions while, on the other, encouraging employee influence over the management process. Perhaps this potential contradiction is best summarized by Mortiboys who states

> A company-wide perspective is essential and must be driven from the top. All directors and managers must be committed to effective

> leadership and cost-effective quality management. The ability to work with employees as teams rather than attempting to control people through systems must be a high priority for managers. (1990, p. 33)

This hard-soft distinction is noted in a number of case studies, especially those carried out by researchers with a qualitative bent. For example, Needham (1990, p. 155) observed that conflicts developed between different managerial interest groups with each attempting to ensure that their version of TQM achieved prominence within the chemical works; some senior managers were devotees of Peters, whereas another specialist team regarded this approach as too generalized and lacking in systems. Conversely, the senior managers felt that the TQM message had not penetrated to any depth because the specialists lacked a real appreciation of involvement and participation. Wilkinson et al. (1991) found tensions between the hard and soft approaches in their studies at Black and Decker and the Co-operative Bank, whilst Seddon (1989, pp. 153–7) observed that management's preoccupation with the hard elements of TQM, to the relative neglect of the soft, had caused employees to become disillusioned with the concept as a whole. As with other problem-solving approaches whereby employees are encouraged to use their skills to resolve organisational problems, they can become immersed into the 'logic' of the market, especially if these are dictated by customer requirements. To some extent, this shows up the potential contradictions between increased employee influence over management decision making, and the limited impact of EI upon underlying organizational structures.

Nevertheless, TQM has clear implications for employee involvement, whether this be in terms of employees taking greater responsibility for quality and having accountability for its achievement, or in terms of the introduction of teamworking principles into organizations. In addition, TQM is different from the two previous examples (suggestion schemes and quality circles) in that it is *compulsory* rather than voluntary, representing part of the job rather than being a supplement to existing activity. It is also supposed to place a greater emphasis on self-control, autonomy and creativity, expecting active co-operation from employees rather than mere compliance with the employment contract (Wilkinson et al. 1991, p. 24). For Hill (1991, p. 400), participation is 'the central mechanism for improving business quality,' one of the five key principles of TQM, alongside harder elements such as statistical process control (SPC).

He argues that 'everyone, from the most senior managers to the ordinary office and shop-floor employee, should participate in the process of identifying and implementing improvements. The task of top management is to design a structure and establish a culture that will maximize the effective participation of all employees in the pursuit of quality.' We will follow through the link between TQM and teamworking rather more in the next chapter, where there is also a consideration of the implications of these 'new' styles for supervisors and junior managers. Now, however, we turn to a discussion of customer care, which may be seen as a variant of TQM used in many service sector organizations.

Customer Care Programmes

Whereas TQM focuses on customers both external and internal to the organization, customer care/service programmes tend to concentrate on those in the former category alone. Usually, the ethos behind these schemes is to improve relations at the organization/customer interface, to encourage staff to treat customers in a more positive way. Often, the shift to place a higher emphasis on this also involves linguistic changes as well; for example, as with British Rail's use of the terminology 'customer' rather than 'passenger', or in some leisure organizations which use the term 'guest-care' as opposed to 'customer-care'. Unfortunately, there has been some slippage in the definitions here, and a recent IDS/IPM (1989) booklet includes team briefing, quality circles, suggestion schemes, and performance-related pay as just some of the possible examples of customer care in the public sector. As with TQM, the notion of customer care comprises both a hard and a soft dimension; the former focuses on the best way to do jobs by setting prescribed standards for practice, whereas the latter is more concerned with employees utilizing their initiative in order to resolve problems which may obstruct the achievement of high quality service. As before, the soft/qualitative element tends to be in tune with the eulogies of American consultants like Peters, who talk of being 'close to the customer' or achieving 'productivity through people'.

The best-known UK example of customer care is the British Airways 'Customer First' programme, and it is not uncommon to find other service sector companies attempting to follow their approach. This involved extensive training for all staff, and a series of workshops designed to increase awareness of customer needs. It was also undertaken in conjunction with the trade unions recognized by the company. In a recent training course, 'To be the Best', staff were given the opportunity to watch videos of other airlines' approach to customer care and were encouraged to make suggestions on how to compete more effectively. In a similar vein, most of the major finance institutions and large retailers have followed similar sorts of programmes, albeit with less publicity and often via highly prescriptive training videos. The tendency to focus on customer care is not just restricted to the private service sector either, and there are examples of local authorities and health districts taking on board equivalent models. For example, the IDS/IPM booklet describes developments at Arun District Council organised around a 'Working For The Public' campaign; this included a message from the Chief Executive, discussions of the Peters' video, *A Passion for Excellence*, and various training sessions. In addition, the Council also introduced an 'employee of the month' competition, in which an employee is nominated by colleagues for having achieved particularly outstanding customer care, and the winner is presented with an award. Although the scheme was greeted with some cynicism at first, it now appears to be rather better accepted by staff.

As with TQM, there are also a number of underlying tensions apparent within customer care programmes between different versions of management style. On the one hand, it emphasizes open and participative approaches to staff, and a preparedness to seek opinions, whereas on the other the tendency is to increase direct control over staff and limit their potential for discretion by putting forward Taylorist models of so-called best practice which are to be observed. Managers have an incentive to ensure that these standards are closely followed because they can also be assessed on how well their staff convey the company image; in the case of supermarkets, this is either done by a regional manager during his or her visits to the store, or in some cases by 'mystery shoppers' who provide reports on specific stores. There is also some concern amongst check-out staff that security cameras which are pointed at the sales area in order to catch or deter shoplifters can also be used to watch over employees. Whether real or imagined, such techniques of surveillance are hardly consistent with employee involvement. Yet, at the same time, some employers are genuinely seeking suggestions from staff about how to improve customer and, because their environments are common, employee care. Research undertaken in a number of retail outlets by Marchington and Harrison (1991) does suggest that staff value a more open approach and believe that employee involvement is more extensive than it was a few years ago.

However, there are doubts as to how far the culture of customer care has actually changed attitudes and behaviour on the sales floor. Ogbonna and Wilkinson (1990, pp. 12–15) provide a range of verbatim quotes from superstore staff which suggest that employees find the message of customer care hard to accept at certain times. The whole process of customer care can degenerate into an 'act' which requires coping skills, and to be successful this has to be managed to cover up real emotions. Moreover, the impact of customer care programmes is further limited by high levels of labour turnover amongst these grades of staff. However, my own studies of food retailing show that even the training videos on customer care often fail to have the desired impact on staff attitudes and behaviour, especially where the participants are mature women who have gained considerable coping skills during periods spent working in the home. Rather than learning how to follow a predetermined script, these women are resentful of management's attempt to impose prescribed patterns of behaviour. This reaction has much in common with that observed by Hochschild (1983) during her research into flight attendants on US airlines, whose work she characterized as 'the managed heart'. This kind of 'emotion work' is directed by 'paid stage managers who select, train and supervise others' (pp. 118–19). The more that the flight attendant learns to 'put on' a smile, the less that this becomes genuine, and the greater the difficulty in coping with work. Consequently, one of the major tests which customer care programmes face is how to preserve the individuality of staff and allow for the exercise of creativity and initiative, whilst at the same time ensuring that the corporate image is satisfactorily conveyed. Effective selection, training and employee involvement can go some way towards maintaining the role of the individual in service sector organizations.

Case Study: Involvement through Customer Care

Multistores is one of the leading supermarket chains in the country, operating in well over one hundred different locations in Britain. The company moved into the superstore market in the early 1960s and, like many in the field, is still growing; the company as a whole now employs well over thirty thousand people. It has placed increasing emphasis on direct communications with the shop-floor (via team briefing) and on customer care campaigns, as manifested in a range of competitions aimed at improving service within the stores. More broadly, following a business review in the mid-1980s, the company introduced a new management ethos, with a more explicit focus on the development and importance of employees; after all, shop-floor workers at Multistores are the principal point of contact with the customer, much closer to them than management.

In general terms, there has been overall market growth during the 1980s, but at the same time an increase in competition between the major retailers for a share of this market. Multistores has been opening up new superstores in different parts of the country, as well as revamping its original shops in order to increase available floor space, develop the range of goods on offer, and update the image of the company as a whole. The company is unlikely to become a market leader but is keen to maintain a presence in the top four or five in the sector.

This has significant implications for employee relations, particularly with regard to the quality of service provided and therefore the recruitment and training of staff employed. The company has introduced a series of campaigns aimed at customer care either on an individual basis (employee of the month), or collectively (store of the year), both of which will be dealt with in more detail below. At the same time, Multistores has also improved its induction training, one aspect of which is to highlight the importance of each customer, and the link between market success and employment stability; posters displayed around the stores indicated this quite graphically. For example, 'A smile or thankyou costs nothing', or 'Think customer first and they will think Multistores first'. One full poster ran as follows:

> Satisfied customers who keep coming back again and again strengthen sales and jobs!
> Our success and security depend upon *every* employee supporting the sales effort through *personal interest* and *good workmanship*.
> CUSTOMERS make pay days possible.

Since the mid-1980s, the company has placed mush more explicit emphasis on the 'people' component in management development programmes, that is not just employees but also customers. It is now company policy to provide all new starters with a handbook, incorporating the new motto on the front, and in which the Managing Director writes of his belief that 'our staff are our most important asset and we will do everything to help you enjoy working with us.' The attempt to be more open, progressive and developmental in relation to employees is a view which found considerable support throughout the echelons of senior management, although it was not always easy to see this style in operation within the stores – especially at times of intense customer pressure.

Two of the major issues facing personnel managers in the stores are completing the 'jigsaw' of ensuring staff availability when required (and by implication labour turnover) and the need to promote employee commitment to the concept of customer service at all times. The solution has been to communicate far more with employees than in the past, in order to increase awareness of the product market pressures affecting the company's fortunes. Labour turnover has been over 50 per cent per year, with 12 per cent of all leavers doing so in the first month. This suggests a 'crisis of induction', which the company has sought to rectify. All new recruits now receive literature on health and safety matters, the company's history, rules and regulations, and details of service-related benefits. In addition to these routine documents the new starter receives full information about the customer service campaign, including a number of regulation-issue booklets. During the induction period employees are meant to complete a number of modules, and the importance of these is such that the company pays part-timers at time and a half to come to the store for these sessions which centre on a video showing examples of poor practice by sales assistants. The scene is then reviewed and each error pinpointed. The second half of the session introduces the five elements of customer service which are subject to performance appraisal – At the Service Counter, Asking for Products, Checkouts, Dealing with Complaints, and General Store Operation. Every employee receives a small plastic card summarising key points for action. 'Acknowledge eye contact and smile at your customer', 'Say Hello/Good Afternoon etc.', 'Help your customer', 'Be smart. Impress your customer', 'Thank your customer and say Goodbye'. The reminder card exhorts 'Remember! Customers always have a choice'.

Multistores also recognizes a trade union for bargaining purposes, and a high proportion of the staff (over 70 per cent) are actually members. The union has no great significance in the stores because so much of its work is done at national level between full-time officials and senior managers; of course, this is the level at which collective bargaining is conducted. Some stores experience great difficulty in persuading staff to take on the role of union representative and, despite formal agreements that stewards should occupy about half the seats on the store councils, this is often not achieved. The stores councils are the equivalent of a JCC in manufacturing industry, and are designed to provide an opportunity once a month for the general manager and his deputy to meet with a cross section of staff representatives from different departments.

The constitution specifies both a consultative and a communications role, and the councils which I observed tended to operate as problem-solving and grievance committees for the most part, as well as giving the general manager a chance to review recent performance. For example, during one meeting, he reminded representatives of the newly-instituted 'employee of the month' competition. This was first mentioned by him at the April meeting, and he indicated that several nominations had already been received for this competition. By June, the general manager was 'disappointed' at the small number of nominations so far, whilst by July, in response to a comment that the staff were not particularly interested in the scheme, he explained

> It's an incentive to maintain customer service. Staff make the difference in the market place. People like going into some stores because of the people. All this is to reward staff who give good service. I'll be disappointed if someone from each department is not nominated by the end of the month. There's only one winner, but it should create an atmosphere, everyone aiming for the same goal and with a happy atmosphere.

The matter was not raised in August since more nominations had been forthcoming, and it did not reappear again during the remainder of the research period.

'Store of the Year' results were reported at the August meeting, with the news that the store had come fifth in the region; 'a bit disappointing' said the general manager, 'basically we are not keeping our costs down. I'm expecting to jump up the league table next time . . . I'm going to try and squeeze us a few points. I'll do my bit, staff must do theirs.' This almost innocent unitarism was also conveyed when he gave out advance information about a new range of confectionery products, with the instruction to 'keep it under wraps so that our competitors can't get hold of it'. The representatives, especially those who were not stewards, seemed to value this information since it made them feel part of the company, and were equally keen on improving store performance because they conceived of their future at the company and in this store. In short, therefore, the stores council tended to be used by management as an ideological device to promote the ethos of customer care, although it was apparent that this message did not always percolate through to the shop floor from the council.

Employee involvement is also practised via the customer care programme, and its associated activities, which constitute the most recent initiative within the company to foster and develop a service orientation amongst employees. In part, this was advanced through quality campaigns, but a key element of the programme are the various competitions which employees can enter for monetary gain; for example, one of the principal tasks of the customer care committee (a non-elected body, but one whose membership encompassed all employees in the store) is to select an 'employee of the month' from a list of nominations. Staff from any part of the store are eligible for nomination, and management went to great lengths to ensure that staff knew that contact with customers did not represent a prerequisite for the award. Committee members other than the general manager and personnel manager voted each month on the candidates, and the winner received a prize of £5. More important perhaps is that the votes cast were carried forward, contributing to the bigger award (£500) for 'employee of the year', something which all the interviewees saw as a worthwhile target.

One of the store personnel managers interviewed described the objective of these initiatives as 'to highlight the customer care issue, and to create models of good employees for others to follow.' Similarly, the customer services manager explicitly linked employee involvement and motivation to the service ethic:

> The customer pays our wages, and is the most important part of the store. We must be the brightest, cleanest, most pleasantly served unit, otherwise all stores are the same. Giving employees a piece of the cake motivates them. The check-out operators were already practising customer care even though they didn't call it that. The campaign just polished it up.

In general, employees at the stores reacted favourably to the notion of customer care, although the cash benefits undoubtedly increased its attractiveness. A number of bogus entries were received, especially for the first competition, but nevertheless there were ten or more serious nominations each month, and the winners appeared to be more satisfied with the accolade from their colleagues than the monetary gain. Employees stressed the intrinsic merits of the scheme, referring to it 'making you feel more involved in the store', or 'making customer care more visible', as well as to specific substantive improvements in service which had evolved from discussions at the customer care committees. Initial assessment of the schemes clearly indicated their potential.

The whole climate of employee relations in food retailing is explicitly and physically market-oriented in that employees are in direct contact with customers on a day-to-day basis, and are consequently aware of the immediate fortunes of their establishment. Thus, competitions such as employee of the month and customer care committees appear appropriate in these circumstances whereas they may be difficult to organize and could look out of place in a manufacturing company.

Conclusions

The key points to emerge from chapter 5 are:

- involvement in problem-solving exercises provides employees with a chance to contribute directly to the achievement of departmental and organizational goals.
- since suggestion schemes offer monetary rewards to individual employees in recognition of their ideas, they acknowledge the instrumental orientation which many people have towards their work.
- quality circles need to be managed with great care and sensitivity in order to ensure that employees wish to join and remain in membership, putting forward ideas which are relevant to the organization.
- both TQM and customer care programmes represent a more integrated approach to EI, and unlike most of the techniques dealt with in this book, they are compulsory rather than voluntary, a part of every individual's job as opposed to a 'grafted-on' element.
- management need to be aware of the potential contradictions between the 'hard' and 'soft' variants of TQM and customer care; whereas the latter conceives of employees as resourceful humans, the former expects them to have limited discretion and follow standard rules and procedures.
- given that the operation of each of these techniques has implications for trade unions as representatives of employee viewpoints, senior managers need to be fully aware in advance of their impact on existing procedures.

The purpose of this chapter has been to review a number of mechanisms by which employees are encouraged to contribute to improving departmental or corporate performance. Some of these – such as quality circles and suggestion schemes – are voluntary, and rely upon the willingness of employees to offer their ideas for improvements at work. Perhaps because of this, neither of these schemes entice more than a small proportion of employees to become involved. In contrast, TQM and customer care initiatives *require* the involvement of employees, as part of their existing jobs, in attempts to improve performance. As such, these systems go rather further than EI alone, and are directed at increasing the effectiveness of management as a whole. In their 'soft' variants, however, EI is a necessary component of both of these approaches, and each has implications for traditional patterns of managing people at work, as well as for supervisory styles. So too can the subject of the next chapter – job redesign – and it is to this we now turn.

6 Job Redesign

Introduction

Much of the discussion in the previous chapter revolved around notions of quality, responsiveness to customers, and the contribution of employees to competitive advantage. In particular, we focused on ways in which staff could offer their ideas – via suggestion schemes, quality circles, TQW, and customer care schemes – in attempts to improve departmental and organizational performance. These themes also underlie most of this chapter, which is concerned with a variety of forms of job redesign. Some of these are rather older in origin, for example based upon the research of Herzberg on job enlargement and enrichment, or Walker and Guest on job rotation. Conversely, others – such as teamworking and attempts to reduce demarcation – have become more widespread since the mid-1980s as employers have sought to gain both greater flexibility and the commitment of employees to organizational goals. As we shall see in the chapter, many of the better-known experiments in job redesign have taken place in the USA or Sweden, although there are a growing number of publicized examples from the UK.

The remainder of the chapter is organized as follows. First, there is a discussion of the rationale for job redesign which illustrates the historical development of ideas in this area and the shift in employer motivation for increasing EI through such schemes; in effect, this charts the move from job redesign as a device for reducing alienation at work, through one which aims to improve employee commitment, and more recently to initiatives which have as their primary aim the goal of competitive advantage. Following this section, the material is structured along the lines of the classification developed by Kelly (1982) of (a) flowline reorganization, (b) vertical role integration, and

(c) flexible workgroups. This is seen as more appropriate than the conventional distinctions between job enlargement, job enrichment, and autonomous workgroups because it is less replete with value judgements about the efficacy for all concerned of these attempts to redesign jobs. It also avoids some of the shortcomings connected with the socio-technical school of job design, in which it is (naively) assumed that both employers and employees automatically and necessarily gain from new methods of working.

While adopting Kelly's threefold categorization, here we will utilize a slightly different terminology which offers a more accurate description of these variants of job redesign. Thus, *horizontal job redesign* will be used instead of flowline reorganization because it conveys the central principle that tasks are extended at the same skill level, and *teamworking* will be used rather than flexible work groups so as to avoid problems of being drawn into the wider debate which has surrounded this and other aspects of flexibility in recent years. *Vertical role integration* will be retained because this seems accurate enough. This approach also allows for a more systematic treatment of differences in job redesign which avoids the temptation to dismiss all schemes as yet more sophisticated attempts by employers to intensify work and achieve an even greater subjugation of workers. Job redesign does have its problems however, and the penultimate section of the chapter examines these, in particular the implications for supervisors/middle managers and workplace trade union organization. Finally, we conclude with a case study on teamworking in the chemical industry.

The Rationale: From Alienation to Competitive Advantage

There appear to be three broad sets of reasons why employers might be attracted to the principle of job redesign, although it should be recalled – as in previous chapters – that each of these may operate at the same time in the same organization.

1 *as a counter to alienation at work*. This was particularly apparent in much of the earlier literature on the subject, including the classic contributions of Walker and Guest (1952) and Blauner (1964), in which 'new' methods of working were seen as an antidote to the repetition, boredom and loss of autonomy which characterized many mass production jobs in industry; in a sense, therefore, job redesign

was viewed favourably as a reversal of Taylorism. At the same time, it is suggested that, as lower levels of unemployment present job seekers with more choice in employment, employers need to find more attractive ways in which to package work. This has clear implications for jobs which demand little of employees' intelligence and initiative. Daniel and McIntosh (1972, p. 3) argue for a restructuring of work to inject some interest, meaning and reward into tasks, because employees regard their work and employers with hostility and resignation, as a chore to be endured. In a similar vein, Kochan, Katz and McKersie (1986, p. 151) note that the job redesign programme in the USA in the late 1960s grew in response to increased absenteeism and increases in shop floor problems (e.g. grievance rates). More recent analyses (e.g. Kelly, 1982) have questioned the extent to which these initiatives were driven primarily by 'personnel-type' motives, and were directed at satisfying employee and employer needs simultaneously, but they did form at least one part of the rationale.

2 *as an attempt to increase employee commitment*. This factor has already been mentioned in previous chapters in relation to other forms of EI, and in particular via the use of problem-solving techniques. With regard to job redesign, Walton's notions of 'control' and 'commitment' strategies are especially relevant, because he specifically refers to two plants within the same chemical company which have different patterns of working. About the latter, he writes:

> (This) divides its employees into self-supervising 10- to 15-person work teams that are collectively responsible for a set of related tasks. Each team member has the training to perform many or all of the tasks for which the team is accountable. The teams have also been thoroughly briefed on such issues as market share, product costs, and their implications for the business. (1985, p. 77)

At the centre of this 'commitment' strategy is 'a belief that eliciting employee commitment will lead to enhanced performance. The evidence shows this belief to be well grounded' (p. 80). Some of the work undertaken by The Work Research Unit in the UK also operates on the assumption that helping to progress 'people-strategies' from 'control' to 'commitment' will improve the effectiveness of organizations in a highly competitive operating environment (see Jones, 1990 for example). Furthermore, an opinion survey undertaken by MORI for the Industrial Society in 1989 suggested that the existence of teamworking was associated with higher levels of job satisfaction and employee commitment to organizational success (Webb, 1989, p. 33). At the same time, however, we also need to remain alert to the fact that it may be difficult for employers to sustain high levels of commitment over long periods of time, especially if economic conditions place increasing pressure on employers to reduce employment levels or unit labour costs. Moreover, Guest (1991, p. 155) has also queried the simplistic equation between EI and commitment.

3 *as a contribution to competitive advantage*. This has been a more prominent feature of recent publications, and it is most explicit in Tom Peters' thesis of *Thriving on Chaos*. In this, he argues, *inter alia*, that 'the chief reason for (US) failure in world-class competition is a failure to tap our workforce's potential' (1987, p. 286). For him, the self-managing team offers a valuable corrective; he asserts that 'wholesale worker involvement must become a national priority if we are to create the competitive strengths necessary just to maintain, let alone improve, our national economic well-being. The self-managing team should become the basic organizational building block' (p. 297). A similar line, albeit delivered in much less eulogistic terms, is also apparent from Dankbaar's analysis of the world car industry. He suggests that the 'new competition' on the world market requires 'the ability to design and change products quickly, to adapt production methods, and to search for new markets constantly. Such capabilities can only be realised if the flexibility of computer technology is combined with the creativity and adaptability of skilled workers' (1988, p. 31). In short, after years of assuming that competitive advantage could be secured only by further subdivisions of labour, senior managers are now being confronted with the argument that jobs need to be expanded and teams need to be created, in order to satisfy customer demand and make the best use of employees' contributions. As we shall see below, there is some debate as to whether or not this actually benefits employees.

Horizontal Job Redesign

Horizontal job redesign relates to the number and variety of operations which an individual performs at the same skill level in the organization, and as such it represents the least extensive form of EI to be dealt with in this chapter. In practice, it can be as little as doubling the number of fairly simple operations which are undertaken by an employee or allowing groups of workers to rotate between different tasks on some prearranged basis. It is built around the concepts of increased variety in working patterns or a lengthening of the work cycle so as to counteract the monotony of repetitive short timescale tasks. It is hypothesized that horizontal job redesign reduces feelings of alienation and increases the degree to which employees identify with the overall product.

Some of the earliest examples of this form of job redesign were seen as an antidote to the worst excesses of Taylorism. For example, on the basis of their studies on assembly line work, Walker and Guest (1952, p. 148) put forward job rotation as a technique to remove the most undesirable features of mass production – such as repetitiveness, minute subdivision of labour, surface mental attention, and lack of choice – by extending the range and variety of tasks which an individual employee undertakes in any one day. In factory work, horizontal job redesign usually means adding different tasks to the existing job or attempts to create 'whole' jobs, the completion of all operations within a work area. At Foodpack, a company studied by the author in the late 1980s, women employees on the packing lines practised their own form of job rotation so as to alleviate the boredom associated with individual tasks; during any one working day, small teams of eight to ten employees would take it in turns to load the packing line, check for quality and weight, operate the labelling machine, pack cartons into boxes, and act as a 'floater' to help out as appropriate on the line. All the women who were interviewed felt that this made work more tolerable, although it hardly constituted any dramatic increase in operator control.

In an office environment, the division of labour between different processes (for example, filing, sorting mail, typing) has increasingly been replaced by divisions between groups of customers such that each employee undertakes all the tasks for a particular client group as required. This form of horizontal job redesign has become commonplace in much of the financial services sector and in many data processing operations. Again, the rationale behind these schemes is a desire to enhance the quality of customer service, and also an attempt to improve the attractiveness of jobs to employees (both current staff and potential recruits). The key words associated with this type of horizontal job redesign are variety and task identity.

Many of the most widely-quoted examples of this form of EI have been in the motor vehicle industry, starting in particular with the attempts by Volvo in the 1970s to move away from mass production techniques. Althogh it was hailed as a radical departure from systems which operated at the time, more recent assessments have been much more cautious, and in retrospect it appears that much of the first wave of changes at Kalmar (the plant in question) were little more than simple job rotation techniques, albeit organized around the concept of cell – as opposed to assembly line – production. As S. Hill (1981, p. 105) notes, teams of 15–20 people worked together in small workshops, and were assigned a wide range of tasks covering the whole operation. Team members arranged the working methods between themselves in consultation with management specialists. So far, so good. However, Hill goes on to argue that 'the content of individual tasks differs little from other assembly operations, and workers merely perform a greater variety of simple tasks than before.' In a more recent analysis of subsequent changes in the European car industry, Pontusson illustrates that these early changes at Kalmar focused around job rotation within work teams, and there was little evidence of any job enrichment or employee influence over management decisions on how to develop the new system. Even indirect tasks, such as quality control, were assigned to team members with longer periods of service or special qualifications (1990, p. 322). In contrast, the second and third waves of job redesign (in the early and late 1980s) have been more specifically concerned with job enrichment, via teamworking, and there has been evidence of increased employee influence over at least some of the design decisions. Unlike the schemes which are being developed elsewhere in the early 1990s, the reduction of labour turnover and absenteeism remains an important feature of job redesign at Volvo.

Given their limited nature, it is hardly surprising that many experiments in horizontal job redesign have attracted considerable criticism over the years. Herzberg is particularly scathing about these forms of EI; he provides a number of examples to support his contention that some job enlargement programmes merely 'enlarge the meaninglessness of the job' (1972, p. 118). Whilst the two examples quoted here are probably amongst the most extreme, others could be produced which illustrate that job rotation may not be much more challenging:

> Adding another meaningless task to the existing one, usually some routine clerical activity. The arithmetic here is adding zero to zero.

> Rotating the assignments of a number of jobs that need to be enriched. This means washing dishes for a while then washing silverware. The arithmetic is substituting one zero for another zero. (Herzberg, 1972, p. 118)

While extending jobs horizontally may cause employees to feel that they have greater variety in their jobs, and reduce the monotony associated with basic tasks, it is unlikely that this will be sustained over longer periods of time. Indeed, it may even be counterproductive, in that employees find they have to pay greater attention to the detail of several boring jobs rather than just one; rather than easing the burden of working life, this may serve to increase the stress associated with it. It also means that employees have to break with established customs and may also be separated from friends at work. Connected with this is the fact that increased EI is normally introduced after the major decisions about technological and organizational systems have been made solely by managers. It has been rare for employees (or their representatives) to be involved at earlier stages in decisions about new designs and layouts.

Many grand claims have been made by job redesign enthusiasts about the success of this form of EI. Aside from the fact that evaluations are often made by consultants or senior managers, as opposed to independent observers, there are also doubts about the contribution which job redesign has actually made to improvements in quality or productivity. Based upon an extensive survey of the literature, plus his own study of flowline reorganization in manufacturing industry in Britain, Kelly (1982, p. 110) argues that a 'substantial part of the total productivity increase can be attributed to the operation of . . . pay rises and incentives, and work-related improvements . . . 'Intrinsic motivation' at best played a minor role in the genesis of productivity improvements.' This demonstrates that there are several problems with the job redesign = improved performance equation. First, it is difficult to disentangle the influence of one variable from among the many which operate within the working environment, and this is especially problematic in that job redesign tends to be introduced as part of a package of changes which also include increases in pay and substantial improvements in technology. Either of these, it is argued, may have a much more potent influence than increased opportunities for staff to rotate between jobs. Second, the equation is also blind to the influence of wider economic and political developments which may again have a more significant influence over productivity; performance improvements over the course of the 1980s probably owe a considerable amount to changes in employee and employer attitudes brought about by high levels of unemployment and a more compliant trade union movement. Third, and more generally with all forms of change in employee relations, there is a benchmarking problem; that is, choosing the base points from which to start and conclude assessments of the degree of change.

A somewhat different explanation of enhancements in performance has been proposed by Parke and Tausky (1975, p. 18) on the basis of their reassessment of horizontal job redesign at AT&T in the USA. Rather than viewing quality improvements as the product of enriched jobs (arguably a positive factor), they suggest on the contrary that these were due to fears that increased visibility and accountability allowed for management to use negative sanctions against employees. They quote two cases: (1) 'mistakes became directly traceable to a specific individual, and management gained the ability to pinpoint performances above or below standard'; and (2) 'responsibility for delay (in passing customers' orders) could be fixed to specific individuals.' In either case, they argue, employees can hardly ignore such accountability unless promotion, merit increases, and job security are of little concern to them.

Vertical Role Integration

There appear to be two different forms of vertical role integration. The first refers to increased employee responsibility for supervisory decisions which was the principal focus of Herzberg's research in the USA. This has been defined by Lawler as 'the degree to which the job holder controls the planning and execution of his/her job and participates in the setting of organization policies' (quoted in Buchanan, 1979, p. 35). It could encompass formal schemes to enhance the involvement of employees in managerial decisions at local level, or it may be a product of informal EI within the workplace. The second variant, to which we return later in the section, is upgrading jobs so that semi-skilled manual workers undertake simple maintenance or diagnostic work in addition to their existing duties, or office staff perform more skilled tasks (such as ordering new stock for example) which does not involve elements of supervisory work.

The former owes much to the work of Herzberg back in the 1950s and 1960s. He identified seven principles of 'vertical job loading' which were applied successfully to a group of staff in a large American organization. These are (1972, p. 119):

- removing some controls while retaining accountability.
- increasing the accountability of individuals for their own work.
- giving a person a complete natural unit of work (module, division, area).
- granting additional authority to an employee in his activity.
- making periodic reports directly available to the worker rather than the supervisor.
- introducing new and more difficult tasks not previously handled.
- assigning individuals specific or specialized tasks, enabling them to become experts.

In Britain, Herzberg's ideas were applied at various locations and with a variety of different groups of employees within ICI by two consultants, Paul and Robertson (1972, pp. 247–63). The groups whose jobs were vertically loaded included design engineers, factory supervisors, sales representatives, and laboratory technicians. A similar project was devised for fitters and process operators, but this was never implemented according to the authors. In each case, control and experimental groups were used, and individuals were questioned about job satisfaction six months to a year after the experiment started. The types of changes introduced included increased opportunites for planning work, writing final accredited reports, implementing training programmes for more junior staff, greater discretion for following up queries, selection of new recruits, greater authority to discipline staff, and greater control over section budgets. The general conclusion to the study was highly positive. For example, for the supervisors, it was felt that – amongst other things – selection had improved, training was handled sucessfully, and disciplinary matters were well dealt with (p. 258). Job satisfaction also appeared to have increased for most of the groups, especially the design engineers.

Nevertheless, there are problems with this study, partly due to the Herzberg methodology and concerns that the questions asked were almost bound to generate distinctions between hygiene factors and motivators in responses by these groups. Equally, the fact that the study was not completed with manual workers, as well as the type of changes which were introduced, also cast doubts on the applicability of vertical job loading to *all* kinds of employee. Finally, in the British cases, many of the evaluations about change were made by managers (Buchanan, 1979, p. 58) rather than by independent assessment. Paul et al. (1972, pp. 262–3) do raise a number of questions about the implications of the findings, and some of these (for example, whether job enrichment for subordinates makes supervision (and supervisors?) superfluous, or whether it releases supervisors to engage in higher order responsibilities) will be addressed later in the chapter. Others, such as whether job enrichment is welcomed by all staff, is dealt with in a less than satisfactory manner. It is argued (p. 261) that

> So long as the changes are presented as opportunities rather than demands, there is no need to fear an adverse reaction. If someone prefers things the way they are, he merely keeps them the way they are, by continuing to refer matters to his supervisor.

This seems a little naive, given that the pressure for involvement may be intense and it may prove difficult to retain existing patterns of work if the culture of the organization is shifting. As Dawson and Webb (1989, p. 236) note, employees are not merely encouraged but *expected* to identify problems, intervene in production and suggest changes. 'The widening of responsibility creates extra stress and makes the experience of work more precarious.'

The second way in which vertical role integration can take place is via the addition of extra skilled tasks to the employee's existing job. The best known examples of this are where semi-skilled assembly line workers in manufacturing plants are expected to take over responsibility for minor maintenance and diagnostic tasks. The 1988 ACAS survey of nearly 600 companies indicated that one-quarter of the sample reported increases in vertical flexibility over a three-year period, although it should be noted that a large proportion suggested there had been little change over this time (1988, p. 15). Flexibility was most extensive in the electrical engineering, metal goods and vehicle manufacturing industries, and least extensive in banking, insurance and finance (p. 16). There have been case study reports of assembly line workers in the car industry undertaking maintenance tasks traditionally done by skilled employees in order to keep production going – for example at Nissan and at parts of what was British Leyland. Similarly, Cavestro (1989, p. 26) records the way in which process operators in cement factories learn to *diagnose* potential problems and *anticipate* random changes or prevent breakdowns by making use of their tacit skills – that is, those which are intuitive, unwritten and sometimes sub-conscious – to maintain output by modifying the process accordingly. He notes that 'they override the automatic computer control system and supervise variations in the process manually; in automated systems, the need for human intervention becomes virtually permanent.' We return to the studies of chemical plants in the next section.

But there are limits to this vertical flexibility, and it is likely that the removal of demarcation lines between craft and production workers is rather less extensive than some commentators appear to imply. Both MacInnes (1987) and Pollert (1988) are sceptical about the degree to which there has been *real* change across industry, and there are suggestions that the flexibility phenonemon has been 'talked up' in order to bolster political claims about the popularity of new working practices. Many of the deals which have paved the way for greater vertical functional flexibility have been 'enabling' agreements designed to facilitate the achievement of change at local level. In such cases, it is harder to ascertain the degree to which semi-skilled employees have become more flexible in reality, as local union organizations may delay the introduction of this in the workplace. Equally, custom and practice serves to limit the spread of vertical role integration on the shop floor or in the office. Moreover, lack of appropriate skills training for production line employees can also prevent the implementation of new methods of working, a problem which is exacerbated when the economy is less buoyant.

Teamworking

Teamworking represents the third and most extensive form of job redesign which is considered in this chapter. It combines both horizontal and vertical additions to existing jobs such that individual employees not only move between different tasks on a particular operation but also take over some or all the responsibilities for managing the team as well. As noted in the introduction to the chapter, the tag 'autonomous' has typically been dropped from the concept of this kind of group, and teamworking provides a more accurate description of their activity. In 'flexible' work groups, as Kelly terms them, 'work is assigned to the group rather than to particular individuals or roles' (1982, p. 119). Buchanan prefers the term 'high performance work design', but the description of activity is much the same: 'a work group is allocated an overall task and given discretion over how the work is to be done. The groups are "self-regulating" and work without direct supervision' (1987, p. 40). Grayson uses the terminology of 'self-regulating work group'; he defines this as:

> a democratic form of work organization which ascribes to the group of workers responsibility for the regulation, organization and control of their jobs, and the conditions immediately surrounding them. It involves the establishment of specific group responsibilities and boundaries of autonomy to undertake defined tasks in a way to be decided within the group . . . Within (these) boundaries, the group is free to make decisions about its day-to-day work. (1990, p. 1)

Ignoring the fact that Grayson tends to underestimate the constraints on these kinds of group, especially with regard to autonomy, the key features of teams – co-operation, task variety, responsibility for a complete operation, and diagnosis – are central to all three definitions.

Examples of teamworking can be found in a number of different industries and countries, but analyses of those in chemicals and vehicle production are predominant. One of the first examples used by Walton to illustrate the nature of a 'commitment' strategy is from chemicals, in which he notes that 'jobs are designed to be broader than before, to combine planning and implementation, and to include efforts to upgrade operations, not just maintain them . . . Teams, not individuals, are often the organisational units accountable for performance' (1985, p. 79). Research by Buchanan and myself has examined the nature of teamworking in different plants in the chemical industry. Buchanan (1986, pp. 71–2) reports on the operation of a new pigments factory at Ciba Geigy in Scotland, on which plant operators were not supervised and rotated jobs on a daily basis. All the operators had been trained for at least one year prior to working on the plant, and they were given responsibility and discretion for how the plant should operate to meet production targets. They had to understand the process, the product and the equipment, and their experience, judgement and initivative were critical to ensure that the plant maintained its output. In addition, they needed to use their tacit skills to override computer messages as appropriate; to keep production going if they 'knew' nothing was wrong, or to close down operations if they recognized a serious fault.

My own studies in the chemical industry paint a similar picture; at Ichem for example (1990, pp. 107–8), process operators on the more automated plants typically worked as teams undertaking a whole range of tasks from the most technologically advanced through to the heaviest and most mundane. Again, as with Buchanan's study, operators underwent long training periods, often achieved externally recognized qualifications, and operated without much direct supervision; indeed, the supervisor operated more as a facilitator for the teams, and a technical officer was also available to assist with more difficult problems. All the operators were qualified to do every task on the plants, and they rotated between manual operations (checking the plant, bagging products, mending minor leaks) through to work in the control room, where they had responsibility for overseeing the process in line with production requirements. The process operators seemed to value the opportunity to undertake a wide range of jobs, especially the 'simple' tasks because this 'makes a nice change'. Increasingly, they are expected by management to take responsibility for the production of a particular batch or process, and they have been well rewarded financially for so doing. At another plant which is renowned for being at the forefront of teamworking in the chemical industry, there is even greater flexibility between process operators and craft workers, and indeed the two jobs have now been merged into a common enhanced grade. Maintenance and repair work, which was previously centralized for the site as a whole, has now become a part of each team's tasks, and craft workers have been assigned to each plant and shift. Again, a key feature of the change process has been a massive investment in new plant and equipment which is bolstered by a high commitment to training. Ultimately, all process workers will gain the capability to undertake any job across the plant, but there is still a tendency for employees to rely upon their specialist area of expertise, especially amongst the ex-craft workers and at times when the speedy resolution of a problem is seen as crucial to maintain prduction. The 'old' role of supervisor has now been removed and instead operations are co-ordinated by a team leader who works in conjunction with plant managers who are themselves part of a much reduced hierarchy. Interviews conducted at both of these plants suggest that employees appear to be satisfied with the new arrangements and are particularly keen about the variety which is now contained within their jobs.

Teamworking is not just restricted to the chemical industry, of course, although a whole range of factors (technological, product and labour market) make it especially appropriate for this sector. Recent studies have shown how teamworking has been developed in computer manufacture and food processing. At the former (Digital Equipment VLSI, in Scotland), small groups (10–12) were set up with full 'front-to-back' responsibility for product assembly and test, fault finding and problem-solving, and some equipment maintenance. Management had to adapt a supportive style, and team leaders were present initially but were expected to withdraw once they had developed a greater sense of autonomy in the groups (Buchanan, 1987, pp. 40–43). A subsequent assessment of the scheme regarded it as successful because of improvements in quality, reductions in work-in-progress, and smaller batch sizes, and employees generally reported satisfaction with the new methods of working. The best features appeared to be greater job interest, variety, and freedom to make their own decisions, and there was overall support for the cell-based approach to work organization. Although attitudes to other colleagues and the company were generally positive, areas of dissatisfaction were also identified, particularly in relation to pay, a lack of adequate training, and management style (IRRR, No 475, 1990). Teamworking was also introduced into RHM Ingredients when a new site was opened in 1989, and most of the features are similar to those already discussed; again, it is interesting to note that team members are *expected* to exercise responsibility for planning and organization, including quality assurance and the co-ordination of maintenance work (IRRR, No 477, 1990).

The motor vehicles industry has also seen a number of attempts to bring in teamworking, especially in Sweden and the USA. In the case of the former, the second and third waves of development at Volvo have extended task-based EI beyond the simple job rotation (horizontal job redesign) experiments of the early 1970s. The second wave of the early 1980s comprised a number of features of both horizontal and vertical job redesign; among the former was job rotation between workers on the assembly lines, whereas the latter included a new mix of tasks – for example, allocating responsibilities for administrative work within the team, such as scheduling vacation times, hiring and training new workers, and rotating the position of team leader on a regular basis (Pontusson, 1990, pp. 322–3). A similar process of teamworking has been introduced at one of Volvo's truck assembly plants, and evaluations by employees four years after the system had been implemented yielded highly positive results; for example, 'jobs at LB (the plant) are considered to be more varied, to involve more responsibility and challenge, and to foster more helpful attitudes.' However, the survey evidence also found many employees still regarded the work as degrading and exhausting (much lower than at a sister plant though) and a large minority suffered from back pains (nearly 40 per cent) and felt there was a strong time pressure (20 per cent) connected with their work. Whilst the new truck plant was consistently seen as better than the others, one of the interviewees commented:

> It is good here if you have something to compare it with . . . It is definitely better than a line . . . but I do not feel any pride about what I do, the work is so monotonous and boring that anyone can do it. (Berggren, 1989, pp. 194–9)

In the USA, the teamwork concept has been introduced in a number of organizations, often as part of a QWL (Quality of Work Life) Programme and sometimes referred to as the 'new industrial relations'. As we shall see below, its implementation has been greeted with differing sets of reactions by different people; on the one hand, it is seen as the key to a more successful future, while on the other it is viewed with alarm as the latest management move to intensify and control labour – 'management by stress' as Parker and Slaughter (1988) term it. One of the first examples of a 'team-concept' plant, according to Kochan et al. (1986, p. 96) was at TRW Inc, a diversified manufacturing firm located in a small community in the mid-west of the USA. Most teams had between eight and fifteen members, and some operated as autonomous work groups, with a team manager – generally appointed from within the team – to oversee its work. The manager was expected to act as a facilitator, and many tasks which would traditionally be undertaken by management were given over (at least partly) to the team members – training or production scheduling, for example. Employees did not work solely on one job, but rotated as appropriate, often after they had acquired the skills to make this effective. Compared with other similar plants in the company, wage rates were low, although they were in the upper half of wage distribution in the local area; incidentally, this represents a somewhat different picture from the British examples from chemicals quoted earlier, where wages were well above average.

The team concept came to the US car industry in newly-opened non-union plants in the south during the mid-1970s, and it was negotiated into the large northern plants in the early 1980s. The stimulus for change was a combination of economic problems in the

American car industry and the growth in international competition, especially from the Japanese, which together led the key negotiators to reach agreements about introducing new methods of working as a way to 'save the industry'. The teamworking systems which were initiated look remarkably similar to those which have been discussed above. However, as Kochan et al. (1986, p. 160) note, compared with traditional methods of job design,

> The operating-team system entails a fundamental reorganization of shop floor labour relations because it integrates changes in work organization with increases in worker decision making. The operating team provides both a reduction in job classification and a broadening of (individual) jobs.

In addition, there is provision for semi-skilled employees to take on maintenance tasks, allocation of work, and inspection, as well as regular team meetings. By the spring of 1988, the team concept was in use or planned for 17 GM assembly plants, in six Chrysler plants, in addition to two Ford plants and all the wholly- or partly-owned Japanese factories (Parker and Slaughter, 1988, p. 4). As an example, Black and Ackers (1990, p. 3) analyse the operation of the 'joint process' at a GM components plant which has a cell-based manufacturing unit known as 'Team Syracuse'. All employees on the team are fully flexible, but in addition, members have responsibility for production start-up, shift scheduling, inspection, statistical process control, machine loading, and tool change. The team area has also been established as a separate accounting base so as to track the efficiency of the unit. Local union representatives were involved in the design of the system, which led one shop committee chair to note that for the first time, local hourly workers had managed to provide an input prior to the assignment of employees to the area (p. 5). Perceptions of work and involvement had changed due to the introduction of the team concept; some were pleased to have more control over their immediate work environment, whereas others felt that the new system did introduce extra stress by having to work faster to cover for absent colleagues and due to peer pressure (p. 11). Even the most stringent critics of teamworking in US car factories acknowledge that at NUMMI (one of the plants where the team concept has made most impact) there have been substantial gains in productivity (Parker and Slaughter, 1988, p. 10). Furthermore, this improvement was achieved at an old plant, with an existing workforce, and without any advanced technology or an overt confrontation with the union.

What are the implications of teamworking, however, for employees, supervisors, and workplace trade union organization? Although there are several reports which suggest that employees find the new methods of working more attractive than traditional techniques (especially in Sweden where teamworking has been introduced jointly with the unions), there are also indications that it produces a more stressful factory environment. Many of the independent studies agree that teamworking, especially on car assembly lines, does induce higher levels of stress among employees. For example, Berggren indicates that workers perceive greater time pressures in the most technologically advanced Volvo plants than in the others (1989, p. 197), and Black and Ackers report a similar finding from studies at GM in the USA (1990, p. 11). Others, and in particular Parker and Slaughter (1988, pp. 16–30), view the whole concept of teamworking as little more than a managerial technique to intensify work yet further, to 'stretch' the production system as far as it will go, and 'manage by stress' (MBS). They illustrate the principle of MBS with reference to an andon board, located over the assembly line, which has red, yellow and green lights. A red light indicates there is a problem and the line needs to be stopped, yellow indicates that an operator is falling behind and needs assistance, whilst a green means that production levels are acceptable and there is no problem. In the traditional US operation, they state, management wants nothing but green lights and would design the system accordingly. However, in the team concept plants (MBS, as they term it) green is not a desirable state because presumably the line could run even faster. Instead, management speeds up the line until the light is mostly on yellow, with the odd red light to pinpoint areas where further improvements can be made. Perhaps Parker and Slaughter's conspiratorial notions of management strategy go rather too far, but this account is a useful corrective to the view that job redesign represents a panacea whereby both managements and employees automatically gain substantial benefits. It also helps us to remember that management's primary interest in new production techniques is not – with the possible exception of some of the Swedish experiments – specifically aimed at increasing industrial democracy and worker participation (Wood, 1986, p. 442).

Vertical role integration and teamworking both have an impact on the traditional supervisory role, and all the studies point to potential problems for this group of staff. In theory, the more that subordinates take over responsibility for running operations (scheduling the line, controlling the process, prioritizing the paperwork) the more that supervisors are released to concentrate their energies on higher level activities; this should then reverberate all the way up the hierarchy. In practice, however, supervisors seem to have seen the situation in a rather different way. The introduction of teamworking is often associated with other organizational changes, especially those to reduce the number of levels in the management hierarchy, and there have been fears amongst supervisors that their jobs will be lost. Even if they do not actually lose their jobs, it has proved difficult for many supervisors to adapt their roles to that of facilitators, people who assist the team to complete their work and act as troubleshooters. Given the fact that most supervisors are promoted from the shop-floor or office, they understandably lack confidence in their abilities to cope with new expectations (see Daniel and McIntosh, 1972, p. 49; Marchington, 1982, Dawson and Webb, 1989, p. 236). Other supervisors are dubious about the advantages of greater operator control and teamworking in any event, viewing this – as part of a drive to develop a strategy of 'responsible autonomy' – as pandering to the workforce, as a misguided approach propagated by 'the long-haired idealists at corporate HQ' (Marchington et al., 1991, p. 112).

The impact of teamworking on workplace union organization is rather more difficult to determine, especially because many of the deals in the US car industry have been the subject of joint union-management agreements and those in Sweden were at least partially instigated by the union movement. On one level, given the number of unionized workplaces in which teamworking has been introduced alongside a desire to maintain the role of the union (at least in formal terms with the continuation of existing agreements), it could be argued that the two can co-exist quite satisfactorily. On the other hand, however, the longer-term implications of teamworking, with its unitary undertones, can spell problems for employee commitment to workplace union organization. This appeared to be happening at the Ichem plant studied by Marchington and Parker (1990, p. 224) as employees identified more with the production processes on which they worked and saw problems increasingly within the context of organizational goals. The situation in the US car industry which is summed up by Wood (1986, p. 439) in the following way, appears to have a wider relevance:

> The aim, at least from management's point of view, is to change the rules of the game, or to substitute one game for another. That is, one in which the union plays a less active role in defining the terrain of contest on the shop floor, the expectation being that it will be the inevitable contingencies of production, as well as the continual search for improvement, which define shop floor controversy.

In addition, teams may be encouraged to compete with one another, with the inevitable consequence that notions of plant-wide solidarity are not achieved or maintained.

Case Study: Involvement through Teamworking

This case study is concerned with the operation of teamworking at one plant of a large American-owned multinational, codenamed Qualchem. The company has outlets all round the world, and it sells high quality specialist chemicals for use in both the domestic and commercial markets. It is one of the leaders in an oligopolistic market, and the major change over the last decade has been the continuing challenge of Japanese companies and products. Indeed, one of the major influences on corporate strategy in recent years, as well as employment policy, has been the perceived threat of Japanese import penetration into the USA plus the more competitive markets in other countries.

Over 100,000 people are employed by Qualchem worldwide, of which nearly 8,000 work in the UK across a number of sites in different parts of the country. The bulk of these are employed at the head office and principal production site, including a sizeable research division and distribution department. Two other sites employ smaller numbers of staff, who are engaged on production of raw materials and products for use in the main factory; in all cases, products are sold in both British and European markets. The site which forms the basis of this case study is the smallest unit in the company in Britain, with just over 200 staff, but the policies which it implements are broadly in line with those adopted at other sites. If anything, however, it is slightly further down the teamworking road because of its size and the nature of the technology employed at the site.

The parent company, Qualchem – like many others in the

chemical industry – publishes a set of corporate principles which is distributed to all employees. The preface to this is written by the UK Chairman, and it states that the booklet 'is an expression of the way in which we intend to manage the company taking account of the external influences which are crucial to our business interests'. He continues by asking employees to 'help make these statements a living commitment, by developing the beliefs into plans for *continuous improvement*'. Qualchem's mission comprises five goals, of which two are particularly relevant for this case; (1) recognize that our people are our most important asset, and (2) adopt quality as a way of life. The 'people' policies and practices are fairly typical of this kind of progressive organization, and include commitments to the best health and safety standards, equity of treatment, effective channels of communication, a superior employment package, stability of employment, and high performance standards from staff. The 'quality' policies refer to visible and reinforced managerial commitment to quality, an emphasis on customers (both external and internal to the organization), quality as a measure of performance, and clarity of employee goals and objectives. The final point has a clear relevance for EI; it states that 'we will create an environment that encourage quality by ensuring that the contribution of all employees to the quality process is maximized by *training, team-building, leadership, and ensuring individuals are responsible for their own processes.*'

Teamworking is one part of a tripos in Qualchem's World Class Manufacturing Strategy, the other two being performance management and statistical process control (SPC). SPC is a key part of the quality improvement programme, and this aims to provide the teams with a mechanism for assessing the quality of production, as well as a methodology which will help them to overcome problems. Ultimately, all operators will be trained in the use and meaning of statistical techniques which are relevant to their part of the operation. Performance management is a system designed to seek and achieve continuous improvement in the key aspects of each individual's or team's work, and it operates according to 'reinforcements of good behaviour'. These reinforcements can be either tangible or social (e.g. visits organized for the team, a contribution to a local charity, a beer bust, a badge, a word of thanks from the plant manager). The crucial point is that they are meant to reinforce actions which management define as good for the business (section, department, plant). According to managers, this appears to have been well received in the US plants, but they are less sure about its general application in Britain – despite some evidence that it has gone down well with certain shop-floor teams – because of differing cultures and traditions. The third strand of World Class Manufacturing is the teamworking concept, and this is being extended across the whole company. This has developed well at the case study site, particularly with process operators on the chemical plants who are now covered by a single grade. As an example, the job profile for a chemical team member on one of the plants is as follows. It will be noted that it is written in a broad way in order to allow for subsequent changes:

Main Challenge of the Job

- supply of (chemical) solutions (to internal or external customers) of the right quality and quantity, at the right time and at the optimum cost commensurate with safe working practices.
- ongoing quality improvements.

Key Job Elements

- work planning and raw material ordering.
- solution preparation to formula.
- quality assessment.
- data recording analysis and decison making.
- problem solving.
- line stop/product release.
- process control and adjustment.
- simple preventative maintenance.
- training.

Contact with Others

- across team, department and division/external customers and suppliers.

Skills and Experience

- full working knowledge of plant products and processes and associated safety implications.
- ability to operate complex chemical processes and computer-based equipment
- knowledge of simple maintenance procedures.
- ability to use a range of mechanical and bulk handling equipment.
- ability to work independently or in a team environment.
- ability to adapt to change.
- ability to coach and train.
- appreciation of and active involvement in a TQC (total quality control) culture.

The move towards World Class Manufacturing has been bolstered by two further employee relations practices. First, the company aims to devote 5 per cent of each employee's time (on average each year) to training and development, and this includes not only technical skills training but also teambuilding exercises as well. An example of the former would be the provision of specific packages, often delivered in conjunction with local technical colleges, for different grades of staff – say multiskilling training for crafworkers, or simple maintenance skills for process operators. Another would be training in how to interpret controls on the plant, their meaning and significance, and their relevance for quality. An example of the latter would be outward bound courses designed to develop team spirit and decision making within groups, and to reduce barriers between different grades of staff. While these sorts of exercises have become more common for managers over the last decade, at Qualchem these have been extended to manual workers as well. The second element which underpins teamworking, and appears necessary for it to work effectively, is a revamped pay package which drastically reduces the number of grades on the shop floor. Under the new system, there are four principal grades; ancillary work/labourer, process operator, craftworker, team leader. Each grade has a 'start' and 'established' rate, although variations are possible due to shift allowances and other fringe benefits. Pay levels for a process operator on shifts are high, not only for the industry but also compared with average wages for many white collar and managerial staff in other sectors.

It should also be noted that employees are represented by a number of unions depending upon their job. The TGWU is recognized for all process operators and other unskilled of semi-skilled staff, and appropriate craft unions (AEU and EETPU) represent the skilled trades. In both cases, about 70 per cent of these groups are union members. MSF is recognized for white collar staff (clerical, technical, professional and administrative), and of those eligible to join about 70 per cent are members. All the unions combine through a Joint Negotiating Committee which meets at least twice per annum, drawing representatives from all sites in the UK.

Conclusions

In many respects, the more extensive forms of job redesign analysed in this chapter – and especially teamworking – represent some of the most interesting developments in EI. They provide the opportunity for employees to become directly and personally involved in a wider range of activities at work, as well as offering a greater width to the tasks typically undertaken. They also break down some of the barriers which have traditionally existed between shop floor employees and their supervisors to the extent that the former exercise limited influence over certain decisions at departmental level and below. Most important of all, perhaps, is the fact that this form of EI becomes part of an employee's day-to-day ordinary work activities, rather than being additional or voluntary (as in the case of quality circles) or at prescribed times of each month (as with team briefing, for example). Yet, at the same time, this centrality is also a source of potential tension, if employees feel that they are required or expected to become more involved in work and help to achieve corporate objectives. The stresses of teamworking may be greater than those associated with more traditional task allocation, and there are concerns that employees may not be able to cope with the pressures of being expected to exercise greater responsibility at work. Some commentators also perceive teamworking as a threat to trade union organization, something which has also been associated with certain forms of joint consultation in the past; this is the subject of the next chapter.

Before turning to this, however, it is worth reiterating the key points of chapter 6:

- experiments in job redesign can serve as a counter to alienation at work, as a stimulus to employee commitment, and as a contributor to competitive advantage.
- horizontal job redesign offers a relatively easy way in which to extend even the most simple of jobs, but it ought to include provision for employees to influence the manner in which tasks are allocated.
- vertical role integration can provide employees with a greater sense of responsibility at work, but individuals need systematic support from management in order to overcome any fears which they might have about widening their jobs.
- teamworking is the most extensive form of job redesign in that it can provide groups with greater control over their jobs, but it needs to be underpinned by extensive training in technical and interpersonal skills.
- the introduction of job redesign techniques (especially teamworking) needs to be carfefully managed given that it can lead to sizeable adjustments to the roles of existing job holders.
- if senior managers are serious about the importance of empowering individuals in the ways analysed in this chapter, the range of decisions over which employees have influence needs to be gradually extended to maintain their interest and commitment.

7 Joint Consultation

Introduction

For a number of years, there has been a continuing debate about the nature and extensiveness of joint consultation throughout British industry. During the last two decades, a variety of surveys have suggested that the number of organizations practising some form of consultation in their workplaces has waxed and waned depending upon various factors – such as management commitment, union organization and product market conditions. As we shall see below, the operation of joint consultative committees (JCCs) is necessarily intertwined with the provision (or non-provision as in the case of non-union firms) of other mechanisms for employee representation. More recently, its role in relation to other forms of direct participation has become more central to discussions, and in particular the degree to which JCCs are able to survive (and work effectively) in conjunction with team briefing, customer care committees or total quality management. For the future, given the likelihood of further developments in EI within EC-owned companies, joint consultation may well find a new lease of life. Probably more important than the debate about the extensiveness of JCCs, however, is the question of its nature, and the variety of forms which consultation can take in different organizations. Employers need to be clear about the objectives which are set for consultation – just as with any other aspect of management, of course – and the extent to which these are being achieved in practice. Indeed, a major part of this chapter will explore the different forms which consultation can take, and provide examples of JCCs in action.

Before doing this, however, we need to provide a background to the current situation via a short history of consultation and some information on the centrality of JCCs to human resource management within Britain. In part, this will focus on the reasons why practitioners have shown an interest in this form of employee involvement. Additionally, a framework will be provided which enables us to analyse variations in the nature of consultation, rather than seeking to argue that all JCCs are similar in form and intent. Finally, a case study is presented of an organization in the hotel and catering industry which operates JCCs at establishment level. This case has been chosen because it represents an environment in which JCCs are used not only to communicate information to staff but also as an alternative to union representation through other mechanisms. Thus, it provides a quite different example to much of the published work on consultation.

History and Development

Joint consultation has a long and somewhat chequered history in Britain, starting with so-called 'common interest' committees in a small number of organizations in the nineteenth century. This idea received a boost towards the end of the First World War through the proposals of the Whitley Committee of Inquiry, and there was a growth in the extensiveness of JCCs during the early part of the 1920s. Indeed, one of the best-known consultative structures of the present day (that at ICI) was first set up during this period, although at that time the system was not based on union channels. JCCs became less popular in the 1930s but increased in extensiveness again during the 1940s, via the institution of JPACs (Joint Production and Advisory Committees) and governmental support. By the end of the 1940s, it was estimated that 73 per cent of managers surveyed reckoned that their own organization had some form of formal consultation machinery (Brannen, 1983, p. 46). During the 1950s and 1960s, the conventional wisdom is that consultation went into decline again, largely due, it was argued, to the development of shop steward organization at workplace level. The proponent of this thesis, McCarthy (1966, pp. 33–4), suggested that shop stewards preferred negotiations to consultation, and would either boycott committees or change their character to make them indistinguishable from negotiating bodies. It was felt that consultation would only retain a primary place in workplace relations where union organization was weak or non-existent. A generation of scholars thereafter accepted that joint consultation was in a state of terminal decline, especially in well organized workplaces (see, for example Guest and Knight, 1979). For a more detailed treatment of this whole period, see Marchington (1989).

The 1970s and 1980s produced a quite different outcome however, and this has reawakened interest in joint consultation as a form of employee involvement. The survey by Brown, undertaken in 1978, showed that over 40 per cent of manufacturing establishments had JCCs, and he estimated that 60 per cent of these had been introduced over the course of the previous five years (1981, p. 76). Daniel and Millward's finding is similar although, given the broader nature of their sample, the absolute figures are somewhat lower; they found that 37 per cent had committees in 1980, 20 per cent of which had been established in the previous two years, and 40 per cent in the previous five (1983, pp. 129–33). Almost half of the JCCs were in workplaces in which there was no union representation, thus indicating the width of coverage, as well as the variety of purposes which may be served by consultation. Most commentators were in agreement that there had been an increase in the extent of formal consultation over the 1970s, although MacInnes dissents from this position, arguing instead that 'the high birth rate and apparent renaissance of consultation is paralleled by an equally high but less visible death rate' (1985, p. 106). Daniel and Millward's finding of an introduction to abandonment ratio of 9:1 between 1975 and 1980 seems to point to some expansion, even allowing for fairly severe lapses of memory (1983, p. 132).

The evidence from the 1984 Millward and Stevens survey indicated no change in the overall proportion of workplaces with a JCC over the period from 1980; it was 34 per cent in both cases (1986, p. 139). However, this does mask a decline in the extensiveness of formal consultation within the manufacturing sector from 36 per cent to 30 per cent of establishment over the four year period. The figures reported by Batstone (1984, p. 254) and Edwards (1987, p. 117) in their separate surveys are much higher than this, but that is largely explicable by the fact that they excluded small establishments, and JCCs are much less likely in smaller firms. A large proportion of these JCCs cover both manual and non-manual workers on the same committee, rather than one group alone, and a substantial minority have JCCs based on non-union channels (Millward and Stevens, 1986; pp. 143–5); that is, unions did not nominate any of the representatives for these committees, although this does not mean that these individuals are not union members. The decline in the number of workplaces with JCCs is due, the authors argue, to structural change (by sector and size of workplace) rather than any tendency for establishments with committees to abandon them (1986, p. 138), a finding reinforced by the panel interviews which they conducted as part of the study. Marginson et al. support this view, and provide further evidence about the extent of multi-establishment JCCs, especially in large organizations which operate in a single sector. Nonetheless, as we shall demonstrate later, they also suggest that 'managerial choice may be a particularly important factor in the use of higher level consultative arrangements' (1988, pp. 114–15).

Two more recent surveys also indicate that joint consultative committees remain an important aspect of EI in Britian. The 1989 CBI study indicates that consultation is still well-established, with over 40 per cent of respondents stating that their organization operated some form of consultative committee, and that this forum – especially those at workplace level – had some influence on decision making (1990, pp. 27–8). As with all the other studies on consultation, JCCs were much more likely in large establishments and organizations, a finding which seems highly logical for any representative structure. The other feature which is relevant for our discussion below is the fact that nearly half the sample reckoned that nominations and elections for the JCCs were not based on union channels; it should be recalled, however, that this does not mean these committees were non-union, and previous studies would suggest that many of the participants were indeed union members themselves. The 1990 ACAS study showed that 40 per cent of the establishments surveyed by its advisory staff used JCCs. Formal consultation was found to be more widespread in manufacturing than services, and once again it was more extensive in larger workplaces (1991, p. 10). Interestingly, the JCCs in foreign-owned companies engaged in discussions covering a wider range of issues than did their UK counterparts (p. 19).

Why should employers wish to introduce or continue with consultative arrangements? Several reasons have been put forward. First, it has been argued that consultation can enhance efficiency by increasing the stock of ideas which are available within the organization because of the wider exposure of an issue or problem. One of the 20 action points suggested by the CBI (1990, p. 72) is to 'consult before decisions are made' on the grounds that this can utilize employee knowledge and allow for the expression of opinions about ideas. Clearly, the likelihood of this taking place depends upon a host of factors, such as the preparedness of managers to encourage debate prior to decisions being taken, the willingness and ability of JCC representatives to contribute to discussions, and the degree to which the business environment allows for meaningful involvement by employees. On the other hand, it is suggested that consultation may actually increase inefficiency by lengthening the time frame for decision making, and causing product market opportunities to be lost; whilst this view may have some merit, it also provides managers with a rationale for legitimizing the non-involvement of their staff, by devising situations when involvement would not be beneficial or relevant to either the employees or the organization – as with the oft-cited case of the hospital consultant asking the porter for his or her views about how to carry out an operation!

Secondly, it has been suggested that consultation may lead to a reduction in industrial action in organizations because there is an opportunity for employees (or their representatives) to express opinions prior to decision making. By providing an avenue for discussion and for the resolution of joint problems, it is likely that the JCC can serve a useful function in helping to smooth over difficulties that may arise in the organization, especially at a time of change. Even though the process of decision making may take longer, it is argued that the consequences of change are less problematic because many of the problems have been aired or resolved at an earlier date. Indeed, in my own research at ICI over the years, this has been a commonly repeated theme. As one manager commented (and this was typical of many more):

> It is particularly useful as a safety valve so that issues come through joint consultation rather than other avenues. If we did not have the system, we would run into lots of industrial relations problems. There would be misunderstandings and that would lead to confusion and resentment.

Irrespective of whether or not this has a basis in fact, it appeared to be an article of faith in the organization, and one which was felt to have contributed to the low levels of industrial action in such a large company.

Thirdly, there is the view that consultation may lead to an increase in employee satisfaction, in the sense that involved staff will feel more committed to the organization and their own jobs. Even if this holds true for participation in general, there must be doubts about its relationship with JCCs, except perhaps for those representatives who actually sit on the committee. Research evidence (see for example, Marchington and Armstrong, 1981; MacInnes, 1985) indicates that the majority of employees have little knowledge of nor interest in the activities of a JCC, and that many do not even know the name their representative or the regularity of meetings. On the other hand, individual employees may be satisfied with the fact that their representative has a place on the JCC, and allow that person to communicate group opinions or respond to initiatives from management. Removal of the JCC might alternatively create dissatisfaction.

Finally, there are some indications that developments in the EC are beginning to have an effect on management organizations in the UK, bearing in mind the publications by the CBI, and more recently the updating of the joint IPA/IPM Code on *Employee Involvement and Participation in the United Kingdom*. In this document, there are a number of specific points relating to consulation (1990, pp. 9–10). These are:

- each organization should establish regular procedures for consulting employees and/or their representatives on relevant issues, so that their views are known and are taken into account by management in making decisions which are likely to affect their interests.
- senior management cannot share their ultimate responsibility for major decisions affecting the organization's continuing viability. They should, however, consult employees and/or their representatives about the organization's future plans, particularly in so far as these may affect job prospects, work organization, and working conditions. Whenever possible, such consultation should allow sufficient time for employees likely to be affected by prospective changes to give their views and contribute their ideas before final decisions are taken.
- organizations should make clear on what matters they will endeavour to have regular consultation with employees and/or their representatives, and the procedures or structures for such consultation.

As we shall see below, the IPA/IPM view is broadly in line with the 'adjunct' variety of consultation practised by some organizations, one in which management aims to encourage participation by an intergrative problem-solving approach. Although the IPA still supports the idea of voluntary arrangements for the development of participation, it called in late 1990 for statutory backing for the Code because of the UK government's negative stance in relation to EC proposals. Similarly, the IPM also gave its support to statutory backing for the provision of information to all staff. Both these developments move us further towards the EC position on EI.

Components of Consultation

There have been a number of attempts to define precisely what is meant by the term 'joint consultation', and it is from these that we can isolate its principal components (for a review of these, see Marchington, 1989, pp. 382–6). Most definitions refer to improvements in the utilization of employee knowledge and experience, to a regular exchange of views, and to matters of common interest which are not subject to negotiation with trade unions. Rather than add to this list of definitions, it may be more appropriate to summarize the key components so that we will be in a better position to compare and contrast differing models of consultation in practice. The five major components are:

1 *objectives*: these may be clear from the constitution of the committee, assuming that this is published and available for inspection, or they may be hidden or implicit in the processes accompanying the JCC. Published objectives tend to refer to the benefits in terms of improved output, greater efficiency, and enhanced employee commitment to organizational decisions, all of which are employer objectives although incidentally employees may also gain from some of these. Some constitutions do stress the mutual benefits which may flow from the consultative processes, as part of the philosophy underlying the scheme. At the other extreme, there are also instances where consultation may be developed as part of a device to prevent union intervention and recognition, but it is hardly likely that such objectives will be comitted to paper.

2 *subject matter*: while most definitions agree that consultation is about issues of joint concern, the precise type of subject matter dealt with is likely to vary between organizations and committees. Some concern themselves with parochial matters of relatively minor importance, such as social and welfare activities, the quality of the canteen tea or reports on new personnel; these are the sorts of committees which are regularly quoted as examples of the marginalization of consultation or those which survive on a diet of anodyne trivia. Alternatively, some JCCs have as their agenda items issues

relating to production and order statistics, commercial matters, and business decisions. Again, the subject matter depends to some extent on the intentions and stances of the parties to consultation, as well as the nature of the business itself.

3 *processes*: the predominant direction in which information flows in a JCC can also vary from one committee to another, and it can be either upward, downward or both. The upward flow of information focuses on the contribution of employees to improving the quality of decision making, and the notion that staff represent a considerable source of ideas, of 'tacit skills', 'feel' and knowledge which otherwise would not be available to management. The downward flow of information predominates in JCCs which are 'educative' in intent, designed to persuade employees (or their representatives) of the merit and so-called logic inherent in management proposals. In this situation, managers are expected to generate commitment to their plans and policies, as well as to the organization, and training in leadership or chairing skills is seen as central to management development. For yet other JCCs, two-way communication is regarded as crucial, and both managers and employee representatives may use the committee as a forum for structuring the expectations of the other party, or for the exchange of views about a forthcoming issue (Marchington and Armstrong, 1981, pp. 13–14).

4 *powers*: the powers of a consultative committee may be stated explicitly in a constitution, or they may be left rather loose and ill-defined. If they are stated explicitly, there is usually some reference to what may not be discussed, and the forum to which such issues should be referred for resolution. Indeed, the clarification of this distinction between negotiation and consultation may be sought by both parties, and both may act as custodians of collective agreements within the company. If it is made explicit that JCCs do not involve joint decision making, this can provide unions (if they are recognized and play an active part within the consultative as well as the negotiating forum) with an opportunity to test out ideas prior to bargaining. Conversely, machinery with no explicit clarification of powers may produce a vagueness within constitutions which can produce and reproduce a greater inequality in power between management and employee representatives.

5 *parties*: the roles of people who actually sit on the JCC can also vary between committees. Employers may be led by line or personnel management, and by high or low status individuals; probably, one of the best indications that employers are not taking consultation

seriously is if the meeting are chaired by a personnel officer, who is the sole management representative on the committee. Conversely, the inclusion and regular attendance of the most appropriate senior line manager on the JCC does suggest that employers are committed to the principle of consultation, and that it is worth the time and effort to become involved. The composition of the employee side of the JCC is potentially more complex because it may consist of manual or white collar staff alone, a combination of the two, and even some relatively senior managers. Sometimes, manual and white collar workers are not prepared to attend the same meetings, and organizations have to run two parallel systems for consultation; as might be expected, this is more likely in situations where more than one trade union is recognized by the employer. Representation on the committees may be by union nomination, via existing representative channels through the shop steward network, or it may be via constituencies determined on the basis of departmental or occupational membership. Although such representatives may be union members themselves, this is not the reason for their election nor are they expected to promulgate a union stance on issues. In firms where the density of union membership is very low, the operation of the JCC may even help to reinforce the view that unionization has little to offer the staff.

Overall, therefore, it can be seen that joint consultation can take a variety of forms and serve a number of interests, depending upon the context in which it operates and the objectives which are sought from it. Clearly, if the JCC has been introduced specifically for the purpose of preventing the development of unionism, it is likely to be markedly different from the situation in which consultation is valued by both parties as an adjunct to the negotiating machinery, as a process preliminary to the bargaining arena. Having outlined the principal components of consultation, we can now move on to analyse four different ideal-typical models which cover the range of JCCs available.

Models of Consultation

An alternative to collective bargaining?

In the first variant, employers initiate and develop consultation in order to resist collective bargaining. This rests upon the assumption that a JCC has the potential of simultaneously allowing for the representation of employee views and the transmission of information from management to the workforce. That this approach has been successful in the past is documented by Clegg and Chester (1954, pp. 329–30) and Hawkins (1979, pp. 40–1), and it still remains a fear on the part of unions, especially in sectors where workplace organization is not well developed – such as parts of the financial services sector or retail and distribution. As we saw above, employee representation for a substantial minority of JCCs is not based upon union channels, but is organized according to departmental constituencies, even in cases where unions are recognized by the employer.

The stance adopted by the employer is essentially unitarist both in practice and philosophy, but it is of the sophisticated paternalist variety, whereby management feels it has a duty to persuade employees of the benefits of its policies. The organization is likely to devote considerable time and energy to the processes of consultation, the central objectives of the system being to promote industrial harmony and 'educate' employees about the business and its environment. Equally, since the JCC doubles up as a grievance procedure, there will also be provision for representatives to indicate areas of concern within the workplace; there may even be a regular agenda item which allows for the expression of these views. Dissent will be seen, in typically unitarist fashion, as an indicator of troublemakers or of inadequate communications skills on the part of management; in the case of the latter, further training is likely to be seen as the answer. The subject matter of the JCC tends to be a mixture of business-related information passed on by the chair of the meeting (who may be a line or a personnel manager) and items of more parochial significance – such as the nature of the car park, projected ideas for use of the social fund, and the quality of food in the canteen. Although these sorts of issue are often dismissed by opponents of consultation as trivial (and at one level, they are), they are also highly meaningful to individual members of staff. In many cases, these items are likely to generate rather more interest than those relating to business or commercial matters. Moreover, to assume that these issues are introduced on to the agenda purely in order to divert attention away from more strategic affairs misinterprets both the nature of management and the workforce in this kind of environment.

Because employees lack independent representation, and may be dubious about the benefits of trade unionism in any event, there is unlikely to be any overt challenge to managerial prerogatives. The desire for more information is either met, or refused on the basis of confidentiality, complexity or inappropriateness, a position which is likely to be accepted by the representatives. Having the opportunity to meet with senior managers and discuss issues of a common interest might even reinforce the belief that these individuals do have the employees' interests at heart. At the same time, however, experience of sitting on a JCC may also lead employee representatives to become more aware of the contradictions and limitations inherent in consultation, and cause them to question the basis on which the committees are established; indeed, it can also lead to demands for union recognition, or to an aggressive reassertion of management prerogatives if there is a challenge to the system (see MacInnes, 1985). But, perhaps more likely, is that the JCC will continue much as before, and expressions of interest and concern by management through the consultative arena will help to reinforce individualism and a commitment to corporate goals.

Marginal to collective bargaining?

This variant describes the situation in which consultation achieves little or nothing for the parties, is marginal to any activity in the workplace, and is in a process of stagnation leading perhaps to the ultimate demise of the system. It is the sort of consultation which is usually seen by critics as typical of JCCs in general, but as will be clear from this discussion it does not provide a total picture. Indeed, this form of JCC may be restricted to situations in which there is little trust between the parties, and management lack any real commitment to meaningful employee development. Whilst the JCC may have achieved quite significant gains in the past, now it is primarily of symoblic value to the parties, only retained because the decision to abolish the system would be interpreted as an act of unnecessary management aggression by employees and their representatives. Eventually, the consultative machinery might fall into disuse. As Clegg and Chester (1954, p. 346) note, 'the formal machinery of consultation may remain in existence for a time or even permanently, but the manager will conduct the meeting without interest.' In a similar vein, MacInnes (1985, p. 104) regards consultation as operating in a circular pattern, in which initial enthusiasm for the concept is sufficient to overcome the looseness of its definition. As time goes by, he suggests, consultation achieves less and less for the parties until one day it eventually peters out altogether, only to be resurrected by a new manager at some future date.

The subjects dealt with at this kind of JCC tend to be mostly 'soft' and parochial in nature, issues which appear on the agenda precisely because they have always been discussed at these meetings; issues such as social or welfare matters, or those concerned with highly localized problems like the discovery of foreign bodies in parts of a chemical plant. Occasionally, more business-oriented items do appear on the agenda, but usually only for the purpose of passing information to the representatives. Meetings will probably be chaired by a relatively junior manager, often from personnel, who lacks authority within the organization. This means that the meetings can be quite informal and friendly in character, but that the JCC system lacks any influence within the decision-making structures of the firm. A good deal of time is taken up with issues which have rearisen over the course of several meetings, and with any other business raised at the meeting itself. Given the chair's lack of status in the organization, it is rare for issues to be resolved at the JCC because they have to be referred elsewhere for further consideration. Membership of the JCC can be a mix of union-nominated and other employees, but what is apparent is the lack of cohesiveness of the representative body and its inability to force management to take action. It is also unlikely that this type of JCC will operate at more than one level within the organization, thus confirming the marginality of consultation yet further. Indeed, the symbolic importance of consultation means that it is a process which needs to be managed by employers in a sensitive and low-key manner if they are keen on maintaining this form of employee involvement. Its substantive importance, conversely, is minimal to the effectiveness of the organization, and this model of consultation is less likely in a company which is attempting to practise HRM.

Competing with collective bargaining?

Within this perspective, joint consultation is seen as being in direct competition with collective bargaining, although in this instance the objective of management is to upgrade the JCC such that negotiations become less meaningful or necessary. A number of authors, such as Terry (1983), argued that consultation underwent a renaissance in the early 1980s precisely because management saw value in making the consultative forum more relevant to employee relations. Rather than dealing with trivia at the JCC, it was suggested that quite the opposite has occurred in these types of meeting, and employers have been prepared to communicate (and maybe discuss) items which are of a more strategic as well as commercially sensitive nature in an open and constructive manner. The kinds of item which constitute the agenda in these 'new, upgraded', JCCs are investment plans, the development of new products, problems of productivity and competitiveness, amalgamation, takeover and rationalization. Occasionally, these items might have emerged during negotiations, but management prefer to deal with these within the realms of consultation given its underlying common interest philsosophy. Some of the Advisory Councils introduced by Japanese companies would probably fit within this category of consultation.

In this kind of situation, not only is shop steward organization and support important for the continuity of the JCC, it is absolutely crucial for its effectiveness. As Terry indicates (1983, p. 56),

> Part of the strategy is an intention to involve stewards . . . more closely in an understanding of the problems and issues confronting the company, and hence of the logic and inescapability of the conclusions and policies proposed by management . . . the logic of this strategy rests upon the maintenance of the representative structure of the workforce, and of its authority and legitimacy, rather than upon its destruction.

In other words, the purpose of consultation is to create a greater awareness amongst representatives of the commercial environment in which the organization is competing, in the anticipation that this will lead them to adopt a more moderate stance in discussions both at the JCC and elsewhere. As the personnel manager at one of the companies studied by Marchington and Parker put it (1990, p. 144), 'it's pushing negotiations down to consultation, and consultation down to communication. You only need do the last two if you get it right, because ultimately there's only one best way of running the business.' In relation to pay and other benefits, it is suggested by managers that negotiations will be conducted with a much clearer view of what the company can afford and the need to secure competitive advantage.

In addition to the steward network, it may be that other employees are also introduced on to the committee structure so that they can hear first hand the issues which are confronting the organization, and be 'educated' into an understanding of proposed solutions. Moreover, because the JCC is chaired by the most senior line manager who is appropriate for the level at which the meeting occurs, there is a greater likelihood that the workforce will accept the prognosis. Combined with this upgrading of consultation, there is often the development of other forms of EI, designed to convince employees of the reasons for managerial actions, and also perhaps apply a brake on steward activity. Each of these techniques is discussed elsewhere in this book, but it includes team briefing, quality initiatives, teamworking, employee reports, and participative payment systems.

There is certainly plenty of anecdotal evidence to support partly the notion of revitalized JCCs and the extension of EI into other areas over the past decade. However, even though the new JCCs may have more high level or strategic items on their agendas compared with a number of years ago, it is less certain whether or not management does anything more than report on such issues, or whether the powers of consultative committees have been extended in any way. For example, while it is true that business plans may be unveiled to representatives, these are not really open to change. Similarly, decisions about rationalization may be communicated to employee representatives after they have been taken, but these may still be contested in the negotiating arena. Although inexperienced stewards may be persuaded by the 'logic' of management explanations even if these do not offer the only solution, those with greater experience and stronger shop-floor organization are unlikely to be convinced merely by more effective selling skills of the JCC Chair. Instead, these representatives can seek to use the information gained at the JCC to help them present a case in the negotiating arena.

An adjunct to collective bargaining?

This final point brings us to the idea that consultation and collective bargaining may operate in tandem with each other, as complementary rather than competing processes in the regulation of workplace employee relations. Within this model, consultation and negotiation are kept strictly separate, although the representatives on the two committees are probably the same people. Collective bargaining is used for wages, working conditions, and aspects of a distributive nature, whereas the JCC focuses on issues of an integrative character –

typically of a high-level nature – and helps to lubricate employment relationships. If asked to choose between them, shop stewards would have no doubt which to go for: collective bargaining. But the two are not seen in competition, and both can provide benefits for employees and the organization for which they work, especially in the context of effective shop floor organization.

Indeed, strong workplace organization may be regarded as a pre-requisite for this model of consultation, given that stewards will be keen to occupy places on both the consultative and the negotiating committees, and will have the potential power to prevent any attempts to undermine the latter by upgrading the former. Stewards argue that by sitting on both bodies, their centrality to regulatory processes is protected, and not only do they receive information which is useful for bargaining but they can also use the JCC to convey their opinions to management, in effect to structure their opinions. Management too can use the forum in this way, and test out ideas within the confines of the consultative committee rather than exposing these to the stewards at a negotiating session. Unlike the previous two variants of consultation, this is not predicated on the assumption that union representatives lack the power to resist management preferences or actions, or moreover that this is management's principal intention. The whole ethos behind the JCC, as with the vast majority of interactions between the parties, is one of problem-solving and integration.

Assuming that management is committed to extending employee involvement within a climate of positive human resource management, and that it is appropriate for the organization to develop consultation, this model has much to offer in both processual and substantive terms. A prescription for increasing the likelihood of success in these circumstances would include many of the following:

- the committee should meet at regular, pre-arranged and adhered-to times.
- meetings should be held on a schedule which is appropriate for the business and allows for meaningful agenda items.
- when established, the Chair could rotate between management and employee representatives.
- meetings should be held at an appropriate time to allow proper discussion.
- management and employee representatives should cover a cross-section of the workforce.
- the agenda should be published in advance, and be the result of informal

discussions between the secretary to the committee and a senior employee representative.

- there should be an opportunity for employee representatives to hold a pre-meeting.
- sub-committees can prove effective in allowing for fuller discussion of items, particularly on a large JCC.
- minutes should be issued promptly, and individuals should be identified to progress specific items.
- any information which requires pre-reading should be circulated in advance, and it should be clear and concise.
- there should be a planned turnover of committee members.
- training in the interpretation of information (for example financial or production matters) and its presentation should be given to all members.
- there should be regular monitoring of JCC effectiveness by committee members, as well as independent assessments of success.

It should be reiterated that this prescription is only appropriate for those organizations which view consultation as an integral part of their EI arrangements, both of a direct and representative nature (via collective bargaining). The action points which are part of the Industrial Society's programme for employee involvement cover a similar sort of ground, though in less detail, and adopt a similar underlying philosophy about the need for management to be genuine in their motives (Webb, 1989, p. 73). Conversely, if the JCC is expected to assist with the achievement of other objectives – such as undermining trade unionism – or if management is happy with a JCC which survives on a diet of trivia and is maintained as a marginal or symbolic component of HRM, then the above list will be of little use, and others need to be substituted for them. At the same time, however, some of this list of action points can also be adapted for the first model which was outlined, especially if the employer is operating in an environment where union membership has typically been low. In this case, the JCC may represent the principal and most extensive form of employee involvement in the organization, a system to which management is positively and fully committed. With this in mind, we can now move on to examine a joint consultative system in the hotel and catering industry.

Case Study: Involvement through Consultation

The case study in this chapter is from a company in the hotel and catering sector, codenamed Four-Star, which constitutes one division within a much larger organization in the leisure industry. Although the parent company is probably best known for its beer, it has now pulled out of brewing altogether in favour of consolidating interests in the hotel and pub trade. Four-Star has over 30 hotels in the UK, including a number of large and well-known establishments in the Midlands and on the South Coast. The company is among the top ten within the industry, certainly in terms of class of hotel (most are at the high quality end of the market), but also in terms of numbers of bedrooms. Given this orientation to high quality and the espoused commitment of the company to employees, the case fits well within the philosophy of this book.

The hotel industry is extremely fragmented, but is beginning to segment along the lines of the food retailing cases discussed in previous chapters. While 70 per cent of hotels have less than 25 bedrooms, and only 4 per cent of units have more than 100 bedrooms, the top ten chains in the industry now have more than 12 per cent of all bedroom space. Profits at Four-Star have been steadily improving since the mid-1980s, as has turnover, and the long-term future for the industry as a whole looks favourable. The product market is highly competitive and operates around the clock, but there are peaks and troughs in demand over the course of week or year. Saturday is the busiest day of the week for functions, while the weekday trade mostly caters for conferences and business travellers. Perhaps even more than in supermarkets, customer care is seen as a key factor in business success.

Four-Star operates with a good deal of autonomy from the parent company, and indeed has its own preferred management style and HRM policies. Given the geographical dispersion of the units within the business, management style in the hotels owes much to the character of the general manager and his or her team, as well as to its location and clientele. A typical unit within the company would employ over 100 people, many of whom would be on part-time contracts, although this figure would exclude contract staff who are brought in to service functions. There is considerable functional flexibility between certain types of staff – including managers who undertake less skilled tasks should there be a shortfall in numbers – but for others there is little chance of this taking place (e.g. chefs). Labour turnover for the industry is high compared with manufacturing, but much of this is due to the seasonal nature of the work, especially in the hotels on the south coast resorts. The Four-Star Personnel Manager is keen to reduce labour turnover, and hopes that developments in EI (along with other changes in benefits) will help to encourage people to remain with the company.

Four-Star has a recognition and procedure agreement with the GMB which dates back to 1982, but this effectively covers solely those issues concerned with grievances and disciplinary matters. At the moment, union membership comprises only about 6 per cent of the workforce, and during discussions with a range of people in the hotels, the subject of unionization rarely surfaced; to say that the union is marginal would be to overstate its influence. Pay rates are determined by the company, and are well in excess of the wages council rate for the industry, as too are the other benefits which have been introduced in recent years. Some of the hotels now have a full-time personnel manager, but the majority of smaller units still make do with a manager who has responsibility for staffing issues. In broad terms, HRM is beginning to develop, but it is still at an early stage compared with some of the giant multinational chemical companies.

Where the procedure differs from a typical recognition agreement is in the area of consultation and negotiation. Here, the company agrees to set up a twice-yearly JCC at national level, which comprises the Group Personnel Manager plus three further management nominees, and the union's National Industrial Officer plus three others. Additional meetings would be set up as appropriate. The ultimate purpose of the JCC would be to discuss any matter concerning the employment of staff, such as the annual wage settlement, and any proposed changes to conditions of employment, benefits and manning levels. Matters specific to one outlet shall not come within the remit of the JCC. However, full recognition (as described above) can only be triggered by membership reaching a level which allows it to be 'broadly and demonstratively representative of the employees concerned'. The trigger is 25 per cent check-off membership and representation by check-off members in at least 50 per cent of all hotels. Given that membership is only 6 per cent this committee has never met.

However, there is also an arrangement whereby JCCs are required at each hotel, and these committees are quite distinct from the national consultation machinery discussed above. The JCCs were introduced into Four-Star in 1984, as part of an attempt to improve communications within hotels and ensure that management got across its message to the staff. Associated with this was a desire to deal with staff grievances at an early stage in order to ensure that the union did not gain the ascendancy in communicating with and representing employees. It was felt that managers had not proved to be good at communicating with staff prior to this. In other words, at least part of the reason for wanting to develop the JCC at hotel level was to prevent the union gaining sufficient members to trigger off the bargaining process. The JCCs also fitted in with the existing channels for communication within Four-Star, in that hotel managers meet once a month at regional meetings which provide some material for the subsequent JCCs. In short, unlike many organizations, senior management was under no immediate pressure to introduce consultation to the hotels, but felt that it would be advantageous for a number of reasons, not the least of which was a formalization of communications within the units.

The constitution of the JCCs has recently been amended, specifically to reduce the required frequency of meetings; this had been monthly, but many of the smaller hotels were finding difficulty in generating sufficient material of a relevant nature, so it had been adjusted to quarterly. However, there was nothing to prevent meetings being held on a more frequent basis, and at some of the larger hotels these remained monthly. Membership of the JCC comprises elected and appointed members, the latter being the General Manager (or Deputy) and other members of the management team, including the personnel manager if appropriate. The elected members are chosen on the basis of departmental constituencies, such as the kitchen or reception areas. Other rules include restrictions on continued membership (no more than two years at any one time), at least twelve months' service for eligibility, and that representatives must come from their own constituency; inevitably, though, given the high degree of labour turnover, it is difficult to maintain these restrictions.

The constitution also requires meetings to be scheduled in advance, for the agenda to be agreed between the manager and a representative, and for a minute-taker other than a manager to be appointed. All of these were adhered to in the hotels where I did my own study, and it was refreshing to read minutes written in a chatty style by a member of staff who seemed unaware of the 'politics' of minute taking. In addition, it is expected that minutes will be posted in the staff rest-room, and that all copies of minutes are sent to the Company Personnel Manager; this is not only done by the hotels, but unusually the minutes are actually read by this person and comments are returned to the hotel in question if there is a query or a mistake in interpreting company policy. This also gives him the chance to monitor the JCCs and pick up any generalized grievances or comments.

The type of items to be discussed at the JCC is also suggested in the constitution, although this is not meant to be an exhaustive list, nor is it meant to imply any order of priority. These are:

- the business of the hotel.
- terms and conditions of employment (not of specific individuals).
- health and safety.
- training.
- housekeeping.
- working methods.
- sports and social activities.

Inspection of the minutes for a number of hotels indicates that the subject matter which formed the basis of the meetings did tend to differ from that suggested in the constitution. At one hotel in particular, both the Deputy General Manager and the Hotel Personnel Manager felt that the JCC was principally concerned with social issues, ideas about work, and grievances ('a chance to let the employees have their say, to raise issues which have not been actioned, to generate ideas from the staff, and for us to put across our thinking to them'). The Hotel Personnel Manager felt that the JCC should be more geared up to increasing awareness of the hotel, to ensuring that there was a shared understanding of the business and for generating a 'sense of pride' in its activities. The JCC at this hotel, which is fairly typical of the company as a whole, is part social committee, part grievance procedure, with the occasional dose of business-related material. This was not something which bothered the Chair, and he felt that it was important to establish a forum for staff to air their views and talk about social issues, rather than about the business. 'I try to keep business information away from here as much as I can. I want the staff to feel that it is a less serious (i.e. high level?) meeting, that it's not a company organ.' The staff themselves also appeared to approve of the emphasis on social issues.

The minutes indicate that there is little discussion of business issues. For example:

- *sports and social issues*: the provision of a football kit; redecoration of the staff block and the purchase of a new TV; ideas on how to raise money for the social fund.
- *health and safety*: problems with rubbish being left in the hotel; new safety booklet just been printed; problems with a carpet.
- *working methods/housekeeping*: off-loading of barrels to protect carpet;

ladies toilets are smelly and a mess; request to purchase new machinery, e.g. glass washer, nappy bags; problems with contractors around the hotel; conversion of snooker room into offices/training room.

- *terms and conditions of employment*: BUPA – clarification of eligibility; request for better quality kitchen shoes and uniforms; evaluation of robo-serve facility for staff canteen; complaint about poor ventilation in the hotel van.
- *business matters*: (only two items during the year) word of thanks from the GM to all those who served breakfasts under difficult trading circumstances the previous weekend; 'Quality Through People' Campaign, and follow-up soon – this happened a couple of months later.

This sort of JCC clearly operates as a safety valve for staff grievances as well as a forum for the sharing of ideas about issues of joint concern. However, some JCCs in the company are more geared up to the provision of business information, as the minutes from another more high profile hotel indicated. These suggested a rather different sort of JCC, and figures were presented each month about the state of forward reservations and bookings for the hotel, as well as advance warning about major events. Financial results were also presented for a three-month period. There was reference to a hotel staff magazine, as well as lots of minor issues and niggles which are similar to those dealt with elsewhere. Again, one of the interesting things about these JCCs, and similar to those observed in parts of the retail sector, is that many of the staff grievances are also those which affect customers as well – e.g. worn carpets, faulty machinery etc.

It is felt by senior management that the JCCs will increasingly move towards the more business-oriented model, especially in the larger hotels, because of the importance of customer care, and staff awareness of and commitment to the success of their own unit. Nevertheless, in the absence of any effective union representation, there will remain a key role for the grievance and social aspects of these committees. It also appears that the JCCs are being supplemented – again, especially in the larger hotels – by other mechanisms for EI, such as a regular hotel newsletter or staff conferences. The former is particularly interesting, because in at least one of the hotels this is edited by a porter, i.e. an employee who is not a member of the management team. Nevertheless, despite these additions to the EI mix at Four-Star, the JCCs are likely to retain a primary place in the structure of workplace employee relations and HRM.

Conclusions

After being written off in the 1960s and 1970s, joint consultation appears to have become more important again within the last decade or so. What is also striking from the more recent studies, is the degree to which JCCs vary between diferent workplaces such that the nature of consultation is anything but uniform. For example, the JCCs used at ICI (long-standing, high profile, multi-level, union-nominated representatives, a prevalence of business information) are of a totally different character from those operated by some organizations in the private service sector (short-lived, marginal, establishment-level only, non-union, social and sports topics on the agenda). They are indicative of quite different power relations in these organizations, and managements have vastly differing objectives and criteria for success in these contrasting cases.

The key points to emerge from chapter 7 are as follows:

- JCCs can be a useful component in the EI mix because they allow for representative participation in a consensual atmosphere.
- joint consultation can lubricate employee relations, fill in the gaps left by other practices, and help to create good working relationships between employee representatives and management.
- the character of joint consultation (powers of the committee, regularity of meetings, principal subject matter discussed) varies widely depending upon the objectives which are pursued by the parties, especially management.
- it is inappropriate to specify an 'ideal' JCC, given that so much depends upon the objectives of the parties; what may be appropriate for a JCC used as an adjunct to the collective bargaining machinery is quite inappropriate for a non-union firm.
- whatever the objectives, however, if a JCC is to satisfy the different interest groups in an organization, committees need to be well chaired and smoothly organised, meet at regular and adhered-to intervals, both sides need to be as open as possible, and action points need to be specified.

The high-level committees are also of interest in relation to EC initiatives on participation, and especially the notions of European Works Councils (EWC) and further attempts to harmonize company law across the Community. Some of the multi-establishment JCCs which currently operate in the UK are of similar order to that proposed for EWCs, albeit restricted solely to one country at the moment. Arguably, companies based upon one industry would have less problem accommodating these EC proposals than would conglomerates with interests in a wide variety of industries and countries, whose financial organization and control is devolved to divisional or unit level. As the proposals currently stand, however, EWCs would only be required for those organizations which are registered in EC countries which have agreed to implement the social chapter of the single market, and then only in specified circumstances. Tax incentives would be offered to persuade organizations to opt for this form of regulation. In a similar sort of way, during the 1980s, UK employers (and employees) have received incentives to initiate or extend share ownership schemes, and this has led to a sizeable increase in their extensiveness. This is the subject of chapter 8.

8 Financial Involvement

Introduction

One of the most significant growth areas of employee involvement in recent years has been in the field of financial participation. Facilitated by several pieces of legislation since the late 1970s, the number of employees and private sector organizations which have taken advantage of share ownership or profit sharing schemes has increased considerably in recent years; this has also stimulated a number of publications. However, there has been a tendency to group each of the different types of scheme together in publications on the subject, and this ignores some sizeable differences between the objectives behind the various systems as well as in their consequences. For ease of clarification, there are basically three types of scheme, each of which has a number of sub-categories. These are:

1) *employee share ownership*: this is where employee ownership is extended, albeit to a small degree, by using part of the profits generated to acquire shares for employees in the company concerned. There are four sub-categories of scheme in this area; approved profit sharing (known as APS or ADST) introduced in the Finance Act of 1978; save as you earn (SAYE), Finance Act 1980; discretionary share option schemes, Finance Act 1984; and employee share ownership plans (ESOPS), which have developed from their USA counterpart, employee stock ownership plans. Each of these will be mentioned again in subsequent sections, but the principal point which binds them together is the notion of share ownership, as opposed to cash bonus.

2) *cash-based profit sharing*: this is where a cash bonus or payment is made to employees based upon the share price, profits or dividend

announcement at the end of the financial year. Whilst this may be seen by some as little more than a further form of payment, and thus quite distinct from other types of employee involvement, it does at least link some part of employee remuneration to the performance of the company as a whole. As we shall see below, that also raises certain problems, but the basic principle behind such schemes is that of trying to associate employee effort with company success. A more recent variant of this type of scheme has been *Profit-Related Pay*; this has its roots in research by Weitzman, becoming law in the late 1980s, and it operates according to the principle that PRP can represent a tax-efficient way in which to finance a part of employees' pay rather than acting as a bonus payment on top of normal salary as with more conventional profit sharing schemes.

3) *plant- or enterprise-wide bonus schemes*: this is where a bonus or payment is made to employees based upon establishment or company performance. Two of these schemes are better known than most; the first is the *Scanlon Plan*, whereby payment is based upon the ratio of total payroll costs to sales value of production; the larger the latter, the greater the bonus to employees. The second variant is the *Rucker Plan*, in which the bonus is related to the value added by the production process or service; thus, there is an incentive to keep down costs as well as increase the overall sales value of products. Either of these schemes can be used in a less comprehensive manner, in that an annual bonus can be paid to employees dependent upon the performance of the unit concerned, or senior management assessments of this – the Multichem plant which formed the case study in chapter 3 provides an example of this.

In addition to the specific legislative provisions which relate to employee share ownership and profit-related pay which have been well documented elsewhere (see for example, Smith, 1986; Duncan, 1988, 1989), there are a number of other developments which have influenced financial participation in general. Section 1 of the 1982 Employment Act, which requires larger quoted companies to provide details of actions taken to maintain or extend employee involvement, includes two features which are relevant: 'encouraging the involvement of employees in the company's performance through an employee's share scheme or by some other means', and 'achieving a common awareness on the part of all employees of the financial and economic factors affecting the performance of the company'. Athough the Act itself has only had a limited direct impact upon organizations, the inclusion of financial involvement is important for the purposes of raising awareness amongst senior managers. It also reflects the Conservative Government's interest in extending financial involvement as opposed to other more radical forms of EI. Profit/gain sharing plans and share ownership are also amongst the points in the joint IPA/IPM Code of Practice and its associated Action Guide. Finally, part of the EC Social Rights Action Programme (Section 1, Article 11) makes reference of employee participation in the capital or profits and losses of the European company. Unlike the current British provisions, however, it goes further in requiring a scheme to be negotiated between the management board of the enterprise and the employees or their representatives. The fate of this part of the programme, as with all other aspects of the Social Charter, hangs in the balance at the time of writing.

Having set the scene, we can now turn to a closer analysis of financial involvement. In the next section, there will be discussion of the way in which profit sharing and share ownership have developed in the UK, tracing their roots back to the late nineteenth century before providing figures on the current extensiveness of various forms of financial involvement. Following this, there will be some examination of management's objectives in seeking an extension of financial involvement, as well as some assessment of the impact of these schemes in practice. This will include an examination of employee and trade union attitudes to these initiatives, as well as some evaluation of the link between financial involvement and organizational performance. This analysis will draw heavily on the research undertaken by Fogarty and White (1988), Poole and Jenkins (1989, 1990) and by Baddon et al. (1989). Finally, the case study for this chapter will report on the operation of an added-value payment scheme in a furniture company, which also incorporates other aspects of employee involvement. This case has been chosen because it represents a somewhat different approach to financial involvement from the profit sharing and share ownership provisions, one which allows the possibility for employees to contribute rather more explicitly to discussions about the performance of their plant or enterprise. In addition, it also serves as a useful complement to the recently published work on share schemes.

History and Development

According to Poole (1989, pp. 8–14), there have been a number of waves of advance in financial involvement, commencing in the 1860s with at least 25 companies, of whom Henry Briggs and Company is probably the best known. Many of these schemes were implemented by employers who, initially at least, had some philanthropic motivation behind their actions, and as such this fitted well with other activities designed to extend welfare provisions in their organizations. Unfortunately, some of the schemes were dropped due to worsening economic conditions, and in the Briggs' case this coincided with industrial action by employees as well as the imposition of wage cuts (Ramsay, 1977, p. 484). The second epoch of development occurred between 1889 and 1892 when no fewer than 88 schemes were initiated, and the most famous of these was at the South Metropolitan Gas Company where one of the most prominent reasons for its implementation was a desire to limit the influence of the emerging general trade unions. In this case, the introduction of profit sharing led to splits not only between union and non-union labour, but also between the union and its members at the company (Lindop, 1989). Because of this and other attempts to introduce profit sharing at times when unions were trying to gain recognition in companies, some trade unions and academic commentators have been hostile to the whole concept; these concerns will be explored in a later section. Other periods of growth occurred in the 1920s (including the scheme at ICI, although it has changed somewhat since then), the 1940s and 1950s, and most recently the period since 1978. Poole is keen to point out that, even though there have been boom periods for the introduction of new profit sharing schemes and associated times of decline, there has been a long-run upward movement in its extensiveness (1989, p. 12).

At no time has this been more apparent than in the last decade. Fogarty and White (1988. p. 5) illustrate this expansion during the early part of the 1980s, particularly with reference to share schemes which almost doubled between 1980 and 1984 to a quarter of private sector establishments employing more than 25 people. This was most marked in certain industries such as financial services (44 per cent of all establishments), distribution, hotels and catering (29 per cent), and minerals and chemicals (23 per cent). Employee share ownership schemes were also more likely, as one would expect, in larger workplaces, with 43 per cent of those employing more than 500 people claiming to operate such a scheme. Nevertheless, about one-fifth of units employing between 25 and 49 people also reckoned to have schemes, so this is less sensitive to size than many other industrial relations practices. Cash-based profit sharing was slightly less extensive than share ownership according to the survey, but even so about 20 per cent of establishments practised these sorts of scheme; again, financial services and chemicals were the most likely to have these, although in this case size of unit was not a significant factor. Value-added bonus systems operated in 15 per cent of all establishments, with the construction industry being most likely to have such schemes (25 per cent of all units) and transport the least likely. If anything, unit size was inversely related to the extensiveness of added-value systems, with small establishments more likely to have them.

A Department of Employment study in 1985 (Smith, 1986; Poole, 1989) extended this research and also assessed the likelihood of different types of scheme following the implementation of legislation on share ownership. This survey found that 21 per cent of the 1,125 firms in the sample had at least one form of profit sharing covering all employees, that is excluding the discretionary, often executive-only schemes. Of these, APS and SAYE were equally the most popular (along with the selective schemes), and cash-based systems were less so. Once again, financial services proved to be the sector with the highest take-up of both any type of all-employee scheme and share ownership, with construction and retail distribution the lowest. For cash-based schemes, it was manufacturing which proved to be the most fertile ground, but at a much lower rate than for employee share ownership. The number of schemes approved by the Inland Revenue shows the continuing rise of APS, SAYE and discretionary (ESO) schemes throughout the 1980s. But, despite the growth in all-employee schemes (over 700 APS and 700 SAYE schemes by the end of the 1980s), the massive take-up of executive share options (nearly 3,000 in the late 1980s) illustrates that financial involement is still skewed towards those with higher salaries and at senior positions in organizations. It also casts doubt on the idea that share ownership, at least in one's own firm, can be seen as an example of people's capitalism.

The most recent survey, undertaken by ACAS advisers during their visits to establishments in the summer of 1988, is rather less comprehensive and capable of generalization. Nonetheless, it does suggest that financial involvement is becoming more extensive, with

37 per cent of all establishments reporting that they operated a profit sharing or share ownership scheme and, contrary to the earlier results, that this was more likely in manufacturing than in the private services sector. The size effect was confirmed however. Plant- or enterprise-wide incentive schemes, such as value-added, were found to exist in 13 per cent of the companies surveyed, again more likely in manufacturing than in the service sector. Moreover, the ACAS advisers reached the conclusion that all types of scheme had become more popular and extensive throughout the 1980s (1989, pp. 18–20).

The Rationale for Financial Involvement

Given that the number of organizations which operate schemes appears to be increasing, it is pertinent to ask why this might be happening (that is, what are managements' motives for initiating financial involvement) and what the reaction of employees has been to this phenomenon. The studies by the Department of Employment (Smith, 1986; Poole, 1989) and by Baddon et al. (1989) each offer insights into these questions. Smith (1986, p. 382) found that, out of a total of ten options, three management objectives seemed to be prominent for the share schemes; 'making employees feel part of the company', 'making employees more conscious of profit', and 'increasing employees' sense of commitment to the company'. Others such as 'helping to hold down wage claims' hardly featured at all in management responses. There was some variarion dependent on whether the scheme was share or cash-based, with profit awareness scoring more highly for the latter type of system and additionally 'ensuring employees benefit from company profitability' featured as a major reason for cash schemes as well.

Poole (1989, pp. 70–2) also reproduces these figures, but on the basis of 303 case studies he suggests five sets of reasons for the introduction of financial involvement; these are (1) moral commitment by employers, (2) staff retention, (3) employee involvement, which encompasses a wide range of factors such as increasing a sense of ownership and commercial awareness and is a form of motivation, (4) improved industrial relations performance, and (5) protection against takeover. One of the problems with this list is category (3), which is so broad and seems to incorporate such a number of different sets of reasons. Also, genuine though managers may be in wanting to extend employee involvement, it hardly seems likely that this is done except as a means to acheive some other objective; for example, to enhance co-operation with management plans for the enterprise. Except in a few special cases – such as Scott Bader – employee involvement is not introduced for altruistic reasons.

Finally, the Scottish study by Baddon and her colleagues also produced a set of management objectives for financial involvement based upon questionnaires to 1,000 companies and in-depth case studies in five organizations. This shows (1989, p. 88) that 'encouraging the co-operation and involvement of all employees in improving the performance of the business' was the principal objective for profit sharing and share ownership, followed by 'giving employees a sense of identification with the company', 'rewarding employees for past performance' and 'creating a sense of business awareness among employees'. Putting these responses (and their categorization, pp. 81–2) together with those from the other surveys, it is possible to suggest a number of major objectives for the implementation of financial involvement. It is probable that several of these objectives will be combined in any one rationale, and it is also likely that initial reasons for introducing financial involvement will not appear as coherent as they appear below. Indeed, it is suggested that these sets of reasons can be more accurately described as post-facto rationalizations of decisions made on less well-researched and possibly more emotive grounds. Nevertheless, with these qualifications in mind, the principal objectives are:

1 *education-based*: concerned with improving employee awareness of the company's position in the market place, understanding the importance of profits for stimulating further investment in the organization, and the need for savings in all modes of operation. In line with several of the other systems for EI already discussed in previous chapters, this perceived need to 'educate' employees about 'the business realities' forms a strong strand in employer motives for employee involvement. In addition, it aims to serve as a powerful legitimizer of management actions taken in the interests of all employed by the company; in other words, it represents a unitary conception of the firm.
2 *commitment-based*: concerned with increasing employee commitment to and identification with the goals of the organization, and enhancing the loyalty of employees to their firm. In a sense, this follows on from the previous category, but it goes further in requiring employees to want to work for the good of the enterprize as a whole, or at least their part of it. Again, this has similarities with many of the other systems of EI, and it is central to current thinking about HRM.

3 *performance-based*: concerned with enhancing both employee and company performance. In the case of the former, this refers to the translation of employee commitment into observed behavioural change – such as increased co-operation with plans for change which are deemed to be necessary for organizational success. It would also incorporate attempts by employers to reduce levels of absenteeism, and improve productivity and efficiency. For the latter, this would include increases in profits or share prices, and in the long-term perceived viability of the firm (see Richardson and Nejad, 1986). The theory behind the financial involvement = performance link is that employees with a stake in the overall success of the unit (plant, division or enterprise) are more likely to work harder for its ultimate success, although this depends to a large extent on the degree to which the link is seen as meaningful to and under the control of employees.

4 *recruitment-based*: concerned with attempts to attract and more particularly retain labour, especially in a climate where competition between organizations for high quality staff is more intense and where senior management view employees as the key to competitive advantage. This helps to accout for the high proportion of companies in the financial services sector which have adopted share ownership schemes during the last decade, as well as the move by the high-quality food retailers in a similar direction. Moreover, this has been a significant factor in the massive growth in selective schemes for senior executives.

5 *defensive-based*: concerned with other issues which may influence the position of the firm, such as an attempt to deter trade unions from gaining recognition or in limiting the development of potentially oppositional workplace union organization; as we have seen, these formed at least part of the rationale for some of the earliest schemes in this country. Within this category could also be included the role of financial involvement in reducing wage claims or persuading employees to be more prepared to accept reductions in the size of the workforce so as to maintain their bonus payments. In the case study, we will see how the operation of a value-added scheme produced some unanticipated reactions from employees, in particular in opposing recruitment or accepting redundancies so as to enhance the employee share of monthly pay-outs, both in the short and the long term.

6 *paternalist-based*: concerned with the willingness of employers to offer shares or other forms of financial involvement because it is seen as the 'right' thing to do, generally for some religious or political reason. Again, some of the early schemes were noteworthy for this, and it is also likely to be at least one part of the rationale for the emergence of ESOPs in both Britain and the USA. Some of this may be less far-reaching, and include a desire 'to reward employees for past performance' whereas other objectives may be more radical both in intent and in practice. As Poole

notes (1989, p. 70), this applies particularly to those companies with non-approved schemes since these reflect the longer-term vision of the founder rather than a tax-efficient way to try and secure employee commitment.

Obviously, in any one case, it is likely that there will be a mixture of motives behind the introduction of schemes, and there may be considerable variation in objectives sought within the organization, especially between different management groups. Indeed, in some (perhaps many) cases, the rationale will be neither explicit nor well thought-through, and Baddon et al. (1989, p. 280) conclude their study by arguing that 'in general the objectives are not well specified, tending to be somewhat woolly in the way they are expressed and without any clear understanding of the way the derived outcomes will be generated by the choice of scheme . . . Financial participation schemes have some resemblance to an "act of faith" on the part of management.' Not surprisingly, therefore, it is rather difficult for employers to evaluate the effectiveness of their chosen scheme.

The Impact of Financial Involvement

Given that profit sharing and share ownership are aimed at individual employees, it is important to assess their reactions to these initiatives, and analyse whether or not financial involvement is thought to have had any impact on attitudes or behaviour at work. Results from the variety of surveys undertaken range from the highly positive and enthusiastic to the more guarded and critical. At the former end is the work by Bell and Hanson (1984) for the Involvement and Participation Association (IPA) who feel that financial involvement is warmly welcomed by employees and that is seen as 'good for the company and its employees' (p. 27). Other responses cast doubt on the impact of schemes on the commitment and loyalty of employees, and indicate that profit sharing is seen more in calculative or instrumental terms rather than those associated with greater employee identification and effort. For example, the Bell and Hanson sample was almost equally split on the question of whether profit sharing strengthened people's loyalty to the firm, and there was a small majority in favour of the proposition that it made people try to work more effectively to help the firm be more successful. There was also some evidence that profit sharing was a minor factor in decisions about joining or leaving the firm (p. 30). Fogarty and White (1988), in their study of share ownership schemes in four companies, report that employees were generally in favour of this form of financial involvement (p. 26), although it must be noted that most employees saw the scheme as a way of saving money (p. 77) rather than as part of a package which would generate greater identification with and loyalty to the company. This is substantiated by fairly lukewarm responses to questions about whether the schemes had reduced the 'them and us' outlook in the company or had increased employee influence within the organization. Nevertheless, there was also a feeling that employees had become more cost-conscious since the introduction of the schemes (p. 35).

The calculative (building up a nest egg) and moral (right for workers to own part of their company) dimensions also figure prominently in the case study conducted by Dewe et al. (1988, p. 10), whereas those factors associated with attitudinal change are much less significant. For example, only a small minority felt that the schemes had reduced feelings of 'them and us' or had succeeded in building up team spirit. Yet more evidence to support the view that employees have a primarily calculative orientation to financial involvement can be gleaned from answers to questions about the drawbacks of share savings schemes; namely, that employees have to wait too long before making money, and a recognition that share price movements are beyond their control (p. 11). The authors also found that there was a link between commitment and share ownership, but only in the sense that employees who exhibited greater commitment to the organization were more likely to join the SAYE scheme; there was no suggestion that share ownership increased employee commitment. The implication of this is quite significant; 'if committed workers were disproportionately more likely to participate, the schemes could have very limited potential. The joiners, by assumption, would already possess the kind of attitudes which the firm wants . . . the schemes would be preaching to the converted.' (Dewe et al., 1988, p. 19).

Poole and Jenkins (1990, p. 50) appear to offer more hope to those who believe that financial involvement can have a positive effect on employee attitudes, both in terms of increased co-operation and in terms of a greater identification with company goals. They also feel that there is some evidence that labour turnover may have been reduced after the introduction of these schemes (p. 95). This leads them to conclude that 'the strategy of improving the climate of management-employee relations by means of economic democracy would appear to be very soundly based' (1990, p. 96). However, a closer inspection of their results leads to a more cautious response, and the overriding conclusion from their study appears to be that any positive effect is minor. Indeed, the vast majority of respondents felt that there had been no discernible change since the introduction of the schemes in the effort they put into work, their satisfaction with the company, feelings of involvement, communication and job security (p. 60). Most individuals felt that profit sharing had not broken down entrenched attitudes, a finding reinforced by the fact that there were few differences between the attitudes of shareholder and non-shareholder employees (p. 56).

That schemes were felt to have had minimal impact on employee attitudes also comes across clearly from the research by Baddon et al., and yet again it is the calculative character of financial involvement which appears most prominent in worker views. They conclude that

> The benefits of most schemes are generally too small to have much prospect of making the kind of impact management would wish. The benefits tend not to be seen by employees as an essential element of pay which would generate commitment but are more typically regarded as 'just another kind of bonus.' (1989, p. 274)

There is enough evidence, the authors feel, that management objectives for financial involvement are not being met due partly to the small size of the benefits but also because of the failure of management to design and implement the schemes in a participative manner (p. 285). This final point is important and, as we shall see from the case study in this chapter, is one which is addressed – if not necessarily overcome – with the value-added bonus system at Kitchenco.

The predominant conclusion from most studies of financial involvement is that it has a minor, albeit slightly positive, impact on employee attitudes and behaviour. What about the link between profit sharing or share ownership and financial performance? Each of the studies suggests that there is a positive relationship between the two factors, although there are doubts about the direction of causality of this association. For example, Richardson and Nejad (1986, p. 247) note that there was a clear and statistically significant link between share price movements and the use of financial participation, although they do suggest that it may be that 'innovating firms introduced or extended financial participation as part of a much wider review of their management strategy . . . employee share ownership schemes may have been merely one new element among many.' Poole and Jenkins (1990, p. 95) come to a similar conclusion about the association between company profitability and the adoption of profit sharing schemes, and suggest that improved profits acts as a trigger for the introduction of these schemes. They accept that there may be a linkage the other way round but doubt that it is direct, a view which is reinforced by the findings from the case study work which supplemented their main survey. These studies show, among other things, that profits are much more likely to be affected by factors other than improved employee performance due to the profit sharing scheme itself (p. 78), and that high profits are essential for maintaining positive employee attitudes to the scheme (p. 85). In short, the impact of profit sharing on company performance is likely to be minor, and poor profit announcements may actually have a negative effect on employee perceptions of management and the organization as a whole.

Studies undertaken in the USA into ESOPs (Employee Stock Ownership Plans) suggests that they tend to outperform their traditionally organized counterparts in a variety of ways; better survival rates, higher productivity, greater employment and sales growth, and higher net operating margins. However, other factors such as return on investment (ROI) and profits performance did not differ (Klein and Rosen, 1986, pp. 397–8). In line with the other writers on financial involvement, they also urge caution in reading too much into these findings on the grounds of both limited generalizability and problems with determining the direction of causality of the association. Like Richardson and Nejad, they suggest that ESOPs may be just one of the many new practices which more proactive managements introduce into their organizations, and that improved performance may be due to a combination of these diverse practices (p. 398).

Given the anti-union motives in at least some of the profit sharing schemes introduced into organizations during the late nineteenth century, we also need to consider the position of trade unions in relation to financial involvement. Because of this, trade unions have traditionally been suspicious about profit sharing, and in 1974 these concerns were summarized in a TUC document. Basically, there were at least three sorts of objection to profit sharing and employee share ownership:

1 schemes do not generally provide any real control because employees are unable to influence the level of profits declared or the quality of management decision making within the enterprise. On the escalator of participation, financial involvement represents a very dilute form of democracy.
2 there is no advantage to working people in investing savings in the firm for which they work because this doubles their insecurity. In other words, should the company go out of business or suffer cutbacks, individuals would not only stand to lose their jobs, they might also lose some or all of their savings as well. This feeling is borne out of previous recessions in the country, and it was dismissed as being unduly pessimistic during the (temporary and uneven) boom conditions of the mid-1980s, the period when share ownership schemes grew at a substantial rate.
3 profit sharing does little or nothing to reduce vast inequalities in wealth, and certainly the majority of schemes only provide for small adjustments to the overall pattern of shareholding in Britain. In addition, individual shareholders are almost totally powerless compared with large institutional investors or senior managers in family-owned firms. There were some attempts in the late 1980s to combine the votes of employee shareholders so as to form a more effective and unified block, as happened at British Airways, but even so this still only accounted for 2 per cent of all equity (Baddon et al., 1989, pp. 48–9).

In addition, some profit sharing schemes include penalty clauses which reduce or prevent pay-outs in the event of industrial action. An Industrial Relations Review and Report study in 1987 pointed to the existence of such clauses at Boots and Hotpoint, and Black and Ackers' research (1988) at Brown's Woven Carpets described a similar situation in this family-owned carpet firm. However, it should also be noted that the inclusion of penalty clauses will not necessarily prevent industrial action given that the level of finacial benefit secured from schemes is not that high. Moreover, the fact that a significant proportion of employees hold shares in a company does not inhibit employees from striking if this seems legitimate, even though they are aware that industrial action might reduce their share value – the example at British Telecom in the late 1980s is a good case in point.

Despite these reservations, the response of unions to specific initiatives in organizations has been lukewarm rather than adversarial, a situation characterised by Baddon et al. (1989, p. 248) as 'neutrality at best, a bored hostility at worst, but even the latter not taking on a high profile such as to make the operation of schemes difficult for management'. Poole (1989, p. 96) also notes a similar response, with little overt enthusiasm for share schemes, but equally little widespread opposition provided they were 'kept away from conventional bargaining channels'. Each of the studies found that profit sharing schemes were just as likely in unionized establishments as in those without unions, and many of the examples quoted are of large, heavily unionized companies – such as ICI where the system has been in operation for over 60 years – or at Jaguar, British Telecom or British Gas, where it was introduced along with privatization. Although unions may be ideologically opposed to the spread of schemes, they have to live with the fact that many of their members see financial involvement as a means of securing more money from their employer, at least in the short term.

Of course, trade union objections do not represent the only reservations about financial involvement, and further concerns relate to the fact that profit sharing fails to comply with the fundamental principles of payment systems. Financial involvement does not link effort to reward in a clear and unambiguous manner, nor is the payout made at regular enough intervals to act as a motivator of staff. Because profits or share prices are affected by many factors other than employee performance, and to a rather greater degree, it is almost impossible to conceive of this as a reward for effort. Indeed, due to factors beyond the control of employees, an individual who has worked extra hard during the year may be 'rewarded' with a negligible profit share, or vice versa. Equally, by the time the share announcement is made, so much time has passed since the beginning of the financial year that it is difficult to recall how hard one had been working. All of these problems are especially marked in multidivisional businesses. This leads to the disembodiment of profit sharing from its alleged motivational base, and leads to the oft repeated statement that shares and bonuses are nothing more than an extra payment which causes more or less satisfaction depending upon the amount. Some would argue that employers would be better advised to use this money to reward *specific* individuals – say, through a performance-related pay scheme – rather than through a standardized, all-embracing system.

Thus far, we have considered the impact of financial involvement in terms which relate to the firm or its employees/unions. More recently, there has been interest in the connection between profit sharing and the performance of the economy as a whole, and this came to the fore with legislation on profit-related pay (PRP) in the late 1980s. PRP has been defined as 'a part of employees' pay which varies in relation to the movement in profits of the business or part of the business in which they work'. (Duncan, 1988, p. 186). It differs from profit sharing in two ways; first, it acts not as a bonus but as a *replacement* for some part of the payment package; second, PRP creates a systematic, automatic and regular pay link with profits in contrast to many profit sharing schemes where payment is at the discretion of the directors. Although PRP is applied at the level of the individual company or profit centre, the Government was interested in its relevance for macro-economic performance, especially in relation to flexibility and unemployment. The government was especially attracted to the ideas of Weitzman (1984, p. 2) that some form of PRP could facilitate the achievement of 'reasonable price stability at the same time as reasonably full employment' via a change in basic compensation arrangements to the share system. This, according to Weitzman (1984, p. 111) offers

> full employment to all at variable pay that may, if it is linked to company revenues or profits, fluctuate somewhat with firm-specific changes in the relative composition of demand . . . If a particular industry is declining so that pay rates there go down, plenty of well paying jobs are always available elsewhere in a share economy.

In the end, the introduction of PRP to Britain was on a much smaller scale; by 1990, just over 1,000 schemes had been registered with the Inland Revenue, which covered nearly a quarter of a million employees. Of these, about 75 per cent of schemes had been introduced within the first year that tax relief was available (that is, by 1988). Many of the objections to PRP centred around the idea that it would be subject to tax relief, thus limiting opportunities for spending government money on other projects. Indeed, Duncan argues that PRP is bound to fail because there are fundamental flaws both in the concept and in the detail of the provisions (1988, p. 197). Some of these have already been alluded to in previous sections of this chapter, especially the view that profit-based systems ignore the fundamental principles of payment system design. Others are more specific but equally problematic, such as the lack of applicability of PRP to the public sector which can only serve to create further tensions about comparability. Despite the legislation, there has been little mention of PRP since it was introduced, and the recession of 1990/91 can only serve to limit its possible application yet further. It should be noted that the marginal impact of PRP is in sharp contradistinction to the way in which legislation served to increase the extensiveness of employee share ownership schemes earlier in Britain and ESOPs in the USA.

Plant-wide Pay Systems and Employee Involvement

Although most of the literature, and indeed the practice as well, has focused on profit sharing and employee share ownership as the principal forms of financial involvement, some organizations have developed other schemes which offer an alternative route to the same goal. In the USA, this has been through both Scanlon and Rucker Plans for gainsharing, while in the UK much of this has been through the Bentley Plan – basically an adaptation of the Rucker Plan, with a very specific participative element attached to it. The case study will present an analysis of the latter scheme, but before moving on to this, there will be a short discussion of the principles behind these different approaches to financial involvement. Each is similar in that it is believed that the workforce represents a reservoir of creativity and experience which needs to be tapped, and that this can be more easily effected if employees are able to share in the gains of the whole unit (establishment, division, enterprise).

The Scanlon Plan is named after its inventor, an ex-union official (albeit with a training in accountancy) who implemented a number of schemes in the US steel industry in the 1930s and 1940s, and who ultimately became a member of staff at the Massachusetts Institute of Technology (MIT) until his death in 1956. Scanlon schemes are based on the ratio of total payroll costs to sales value of production (estimated as a norm from inspection of figures over a representative period prior to the introduction of the technique. The smaller the ratio, the higher the bonus. The payment aspect of Scanlon Plans is supplemented by a participation element traditionally incorporating both a suggestion scheme and some form of committee structure at both departmental and unit level.

Some of the earlier proponents of the schemes were highly enthusiastic about its benefits, both to employers and to employees in a whole range of ways, and in bad times as well as good (Lesieur and Puckett, 1969, p. 118). Among the claimed benefits were (a) greater preparedness by employees to accept and even push for change, (b) managers feeling more able to discuss issues with workers and stress quality, (c) greater productivity and efficiency, and also (d) higher levels of job security (pp. 116–18). For Lesieur and Puckett (1969, p. 118), probably the most important aspect of the scheme is that 'everyone in the organization *knows* management wants to work with employees to improve operations' (my emphasis). Schuster (1983) produces evidence of increased productivity in most of the cases he reviewed in a longitudinal study, as well as stable employment figures and satisfactory relations – however, as we see below, this was not always the case. Although many other publications have also been highly enthusiastic about the achievements of the Scanlon Plan (see White (1979) for a review), some reports have been rather less convinced of its merits, particularly in certain situations. For example, Gray (1971, p. 311) felt that the plan at Linwood (at a Chrysler plant in Scotland) 'failed to cure restrictive practices, reduce absenteeism or apparently improve the industrial relations climate'. This could have been caused partly by inadequate bonus levels, but he felt that the problems went much deeper into the poor quality of relations between management and workers at the plant. At one of the sites studied by Schuster (1983, p. 425), a similar situation arose and the scheme was eventually dropped because of a lack of bonus payments, at least partly brought about by management decisions. But, low bonus announcements need not wreck a plan, as Thornicroft (1991) has recently shown in a North American study, and in his case all parties remained committed to the scheme because of associated shifts toward greater employee involvement. Indeed, in all published examples, this feature continually recurs, and it is clear that employers who initiate such gainsharing schemes need to be aware that more open management styles are central to potential success.

The Rucker Plan (and its UK variant, the Bentley Plan) is similar in many respects, but the wage calculation is based on the ratio of payroll costs to production value added (PVA), that is the difference between the sales value of output and the cost of materials, services and supplies. It represents the commercial value of the process of conversion from raw (or bought-in) materials to the finished product, so that value added is then available for the payment of all internally controllable costs such as wages, profits and investment. The amount which constitutes wages is a proportion of the value added, fixed at a rate determined after inspection of records over the preceding years.

Perhaps the easiest way to illustrate the concept of value added is by the use of a hypothetical case: say, for example, that of every £200 received for the sales value of output, £100 is spent on the cost of materials, supplies and services. The £100 which remains is the production value added. An inspection of previous accounts suggests that labour's share of PVA is 40 per cent, that is wages have typically taken £40 of the £100 value added. Wages will then increase or decrease in future depending upon the absolute size of PVA, and this can be increased by greater sales value of output or lower costs of services, supplies and materials. Either of these will increase the amount available for distribution as wages, profits and investment. Increasing the sales value of output can be achieved by higher sales or prices, and costs of materials etc. can be reduced – among other actions – by greater control over their usage, a higher proportion of output which is 'right first time', more efficient utilization of energy, and so on. The incentive for employees to improve these aspects of their work is therefore recognized in an explicit manner and can be rewarded by higher payments; gainsharing is therefore institutionalized and becomes a non-negotiable bonus for the employee. In addition, to protect workers against loss-sharing, minimum wage levels are set, and a reserve account is set up to cope with this eventuality.

But the payment part of the system is only one side of the equation, and the scheme is underpinned by a structure which enables employee representatives to contribute to decision making via a works council or JCC arrangement. Each month, employee representatives meet to hear the bonus announcement, to listen to explanations about the derivation of the figures, to question management about the factors which have influenced these, and to put forward suggestions about how things might be improved. Managers are charged with the responsibility of ensuring that employees understand the figures and with listening to worker suggestions about the operation of the system and the establishment. Therefore, a key feature of the scheme is

> the formalization of the relationship between employee participation in decision making, organizational efficiency and individual reward. By integrating the opportunity to participate explicitly with the rewards for participating, a greater degree of congruency can be achieved than with other traditional payment systems. Equally, the calculative involvement of the individual is recognized and placed within a participative context. (Marchington, 1980, p. 38).

Of course, this is not to say that these forms of plant-wide incentive and participation systems are free from problems. At least four have been identified in the literature, and all are apparent in the case study:

1. although gainsharing plans are implemented on the assumption that employees can see the connection between their own efforts and the rewards which are generated by the scheme, in many cases they have little control over the size of the bonus. External factors such as increased costs of raw materials or services may limit the bonus, as too may management decisions to delay an increase in prices due to competitive pressures.
2. rather than encouraging co-operation between different groups in the organization, the schemes may increase inter-group hostility and recriminations if the bonus levels fail to meet employee expectations. Not only can this be problematic for employers and run counter to their objectives, it can also create conflicts within and between unions.
3. some unions fear that gainsharing plans will lead to a progressive marginalization of their role, either because collective bargaining will become less important in determining wage levels, or due to the fact that employees will develop greater commitment to the goals of the company and 'give away' hard fought-for gains.
4. probably most important of all, some schemes fail because managers are not prepared to accept a modified role, listen to employee suggestions for improvements, and act upon these ideas; a reassertion of managerial prerogatives is likely to undermine employee commitment to the scheme.

Case Study: Involvement through Financial Participation

The case study in this chapter is drawn from a company which operates in the knock-down (DIY) kitchen furniture industry. The company, which has been codenamed Kitchenco in previous publications [see Marchington (1980) for a much fuller investigation of participation at this site], employs about 700 people, of whom just over 500 work on the shop floor. It is located in the West Midlands on a large industrial site which has a long history of factory employment. Kitchenco is a subsidiary of a larger organization with interests in other parts of the furniture trade as well as in steel and iron products. Although subject to financial controls from the centre, each part of the group has a high degree of autonomy in terms of operational decisions, and especially in relation to HRM, production management and marketing. Indeed, given the highly volatile and competitive market within which Kitchenco operates, strongly centralized control and direction could well be counterproductive, and there is little in the way of corporate policies or philosophies for managing people at work.

Kitchenco is among the top ten in the industry with an 8 per cent share of the market, although the size of this share and of the market as a whole is highly variable, and a source of some insecurity to those employed at the factory. Operating in a fashion-oriented market also poses problems for the maintenance of consistent production schedules, and orders vary significantly on a week-by-week basis. In addition, designs are regularly updated, and this too introduces frequent shocks into the system. Indeed, the whole product market environment is characterized by change, instability and insecurity. The technology employed varies between different parts of the factory, with some specialist machinery in the manufacturing areas combined with highly manual operations elsewhere, especially in packing and distribution. Nevertheless, the production system is very interdependent, and the flow of material through the factory is easily disrupted by problems in any one area. Two unions are recognized for the manual workers (TGWU for the 18 drivers and FTAT for the remainder) and one (GMB-APEX) for the clerical staff. All shop floor employees are expected to join the appropriate union which means that membership is at a high level. Collective bargaining takes place at site level, although Kitchenco is part of the employers' federation and thus bound to pay at or above nationally negotiated rates. Management style at the company tends to be open and informal, especially between those in production and personnel and the people employed in the manufacturing and assembly areas, and contact is also reinforced through the sports and social activities at the site.

For a number of years, management had been experiencing problems with a payment-by-results system which, due to regular changes in the technology employed, had resulted in massive pay inequalities between different groups of workers and in extremely high wages for a few. A team of consultants was brought in to overhaul the system and, not surprisingly, suggested that their own scheme might be appropriate. This, the Bentley Plan, is a value-added scheme which operates in close conjunction with a framework which enhances employee participation and a more open management style; in many ways, it is similar in concept though not in detail to the Scanlon Plans dealt with in the previous section. A steering committee comprising managers and employee representatives (mostly though not exclusively shop stewards) met over a period of six months to assess the merits and applicability of the scheme for Kitchenco, with the consultant acting as an adviser to the group. Eventually, following the involvement of national union officials and trips to other companies which used the scheme, detailed proposals were put to a referendum of all employees. This resulted in a vote in favour of the scheme, and it has now been operating for five years. It is interesting to note that although the initial decision to call in consultants was specifically targeted at an overhaul of the pay system, once the first moves had been made the emphasis shifted to one of enhancing employee commitment to the company as well. From the early stages therefore, the link between payment and employee involvement was established, at least in the minds of senior mangement.

The payment side of the system is simple in concept, although rather more complicated in detail. Following a review of the previous five years' accounts, the consultant decided that the ratio of wages to other factors in the value-added equation should be set at 34.51 per cent that is for every £100 which the company makes in value added, £34.51 is the share which goes to employees. This ratio varies substantially depending upon the firm and the type of technology employed, and in the schemes introduced by the consultants it varies from under 20 per cent in a capital intensive industry to about 60 per cent for a more labour intensive operation. A bonus is paid if the basic wages are less than £34.51 for each £100 of value added, and the majority of this is paid out on a monthly basis (25 per cent is kept in reserve until the end of the financial year, with any excess being distributed to employees as a supplement, and any loss being written off by the company). Over the five years that the scheme has been in operation, bonuses have been payable most (thought not all) months, and on a few occasions the bonus payment has supplemted wages by over half as much again; that is, the bonus has been 50 per cent of the basic wage. At other times, the company has gone several months without declaring a bonus, but even so, employees appear to remain committed to the concept of the scheme, and feel that it is much more attractive than conventional payment systems. Perhaps this has been assisted by the fact that, apart from one six-month period, earnings have been well above the rate for the industry as a whole.

However, the gainsharing programme is only one side of the equation, the other being the Works Council and departmental committee structure. The former operates at company level, comprising the managing director or works manager as chair, the personnel manager as secretary, the finance director and four other members of management, typically from production and engineering. Employees are represented by individuals nominated by each constituency in the works (19 representatives) plus the senior shop steward as an ex-officio member. Just over half the representatives are stewards, and this is a continuing point of friction for the employee side of the council, with some departments being committed to the idea that all representatives should be stewards, and others steadfastly opposed to that principle. The constitution of the council specifies that representatives alone are entitled to vote, and that managerial members are only present to respond to questions and report back on initiatives, although in practice managers play a much more influential role in what goes on. Indeed, there have been several occasions when the Chair has refused either to allow or to accept a vote if this conflicts with his assessments of the situation.

The stated objectives of the Council, which meets monthly at predetermined times, are broad:

1 to receive and discuss the results of the Plan.
2 to receive and discuss the Chair's report, which shall cover:
   (a) factory performance.
   (b) order and market position.
   (c) new projects.
   (d) new work layouts for the factory.
3 to review the activities of the departmental committees.
4 to discuss ideas for increasing productivity.

Clearly, the wording of these terms of reference is broad and open to some degree of interpretation, a fact illustrated by the wide range of items which are dealt with at the council. For example, because any regrading, redundancy, or recruitment can affect the distribution of the employee share of the value-added pool, these issues tend to be considered in some detail by the council. Often, in fact, it leads to unusual stances being taken by the representatives who may be more prepared to accept a reduction in staff than would typically be the case, but more resistant to increasing the size of the workforce for fear of lower benefits to individual employees. Similarly, management is expected to report on new ventures to a rather greater degree than would be the case in traditional workplaces, and this leads them to prepare much more carefully before outlining their proposals to the representatives. Many of the other features observed at Kitchenco are remarkably similar to those already discussed in the previous section, (a) the lack of employee control over external factors which affect the determination of value added, (b) the effect on group solidarity of the gainsharing programme, (c) a more open management style called for though not necessarily achieved, (d) some union concerns about being incorporated into management decision making. It is also apparent that employees are more prepared to become more functionally flexible by undertaking work from other departments when required in order to meet production targets.

Despite some of these problems, however, employee commitment to Kitchenco and the continuation of the scheme is at a high level, and most employees who were interviewed expressed their desire to remain there. In addition, employees and their representatives were prepared to put forward ideas for the future, and were very interested in the performance of the company. Undoubtedly, there is a danger that this reinforces an instrumental orientation to work and runs counter to some of the ideas which underpin concepts such as total quality management. Perhaps the group which find the scheme most difficult to cope with are the middle managers and supervisors who have lost some of their traditional prerogatives and are resentful of both the amount of money which employees can earn from the Plan, as well as the access to senior managers which the participation system affords to representatives.

Conclusions

Financial involvement has become considerably more widespread during the last decade, especially in certain sectors of the economy. This has been stimulated by Governmental encouragement via a series of legal changes which have provided tax relief for approved schemes. In addition, the ideas behind financial involvement fit well with the 1980s' emphasis on 'people's capitalism' and 'enterprise culture'. At the same time, it should be recalled that some of the anticipated benefits to be gained from financial involvement are not always easy to secure in practice, and there are doubts as to whether profit sharing or share ownership schemes actually fulfil the principles of payment system design. Equally, the absolute amount to be gained from these schemes can be small compared with other components of the total reward package. Similarly, despite continued exhortations from various quarters, it should be recalled that financial involvement is only one form of EI, and in many respects it is very dilute in comparison with the other techniques discussed in this book.

Nevertheless, the major points to emerge from chapter 8 are:

- there are a number of different types of financial participation scheme available to organizations, and managers need to choose which of these are most appropriate in the cicumstances.
- schemes may be introduced for a variety of motives, ranging from a desire to gain the commitment of employees or improve their performance, through to incentives which encourage recruitment and retention.
- most studies indicate that share ownership and profit sharing have a minor, albeit slightly positive, impact on employee attitudes and behaviour.
- unlike profit sharing and employee share ownership, plant-wide incentive systems may be useful to organizations because they enable employees to make links between their own performance and that of the establishment or unit for which they work.
- the growth of financial involvement does not appear to have stimulated a great deal of interest among employees in wider levels of shareholding, other than in the newly privatized industries.
- it should be borne in mind that the amount to be gained from financial involvement schemes is often small when compared with other bonuses or fringe benefits.

9 Conclusions

Introduction

Having reviewed a range of forms of EI, my purpose in this final chapter is to summarise briefly the major arguments in the book and suggest a few more general conclusions to the study. As with the other chapters, this is supplemented by a short case study of employee involvement in a UK company, in this instance one which utilizes most of the techniques analysed in the book. The case study provides a vehicle for drawing out a number of issues, namely how EI can be found in a variety of forms in the same workplace, how its operation needs to be considered in relation to other features of the organization and its environment, and what is the future of EI in Britain. Before moving on to discuss these issues, there is a brief summary of the book.

Summary

There is little doubt that the 1980s saw an increase in the extensiveness of managerially-initiated forms of EI in Britain, and indeed in many other countries as well. There are several reasons for this growth in EI, but most relate to the attempted attainment of employer objectives, such as 'educating employees about the realities of business', gaining their commitment to corporate goals, and developing employee contributions to improved efficiency, productivity and customer service. Others are concerned with improving the organization's reputation in the labour and product market, and with greater controls over the day-to-day activities of both managers and union representatives. Rarely is the 'new' EI aimed directly at satisfying employee objectives, although it needs to be stressed that this may be a by-product of employer objectives. In addition to illustrating the extensiveness of these different forms of EI, as well as the reasons for their introduction, the book also addresses the consequences of EI for employees, managers and trade union organization. In short, the book focuses on the interrelationship between extent, motive, and impact.

In the introductory chapter, the link between EI and human resource management (HRM) was explored, in particular that relating to conceptions of employees as 'resourceful humans'. Although there are several variants of HRM, those which focus on strategic integration and the search for employee commitment are of most value for the purposes of this book. These tend to view EI as an important component of an organization's attempts to create a positive employee relations policy which can be integrated with the employer's strategic objectives. If, as some company's mission statements suggest, 'employees do make the difference', there is a clear need to develop EI within employing organizations. This is not to argue that all employers should implement the same mix of EI techniques in each and every case, but that some form(s) of EI are likely to be relevant to all workplaces. Of course, there are problems with this as well, especially when economic, legal and political circumstances make it difficult for employers to sustain a more progressive approach to employee relations. But, as we have seen in the book, some employers have been able to maintain their support for EI irrespective of contextual changes.

Chapter 2 presented a brief literature review which combined a short historical summary with some attempt to categorize and classify the material which was covered in the remainder of the book. The concepts of *degree of involvement*, *form*, *level at which EI takes place*, and *the range of subject matter* covered by EI were introduced, and some reference was made to the 'escalator of involvement'. This suggests that EI can be differentiated along a continuum stretching from one-way information passing through to workers' control, the degree of involvement clearly being greater at the latter stages of this. The idea of an escalator is useful for two reasons; first, it implies that EI can evolve from the more dilute through to more radical forms of involvement as employees gain in knowledge and experience, as well as in expectations. Thus, the receipt of information can be seen as a necessary prerequisite for more effective two-way communication, which in turn can help to create the conditions for more effective consultation, and so on. Secondly, the more severe incline at the top of the escalator suggests that it is more difficult to progress from codetermination to control than from information to communication; in the UK, this incline is particularly marked given management attitudes to more extensive forms of participation and democracy.

The remaining chapters then dealt with a variety of different forms of EI, broadly in line with the escalator principle. In chapter 3, written and audio-visual forms of information-passing were analysed, and there was a case study of a retail firm which is well-known for the quality of its house journal. A number of suggestions were made about how these forms of EI could be made more effective, but the principal underlying theme was that managements should ensure that their espoused commitment to employees as a valuable resource is actually met in practice. Given the lack of resources and time which is typically given to written forms of EI – especially company newspapers and house journals – this does not seem to be the case. Chapter 4 analysed face-to-face communications, with a particular focus on team briefing and associated formal communication devices which have become much more extensive over the course of the last decade. Although a wide range of benefits are identified for team briefing by its adherents, studies show that these are not always easy to achieve in practice. For example, there are doubts as to whether briefing leads to increases in employee commitment to the organization or to a greater acceptance of change by employees. The success of these techniques relies to a large extent upon the ability of supervisors to communicate information in an effective manner, and to the context in which briefing takes place. Arguably, rather than enhancing commitment (or whatever), poorly handled briefing sessions may result in supervisors having less status in the eyes of their subordinates, and a weakening of managerial influence.

In chapter 5, the emphasis shifted from an analysis of top-down communications to those forms of EI which are aimed at improving the flow of ideas up the hierarchy, and enhancing the contribution of employees to management decision making. The techniques analysed included those which are voluntary in nature – such as quality circles and suggestion schemes – as well as those which are becoming a compulsory part of the individual's everyday activities – such as TQM and customer care drives. All of these techniques are geared up to improving performance, at departmental level or above, and to the enhancement of customer service. It was stressed that the rationale for all these forms of EI was principally production- or service-oriented rather than directed at increasing job satisfaction or responding to employee demands for more involvement. Again, a number of problems were highlighted here, especially regarding the centrality of quality circles to those organizations which have introduced them. In addition, there were concerns that some of these new techniques actually reduced the opportunity for employee involvement, rather than extending it, by prescribing work operations in yet more detail. For example, the 'smile campaigns' practised by some service sector organizations took Taylorist work organization one stage further by aiming to manage people's emotions, as well as their physical contribution to the enterprise.

The notion of compulsory, as opposed to voluntary, EI also emerged in chapter 6 where the subject was job redesign. This chapter examined a variety of different forms of task-based EI, from the relatively minor changes associated with job rotation, through various forms of vertical role integration (often known as job enrichment), to issues concerning teamworking. The more extensive forms of job redesign offer the potential for increased operator control over their own jobs, greater responsibility for decision making, and more variety at work, as people move around between different tasks as appropriate. On the other hand, many of the teamworking structures have been introduced along with reductions in numbers employed, often as part of a wider programme to ensure the survival of a specific site or industry. In the USA, in particular in car factories, there have been doubts about whether teamworking represents a further attempt by management to intensify work, as opposed to improve its character, with the consequence that stress levels are increased. Additionally, some analysts are convinced that teamworking offers a considerable threat to the future of workplace trade union organization.

Indirect EI was the focus of chapter 7, where joint consultation was analysed in more detail, and there was some reference to company and works councils. Joint consultation has a long history, and there has been continued debate about its role, character, and implications, as well as its extensiveness throughout industry. The argument presented here is that JCCs vary significantly across the economy, with some operating in conjunction with collective bargaining and shop steward organization, whereas others are designed to minimize (and possibly inhibit) the influence of trade unions. Yet others have the consequence, if not the objective, of weakening trade unions at the workplace so that union leaders are 'incorporated' by management and 'won over' by the so-called logic of employer explanations in these common-interest committees. JCCs are also relevant to the discussion of EC initiatives on information, consultation and participation, principally through the long-running debate about higher-level forms of EI, the most recent expression of which is the idea of European works councils. For most 'ordinary' employees, however, JCCs are remote from their everyday experiences at work, and they are often unaware of their existence or powers.

Financial EI, by contrast, is rather more obviously relevant to individual employees, and it also relates to the instrumental and calculative aspects of motivation at work. This has been a major growth area of the 1980s, stimulated by favourable legislation and sustained Government exhortation about the benefits of the enterprise culture. Not surprisingly most employees find the idea of financial involvement, such as through profit sharing or employee share ownership, very attractive. Rarely, however, does this have anything to do with any philosophical commitment to the notion of people's capitalism. On the contrary, a large proportion of employee shareholders view their ownership as no more than an fortuitous 'cash windfall' or an additional 'form of savings'. Value-added bonus schemes represent an alternative to these share-based systems, with the extra facet of linking employee gains to establishment or corporate peformance. At the same time, though, these too suffer from similar problems to other forms of financial EI; that is, remoteness and a lack of employee control over the absolute level of gains to be shared out.

One feature which emerges from this analysis is that EI often takes a number of different forms in any one organization, and that it is useful to conceive of an *EI mix* (Marchington et al., 1992, chapter 3). This mix of EI practices can vary from one organization to the next, depending upon a whole range of factors, and it can also change over time as well. It is also apparent that different forms of EI often come in a series of waves reflecting different stages in the history of the site or company in question. For example, in one organization, virtually all the forms of EI which have been examined in this book may be in existence at the same time, whereas in another some may have disappeared as new forms come to prominence. In others, just one or two different forms of EI may be in operation, and even then these may play only a minor role in employee relations within the organization. Some employers may have introduced a number of new techniques at much the same time, with the result that employees become confused about what management is actually trying to do.

In general, though, except in the very smallest organizations, there is likely to be a range of different EI techniques in operation, and the case study in the next section provides an example of this.

Case Study: Integrating Employee Involvement

Photochem is part of a large American-owned chemical company which employs over 70,000 people world-wide and has interests in a number of different areas of the industry. Photochem was only recently acquired by this firm, having previously been part of another foreign-owned chemical company. It is one of the market leaders in the photography industry, and less than 12 per cent of total sales are in the UK. Its major competitors are from Europe, the USA and Japan. The recent acquisition of Photochem has now enabled the new parent to broaden its market base as well as build up a manufacturing and R&D presence within the UK.

Photochem operates on a number of sites throughout Europe, but the focus for this case study is its sole UK manufacturing unit. The company employs nearly 3,000 people on four sites within the EC, with the British establishment employing about half of these (1,400). As with most manufacturing organizations, this represents a reduction since the 1960s, when 6,000 were employed on two separate sites in the UK, but the closure of its southern factory in the late 1970s accounted for most of this rationalization. Indeed, the northern site has experienced continued growth and been the recipient of massive capital investment over the last two decades as the sole manufacturing facility in the UK. Photochem employs a wide range of staff from highly qualified research chemists and physicists, a fifth of whom have doctorates, through to general labourers and ancillary employees. The technology employed in some areas is highly capital intensive, with small teams of employees responsible for managing the processes (in coating, for example). In others, such as finishing, work is undertaken more on an individual basis in certain sections, and all these jobs have to be done in the dark given the nature of the product. Some of the original buildings are still in use, but a large proportion of the site is relatively new, reflecting the company's growth since the 1970s.

The management style in the company is similar to that previously described for Multichem, with an emphasis on teamwork, cooperation, and openness, and it is one of the few organizations in the UK which operates with a human resource function. In addition, the Head of Human Resources is a member of the Board. The corporate principles of Photochem, which are contained in a handbook distributed to all employees, refer to the goal of 'market leadership' and the importance of everyone contributing to this objective, as well as to 'the encouragement of participation', 'promotions from within', 'employee development', and 'social responsibility'. At the same time, there are indications that the style is not necessarily sustained, and an ACAS survey in the mid 1980s reported that many managers were seen as remote, arrogant and autocratic. Employees who have been interviewed by the author report that recent years have seen changes to a more open style, exemplified by more senior management's 'walkabouts' and interaction with employees. Indeed, following the ACAS survey, the Head of Human Resources has worked hard to persuade his senior colleagues to tour the plant on a more regular basis, with some though not complete success.

Five separate trade unions are recognised at Photochem, each of which has a distinct sphere of bargaining rights and influence. The major union is the GMB which represents all production and related workers (500), while the remainder is organized into the AEU and EETPU (with 90 members between them), APEX-GMB and MSF (each of which has about 250 members, covering clerical grades, technicians, some supervisors, and research chemists among others). The GMB senior steward is also the Chair of the Joint Shop Stewards Committee, which includes both white and blue collar unions, and he works three days per week on union duties. Collective bargaining takes place at plant level, and wages are competitive for the area, although not as high as at some other firms in the chemical industry.

There is a wide mix of forms of employee involvement at Photochem, some of which are of recent origin whereas others have a longer history. The JCC machinery was introduced in the early 1970s, at that time feeding into the company-wide, multi-plant structures across the various sites in the UK. In its early stages, the JCC was chaired by the Head of Production who was then employed at the other major site in the UK, but by the end of the 1970s the chair was taken by the General Manager at the site. Meetings continued to be held on a monthly basis until the mid-1980s when the system was reformed; since then the JCC has met quarterly, although there is provision for more regular meetings should the parties deem this necessary. The terms of reference for the 'new' JCC state that 'it is important to provide a forum for union representatives to participate in an open exchange of views relating to significant matters, the intention being that both the company and employees benefit from such an arrangement'. The major items for consideration at the JCC are quality, productivity, employment, the volume of work, and the impact of longer term capital investment plans on people. The committee is now chaired by the Head of Operations (Managing Director), and membership includes the Head of Human Resources and the senior shop stewards. Although the formal structures for consultation remain intact, albeit with less frequency, the JCC is now less central to activity at the company. For example, the meetings which used to last for a whole morning are now often over within an hour, the minutes are not circulated until a few weeks after the meeting, and the main item of interest on the agenda is the Chair's report on future business prospects. Arguably, the more effective development of direct and extensive communications from management to staff has rendered the formal meetings less necessary for all concerned. However, it would be incorrect to assume that the JCC is now worthless, as both managers and stewards appeared to regard it as a useful vehicle for exchanging views.

Photochem uses two parallel systems for briefing information to staff; firstly, each month, information about performance (sales against budget, earnings before interest and tax) and other matters (e.g. statement about disciplinary action and change to the sickness scheme) is cascaded down the management chain starting with the Board. Although managers are not formally required to hold briefings, it is expected that they will do so. For those that do, the information has to be passed on within two weeks to all staff – a longer period than that specified by the Industrial Society, largely because shift working makes a shorter period untenable. The second method – quarterly briefs – is more comprehensive, is compulsory, and contains a large amount of financial and performance-related information which relates to the outlook for the whole company and the plant.

Sometimes, there are special items, such as in 1990 when the focus was on environmental protection (identifying responsibility for disposal of specific materials) and proposals for the consolidation of manufacturing capacity within the company as a whole. The need for 50 per cent (at least) local information is repeated on the briefing notes, and briefers are requested to convey feedback on questions and answers within one month; these are then summarized and submitted to the MD for inspection.

Across the site, there are variations in the quality of these briefing sessions, with the R&D department proving particularly innovative. In addition to the briefings, there are monthly seminars and reports about technical developments, bi-monthly consultative committees for R&D alone, 'bumper bundles' of information which pass around the department, social evenings at people's homes, and eight communication events per annum. In other departments, the briefs do not seem to work so well. For example, there are problems sustaining briefing in some production areas given shift patterns and other work pressures, and in some cases respondents to my interviews reported that the language and material used tended to be at too high a level: 'we're not all graduates, you know!'

The company produces a newspaper which is published every two months. It is an eight-page tabloid, containing mostly social and general information, with little material of an explicit financial or performance nature. Understandably, given the nature of the product, much is made of photographs. There are items relating to specific developments on the site – again usually with photos – such as TQM or Materials Resource Planning 2 (MRP2); in fact, the latter was the subject of a special pull-out section of the paper recently. An unusual but potentially advantageous feature of the paper is that the company has a 'correspondent' for each department, who is named in the paper and is expected to contribute to each issue.

Photochem has had a suggestion scheme for a number of years, the purpose of which is 'to encourage all employees to put forward ideas for increasing productivity and improving efficiency and conditions within the company'. Management is particularly keen on receiving suggestions on how to reduce waste and cut down on costs, improve safety, systems, procedures and environment, as well as ideas for new products. The reward is a maximum of £1,500. The scheme is administered by a committee chaired by the Head of R&D (Board member) and comprising the Head of Production with managers drawn from engineering, distribution and productivity services. Help is offered to those who wish to put forward a suggestion.

The most recent development at Photochem is a massive organizational change programme which relates to all aspects of employee relations, but has at its core the concepts of involvement and communications. The programme uses the metaphor of a sunflower to convey the image that EI is the centre of a series of interlinking issues – organization planning, training, reward structures, trade union relationships, terms and conditions of employment. The process by which the change programme is being introduced is also highly relevant for this book because it involves a combination of high level representative involvement in the planning stages, through to direct communications, an emphasis on team working, and a requirement for managers to gather feedback from their staff at each stage in the programme.

The initial brief about the programme comprised a 22 page set of notes for briefers (departmental managers), plus a set of slides and a letter for all employees from the MD. The message was very clear, attendance at the briefs (two-hour minimum) was mandatory, feedback was required from presenters, and it was specified that a quiet room, free from interruption, should be sorted out. It was stressed that the programme was to be participative (two-way communication, active participation encouraged), and that union involvement was agreed and welcomed. Other key points of the brief were as follows:

- profitability is critical to business success, which in turn will lead to greater security of employment and improved conditions of employment.
- key business aims are customer satisfaction, efficiency, effectiveness, and profit.
- key business goals are increased sales, the elimination of failures, improvements in productivity (but not through job cuts), reinvestment, teamworking, and innovation and flexibility – in a wider range of skills, more employee responsibility, and a new pay structure 'which relates the money that one earns to the level of responsibility and the skill used to perform our jobs. It is the company's intention to give everyone the opportunity of earning more on the basis of how well they do their job.'
- business confidence comes from people; 'people are Photochem's unique asset – no-one else has them and it is what our people can achieve that will make all the difference. We have a vast fund of knowledgeable people working for the company at all levels. We must ensure that this knowledge is put to good use and ensure that everyone feels that they can use those skills.'
- a high trust environment is to be created, where pride, motivation and contribution are developed.
- the unions are to be involved in the process of change. Reassurances are

given that the company expects the plant to remain a multi-union site, that the company would like to see single table bargaining, and that moves should continue towards the development of a 'problem-solving' relationship between management and unions.

At about the same time as the initial brief to all employees, a project team was also established to develop the programme which comprised seven people, plus the Head of HR who is its sponsor. The team meets once a week until the project is completed. The members of the team are three line managers, three from the HR function, and a senior steward. This latter development is interesting because, although project teams have been set up on an *ad hoc* basis for many years, this is the first time that there has been any union presence on them. Initially, the unions were wary about the implications of being involved at the planning stage in a project, especially one which might lead to major modifications to the pay system (and perhaps performance-related pay). After some discussion, it was felt that a contribution should be made, partly because the unions would have some influence over the direction of the project team, but also because they felt that non-involvement would seal their fate for the future by providing management with a rationale for reducing their role in employee relations.

After the initial brief, and alongside the project team meetings, the programme continued to be discussed within departments through a series of meetings during working hours; many of these lasted for several hours. At one of these, on a day specifically set aside for training on the coatings plant, the manager introduced the session by laying out his vision of the future including quality, flexibility, training, ideas for a new reward policy, teamworking, and how to minimize breakdowns. He then fielded questions from the process operators on the shift, and attempted to develop a more 'open' atmosphere on the plant by reassuring employees that improvements would only come about if both parties were prepared to accept advice and ideas from the others. The employees then broke up into syndicates, under the loose leadership of a named individual – usually a supervisor but not in every case – to discuss the issues raised and then report back to the group as a whole. This tends to be a fairly standard short course format for management training sessions, but it also appeared to generate a wide range of responses from this group of manual workers; in other words, the process seemed to work well with a group less accustomed to this sort of approach.

Managing Employee Involvement

This final case study of Photochem is valuable because it highlights a number of issues which have been addressed in the book as a whole. First, it illustrates that it is perfectly feasible for employers to utilize a mix of EI techniques, ranging from the most dilute (such as the company newspaper) through to the more significant (such as trade union representation on high-level project teams). Even though some of these arguably have little effect on the way in which the organization is managed or upon its staff, they nevertheless perform a useful function in ensuring that information is disseminated to employees on a regular basis. The provision of briefing sessions and the availability of suggestion schemes also allows for the continued involvement of employees in aspects of their work. Arguably, the more progressive and far-reaching developments would have been difficult to achieve without having first laid the foundations with a greater commitment to information-passing and some development of problem-solving techniques. The senior stewards at Photochem, despite having some reservations about becoming involved in top-level policy-forming bodies, were at least sure that this was an extension of previous practice and an indication of the management's commitment to EI. The Head of Human Resources certainly saw this as a 'natural' progression from earlier activities.

The context in which the case study is set is also important for wider discussions of employee involvement and industrial democracy. The chemical industry appears to be at the forefront of many developments in EI, and there are a number of reasons for this, (a) exposure to international competition and ideas about management, (b) highly-qualified managers, (c) strong internal labour markets and employees with lengthy periods of service, (d) close co-operation between management and trade unions, (e) a technology which facilitates team-working and functional flexibility, and (f) the relatively low cost of labour in relation to other aspects of the business. Not only do the circumstances in which the business operates suggest that EI offers an appropriate component of employee relations (making the best use of resourceful humans), but the conditions also facilitate its development because there is more time to communicate with and consult staff as well. The contrasts with food retailing, for example, could hardly be greater; here, there is constant and immediate pressure from customers, skill levels of staff tend to be low, there are high levels of labour turnover, and very few managers have high-level qualifications. In addition, as with the majority of retailing outlets, staff are only employed for the busy periods of the day or week. Not only does the product and labour market environment make it difficult to develop formal schemes for EI, managers also perceive this as hard to achieve during normal working hours. Perhaps senior management could demonstrate its commitment to EI by paying staff to attend briefings outside their contractual hours, but there are seen to be problems with this, both with higher wage costs and the fact that part-timers tend to have obligations other than to paid employment. Overall, though, this contextual analysis does suggest that the precise mix of EI techniques which management chooses to adopt does depend on the circumstances in which the organization operates. On the other hand, this is not to support the idea that employers should be free to ignore all forms of EI because it suits their own prejudices and predilections.

There are a number of general points which can be suggested in conclusion. Most of them have been made elsewhere here and also in a number of other texts, but they still seem to be ignored or overlooked on too many occasions. All of the points are extremely simple, but nevertheless vital to organizations which are serious about developing employee involvement. To borrow from a Herzberg phrase, 'one more time, how do you make EI work?'

- if an organization is not prepared to invest sufficient time and resources in a specific EI initiative, it is probably better not to introduce it in the first place.
- the experiences of other organizations, both in the UK and elsewhere, should be evaluated *before* implementing a new scheme, and an assessment made of its applicability to specific workplaces.
- most organizations appear to use a mix of EI techniques, but the precise choice should be made so as to ensure complementarity rather than competition between them.
- EI should not be regarded as a 'bolt-on' activity, peripheral to the organization, but as an integral part of its whole activity in line with broader business objectives.
- managers have to be ready for changes in their style of operating, especially those skills related to presenting information and answering questions in a clear and unambiguous manner, listening to employee views, developing consensus, acting on agreed ideas from the team, and delegating more responsibility to their staff.
- while the objectives for any organization introducing a new EI technique may vary, these have to be clarified at the outset and agreed by the management team.

- any scheme must be carefully conceived and implemented since first impressions are a critical factor influencing the subsequent success of EI.
- money and time saved by inadequate training schemes for the managers who have to run EI schemes is a false economy, and is only likely to lead to poor results at a later date.
- EI activities – just like any other aspect of management – need to be monitored, reviewed, and if necessary revised at regular intervals, if at all possible by independent analysts as well as internal consultants.
- well-written policy statements on EI are meaningless without well-operated practices, and many a scheme has foundered because of ineffective management behaviours which cause employees to question the organisation's true commitment to involvement and participation.

This leads us finally to the future of EI, and here much depends upon developments in the social arena at EC level. Given the opposition of the Conservative government to any compulsory initiatives in this area, there will be little overt pressure upon employers to introduce new forms of EI. Alternatively, a future Labour government would aim to enact directives on EI, and extend the obligations on UK employers. Given what many organizations have been doing in this area in the last few years, this may prove to be less of a problem than is typically argued; for example, it is only a short step from enterprise-level JCCs to European Works Councils, and companies in other EC countries do not seem to have encountered insurmountable problems with these forms of indirect EI. Furthermore, irrespective of these sorts of developments, there is no reason to suppose that direct EI will fade away, especially if it is seen to facilitate the effective management of successful organizations. There is an increasing amount of anecdotal and case study material – from overseas as well as the UK – which suggests that EI can make a contribution. As ever, of course, so much depends on the commitment and ability of managers to make EI work; will they be prepared to exercise this responsibility?

Bibliography

Advisory Conciliation and Arbitration Service (1982), *Workplace Communications*. ACAS, London

Advisory Conciliation and Arbitration Service (1988), *Labour Flexibility in Britain*. ACAS, London

Advisory Conciliation and Arbitration Service (1989), *Payment Systems*. ACAS, London

Advisory Conciliation and Arbitration Service (1990), *Consultation and Communication*. Occasional Paper 49

Advisory Conciliation and Arbitration Service (1991), *Consultation and Communication*, ACAS, London

Armstrong M. (1987), 'HRM: A case of the Emperor's new clothes', *Personnel Management*, August

Armstrong P. (1989), Limits and possibilities for HRM in the age of accountancy', in Storey J. (ed.), op. cit., pp. 154–66

Baddon L., Hunter L., Hyman J., Leopold J. and Ramsay H. (1989), *People's Capitalism*? Routledge, London

Baird L. and Meshoulam I. (1988), 'Managing two fits of strategic human resource management', *Academy of Management Review*, vol. 13(1), pp. 116–28

Batstone E. (1984), *Working Order*. Blackwell, Oxford

Beer M., Spector B., Lawrence P., Mills D., Walton R. (1985), *Human Resource Management: a General Manager's Perspective*. Free Press, New York

Bell D. W. and Hanson C. (1984), *Profit Sharing and Employee Shareholding Attitude Survey*. Industrial Participation Association, London

Benson J. (1979), 'Briefing Groups and the Development of Employee Participation', in Guest D. and Knight K. (eds), *Putting Participation into Practice*. Gower, Farnborough, pp. 80–95

Bentley D. (1975), *A Dynamic Pay Policy for Growth in Productivity, People and Profit*, Bentley Associates, Brighton

Berggren C. (1989), 'New Production Concepts in Final Assembly – The

Swedish Experience', in Wood S. (ed.), *The Transformation of Work?* Unwin Hyman, London, pp. 171–203

Black J. and Ackers P. (1988), 'The Japanisation of British Industry; A Case Study of Quality Circles in the Carpet Industry', *Employee Relations*, vol. 10(6), pp. 9–16

Black J. and Ackers P. (1990), *Voting For Employee Involvement at General Motors*, paper presented to the 8th Labour Process Conference, University of Aston, March

Blauner R. (1964), *Alienation and Freedom*. University of Chicago Press, Chicago

Blumberg P. (1968), *Industrial Democracy: the Sociology of Participation*. Constable, London

Bradley K. and Hill S. (1983), 'After Japan; The Quality Circle Transplant and Productive Efficiency', *British Journal of Industrial Relations*, vol. 21(3), pp. 291–311

Bradley K. and Hill S. (1987), 'Quality Circles and Managerial Interests', *Industrial Relations*, vol. 26(1), pp. 68–82

Brannen P. (1983), *Authority and Participation in Industry*. Batsford, London

Braverman H. (1974), *Labour and Monopoly Capital*. Monthly Review Press, New York

Brossard M. (1990), 'Workers' Objectives in Quality Improvement', *Employee Relations*, vol. 12(6), pp. 11–16

Brown W. (ed.) (1981), *The Changing Contours of British Industrial Relations*. Blackwell, Oxford

Buchanan D. (1979), *The Development of Job Design Theories and Techniques*. Saxon House, Farnborough

Buchanan D. (1986), 'Management Objectives in Technical Change', in Knights D. and Willmott H. (eds), *Managing the Labour Process*. Gower, Aldershot, pp. 67–84

Buchanan D. (1987), 'Job Enrichment is Dead: Long Live High-Performance Work Design', in *Personnel Management*, May

Cavestro W. (1989), 'Automation, New Technology and Work Content', in Wood S. (ed.), op. cit., pp. 219–34

Clarke R., Fatchett, D., Roberts, B. (1972), *Workers' Participation in Management in Britain*. Heinemann Educational Books, London

Clegg H. (1979), *The Changing System of Industrial Relations in Great Britain*. Blackwell, Oxford

Clegg H. and Chester T. (1954), 'Joint Consultation', in Flanders A. and Clegg H. (eds), *The System of Industrial Relations in Great Britain*. Blackwell, Oxford

Collard R. (1989), *Total Quality: Success Through People*. Institute of Personnel Management, London

Collard R. and Dale B. (1989), 'Quality Circles', in Sisson K. (ed.), *Personnel Management in Britain*, pp. 356–77

Confederation of British Industry (1990), *Employee Involvement – Shaping The Future For Business*. CBI, London

Cressey P., Eldridge J. and MacInnes J. (1985), *Just Managing*. Open University Press, Milton Keynes

Crosby P. (1984), *Quality without Tears*. McGraw Hill, New York

Dale B. and Plunkett J. (eds) (1990), *Managing Quality*. Philip Allan, London

Daniel W. and McIntosh N. (1972), *The Right to Manage?* Macdonald, London

Daniel W. and Millward N. (1983), *Workplace Industrial Relations in Britain*. Heinemann, London

Dankbaar B. (1988), 'New Production Concepts, Management Strategies and the Quality of Work', *Work, Employment and Society*, vol. 2(1), pp. 25–50

Davis L. and Taylor J. (1972), *Design of Jobs*. Penguin, London

Dawson P. and Webb J. (1989), 'New Production Arrangements: The Totally Flexible Cage?', *Work, Employment and Society*, vol. 3(2), pp. 221–38

Deming W. (1986), *Out of the Crisis*. MIT Centre for Advanced Engineering Study, Cambridge, Mass

Department of Employment (1989), *People and Companies: Employee Involvement in Britain*. HMSO, London

Dewe P., Dunn S. and Richardson R. (1988), 'Employee Share Option Schemes; Why Workers are attracted to them', *British Journal of Industrial Relations*, vol. 26(1), pp. 1–21

Duncan C. (1988), 'Why Profit-related Pay will fail', *Industrial Relations Journal*, vol. 19(3), pp. 186–200

Duncan C. (1989), 'Pay and Payment Systems', in Towers B. (ed.), *A Handbook of Industrial Relations Practice*. Kogan Page, London

Edwards P. (1987), *Managing The Factory*. Blackwell, Oxford

Elliott J. (1978), *Conflict or Co-operation: the Growth of Industrial Democracy*. Kogan Page, London

European Industrial Relations Review and Report (1990), *Employee Participation in Europe*. IRS, London

Feigenbaum A. (1983), *Total Quality Control*. McGraw Hill, New York

Fidler J. (1981), *The British Business Elite*. Routledge and Kegan Paul, London

Fogarty M. and White M. (1988), *Share schemes – as Workers see them*. Policy Studies Institute London

Fombrun C., Tichy N. and Devanna M. (eds) (1984), *Strategic Human Resource Management*. Wiley, New York

Foulkes F. (1980), *Personnel Policies in Large Non-union Companies*. Prentice Hall, New Jersey

Fowler A. (1987), 'When chief executives discover HRM', *Personnel Management* March

Fox A. (1985), *History and Heritage*. George Allen and Unwin, London

French J., Israel J. and Aas D. (1960), 'An Experiment in Participation in a Norwegian Factory', *Human Relations*, vol. 13, pp. 3–10

Friedman A. (1977), *Industry and Labour*. Macmillan, London

Gold M. and Hall M. (1990), *Legal Regulation and the Practice of Employee Participation in the European Community*. European Foundation for the Improvement of Living and Working Conditions, Working Paper, Dublin

Goldsmith W. and Clutterbuck D. (1985), *The Winning Streak*. Penguin, Harmondsworth

Goldthorpe J., Lockwood D., Bechofer R. and Platt J. (1968), *The Affluent Worker: Industrial Attitudes and Behaviour*. Cambridge University Press

Gorfin C. (1969), 'The Suggestion Scheme: A Contribution to Morale or an Economic Transaction?', in *British Journal of Industrial Relations*, vol. 7(2), pp. 368–84

Gowler D. and Legge K. (1986), 'Images of employees in company reports – Do company chairmen view their most valuable assets as valuable?', *Personnel Review*, vol. 15(5), pp. 9–18

Gray R. (1971), 'The Scanlon Plan – A case study', *British Journal of Industrial Relations*, vol. 9(3), pp. 291–313

Grayson D. (1990), *Self-Regulating Work Groups – an Aspect of Organisational Change*. ACAS Work Research Unit Occasional Paper No 46, July

Griffin R. (1988), 'Consequences of Quality Circles in an Industrial Setting: A Longitudinal Assessment', *Academy of Management Review*, vol. 31(2), pp. 338–58

Grummitt J. (1983), *Team Briefing*. Industrial Society, London

Guest D. (1987), 'Human resource management and industrial relations', *Journal of Management Studies*, vol. 24(5), pp. 503–22

Guest D. (1989), 'Human resource management; its implications for industrial relations', in Storey J. (ed.), *New Perspectives on Human Resource Management*, Routledge, London, pp. 41–55

Guest D. (1991), 'Personnel Management; The End of Orthodoxy', *British Journal of Industrial Relations*, vol. 29(2), pp. 149–76

Guest D. and Fatchett D. (1974), *Worker Participation: Individual Control and Performance*. IPM, London, 1974

Guest D. and Knight K. (eds) (1979), *Putting Participation into Practice*. Gower, Farnborough

Hawes W. and Brookes C. (1980), 'Change and Review; Joint Consultation in Industry', *Employment Gazette*, April, pp. 353–60

Hawkins K. (1979), *A Handbook of Industrial Relations Practice*. Kogan Page, London

Hebden J. and Shaw G. (1977), *Pathways to Participation*. Associated Business Press, London

Heller F. (1983), 'Introduction', in Crouch C. and Heller F. (eds), *Organisational Democracy and Political Processes*. International Yearbook of Industrial Democracy, Yearbook 1, Wiley, London

Hendry C. and Pettigrew A. (1986), 'The practice of strategic human resource management', *Personnel Review*, vol. 15(5), pp. 3–8

Herzberg F. (1972), 'One More Time; How Do You Motivate Employees?', in Davis (ed.), op. cit., pp. 113–25

Hill F. (1986), 'Quality Circles in the UK: A Longitudinal Study', *Personnel Review*, vol. 15(3), pp. 25–34

Hill S. (1981), *Competition and Control at Work*. Heinemann, London

Hill S. (1990), 'Why Quality Circles had to Fail but TQM Might Succeed', *London School of Economics, mimeo*

Hill S. (1991), 'How do you manage a Flexible Firm? The Total Quality Model', *Work, Employment and Society*, vol. 5(3), pp. 397–415

Hilton A. (1978), *Employee Reports: How to communicate financial information to employees*. Woodhead Faulkner, Cambridge

HMSO (1986), *Profit-Related Pay: A Consultative Document*. HMSO, London

Hochschild A. (1983), *The Managed Heart: the Commercialisation of Human Feeling*. University of California Press, California

Homer J. (1987), *The House Journal*. Unpublished MSc dissertation submitted to the University of Manchester

Hussey R. and Marsh A. (1983), *Disclosure of Information and Employee Reporting*. Gower, Aldershot

Ichniowski C., Delaney J. and Lewin D. (1989), 'The new human resource management in US workplaces', *Relations Industrielles*, vol. 44(1), pp. 97–119

Incomes Data Services/Institute of Personnel Management (1989), *Customer Care: the Personnel Implications*. IDS/IPM, London

Industrial Relations Review and Report (1989), 'Suggestion Schemes; Exploiting Employees' Ideas', *IRRR, IRS Employment Trends, Number 450* 24 October

Industrial Relations Review and Report (1990), 'Change to Cell-based Working, Multiskilling and Teamworking at Digital Equipment VLSI', *IRRR, IRS Employment Trends* 2 November

Industrial Relations Review and Report (1990), 'Moving to Autonomous Work Groups at RHM Ingredients', *IRRR, IRS Employment Trends* 7 December

Institute of Personnel Management (1988a), *Annual Reports – Employee Involvement Statement*. IPM, London

Institute of Personnel Management (1988b), 'Suggestion Schemes', *Personnel Management*. Factsheet 11, November

Institute of Personnel Management (1989), 'House Journals', *Personnel Management*. Factsheet 14, February

Institute of Personnel Management (1990), 'Producing a Video', *Personnel Management*. Factsheet 26, February

Involvement and Participation Association (1991), EC Newsletter No 6, March

Involvement and Participation Association/Institute of Personnel Management (1990), *Employee Involvement and Participation in the United Kingdom: the IPA/IPM Code*. IPM/IPA, London

Jones G. (1990), *State of the Art Technology and Organisational Culture*. ACAS Work Research Unit Occasional Paper No 47, November

Juran J. (1984), *Juran on Leadership for Quality*. Free Press, New York

Keenoy T. (1990), 'HRM: A Case of the wolf in sheep's clothing', *Personnel Review*, vol. 19(2), pp. 3–9

Keep E. (1989), 'Corporate training strategies: the vital component?', in Storey J. (ed.) op. cit., pp. 109–205

Kelly J. (1982), *Scientific Management, Job Redesign and Work Performance*. Academic Press, London

Klein K. and Rosen C. (1986), 'Employee Stock Ownership in the United States', in Stern N. and McCarthy S. (eds), *The Organisational Practice of Democracy* Wiley, New York, pp. 387–406

Knights D., Willmott H. and Collinson D. (1985), *Job Redesign: Critical Perspectives on the Labour Process*. Gower, Aldershot

Kochan T. and Chalykoff J. (1987), 'Human resource management and business life cycles: some preliminary propositions', in Kleingartner A. and Andersen C. (eds), *HRM in High Technology Firms* Lexington Books, Mass., pp. 183–200

Kochan T., Katz H. and McKersie R. (1986), *The Transformation of American Industrial Relations*. Basic Books, New York

Lawler E. and Mohrman S. (1985), 'Quality Circles after the Fad', *Harvard Business Review*, February, pp. 65–71

Legge K. (1989), 'Human resource management: A critical analysis', in Storey J. (ed.) op. cit., pp. 19–40

Lesieur F. and Puckett E. (1969), 'The Scanlon Plan has Proved Itself', *Harvard Business Review*, vol. 47(5), pp. 109–18

Lindop E. (1989), 'The turbulent birth of British profit sharing', *Personnel Management*, January

Loveridge R. (1980), 'What is Participation? A Review of the Literature and Some Methodological Problems', *British Journal of Industrial Relations*, vol. 18(3), pp. 297–317

Lukes S. (1974), *Power: A Radical View*. Macmillan, London

MacInnes J. (1985), 'Conjuring Up Consultation', *British Journal of Industrial Relations*, vol. 23(1), pp. 93–113

MacInnes J. (1987), *Thatcherism at Work*. Open University Press, Milton Keynes

Marchington M. (1980), *Responses to Participation at Work*. Gower, Farnborough

Marchington M. (1982), *Managing Industrial Relations*. McGraw Hill, Maidenhead

Marchington M. (1987), 'Employee Participation', in Towers B. (ed.), *A Handbook of Industrial Relations Practice*. Kogan Page, London, pp. 162–82

Marchington M. (1989), 'Joint Consultation in Practice', in Sisson K. (ed.), *Personnel Management in Britain*, op. cit., pp. 378–402

Marchington M. and Armstrong R. (1981), 'A Case For Consultation', *Employee Relations*, vol. 3(1), pp. 10–16

Marchington M. and Armstrong R. (1985), 'Involving Employees Through the Recession', *Employee Relations*, vol. 7(5), 1985, pp. 17–21

Marchington M., Goodman J., Wilkinson A. and Ackers P. (1992), *New Developments In Employee Involvement*. Employment Department, Research Series Number 2.

Marchington M. and Harrison E. (1991), 'Customers, Competitors and Choice: Employee Relations in Food Retailing', *Industrial Relations Journal*, vol. 22(4), pp. 286–300

Marchington M. and Parker P. (1990), '*Changing Patterns of Employee Relations*', Wheatsheaf, Hemel Hempstead

Marchington M., Parker P. and Prestwich A. (1989), 'Problems with Team Briefing in Practice', *Employee Relations*, vol. 11(4), pp. 21–30

Marginson P., Edwards P., Martin R., Purcell J. and Sisson K. (1988), *Beyond the Workplace; Managing Industrial Relations in the Multi-Establishment Enterprise*. Blackwell, Oxford

Martin P. and Nicholls J. (1987), *Creating A Committed Workforce*. Institute of Personnel Management, London

McCarthy W. (1966), *The Role of the Shop Steward in British Industrial Relations*. Royal Commission Research Paper Number 1, HMSO, London

McCarthy W. and Ellis N. (1973), *Management by Agreement*. Hutchinson, London

McGregor D. (1960), *The Human Side of Enterprise*. McGraw Hill, New York

Miller P. (1987), 'Strategic industrial relations and human resource management – distinction, definition, and recognition', *Journal of Management Studies*. vol. 24(4), pp. 347–361

Millward N. and Stevens M. (1986), *British Workplace Industrial Relations; 1980–1984*. Gower, Aldershot

Mitchell F., Sams I. and White P. (1986), 'Employee involvement and the law; section 1 of the 1982 Employment Act', *Industrial Relations Journal*, vol. 17(4), pp. 362–7

Mortiboys R. (1990), 'Quality Management for the 1990s', in Dale and Plunkett (eds), op. cit., pp. 33–43

Needham A. (1990), *A Study of the Relationship between Quality and Safety in the Light of Organisational Culture in a Manufacturing Organisation*. MSc dissertation, University of Manchester.

Oakland J. (1989), *Total Quality Management: a Practical Approach*. Department of Trade and Industry, London

Ogbonna E. and Wilkinson B. (1990), 'Corporate Strategy and Corporate Culture; the View from the Checkout', *Personnel Review*, vol. 19(4), pp. 9–15

Ostell A., MacFarlane I. and Jackson A. (1980), 'Evaluating the Impact of a Communications Exercise in an Industrial Works', *Industrial Relations Journal*, vol. 11(2), pp. 37–48

Parke E. and Tausky C. (1975), 'The Mythology of Job Enrichment: Self Actualization Revisited', *Personnel*, September/October

Parker M. and Slaughter J. (1988), *Choosing Sides: Unions and the Team Concept*. South End Press, Boston

Paul W., Robertson K. and Herzberg F. (1972), 'Job Enrichment Pays Off', in Davis and Taylor (eds), op. cit., pp. 247–63

Pateman C. (1970), *Participation and Democratic Theory*. Cambridge University Press

Peters T. (1988) *Thriving on Chaos*. Macmillan, London

Peters T. and Waterman R. (1982), *In Search of Excellence*. Harper and Row, New York

Pollert A. (1988), 'The Flexible Firm: Fixation or Fact?', *Work, Employment and Society*, vol. 2(3), pp. 281–316

Pontusson J. (1990), 'The Politics of New Technology and Job Redesign: A Comparison of Volvo and British Leyland', *Economic and Industrial Democracy*, vol. 11, pp. 311–36

Poole M. (1975), *Workers' Participation in Industry*. Routledge and Kegan Paul, London

Poole M. (1986), *Towards a New Industrial Democracy: Workers' Participation in Industry*. Routledge Kegan Paul, London

Poole M. (1989), *The Origins of Economic Democracy: Profit Sharing and Employee Shareholding Schemes*. Routledge, London

Poole M. and Jenkins G. (1990), *The Impact of Economic Democracy: Profit Sharing and Employee Shareholding Schemes*. Routledge, London

Purcell J. (1989), 'The impact of corporate strategy on human resource management' in Storey J. (ed.) op. cit., pp. 67–91

Ramsay H. (1977), 'Cycles of Control; Workers' Participation in Sociological and Historical Perspective', *Sociology*, vol. 11, pp. 481–506

Ramsay H. (1983), 'Evolution or Cycle? Worker Participation in the 1970s and 1980s', in Crouch C. and Heller F. (eds), op. cit., pp. 203–26

Ramsay H. (1985), 'What is Participation for? A Critical Evaluation of "Labour Process" analyses of Job Reform', in Knights et al. (eds), pp. 52–80

Richardson R. and Nejad A. (1986), 'Employee Share Ownership Schemes in the UK – an Evaluation', *British Journal of Industrial Relations*. vol. 24(2), pp. 233–50

Robson M. (ed.) (1984), *Quality Circles in Action*. Gower, Aldershot

Rogaly J. (1977), *Grunwick*. Penguin, Harmondsworth

Ross T., Hatcher L. and Adams D. (1985), 'How Unions View Gain-sharing', *Business Horizons*, July–August, pp. 15–22

Schuller T. (1985), *Democracy at Work*. Oxford University Press, Oxford

Schuster M. (1983), 'The Impact of Union-Management Co-operation on Productivity and Employment', *Industrial and Labor Relations Review*. vol. 36(3), pp. 415–30

Seddon J. (1989), 'A Passion for Quality', *The TQM Magazine*, May, pp. 153–7

Shuchman A. (1957), *Codetermination: Labour's Middle Way in Germany*. Public Affairs Press, Washington

Sisson K. (ed.) (1989), *Personnel Management in Britain*. Blackwell, Oxford

Smith G. (1986), 'Profit Sharing and Employee Share Ownership in Britain', *Employment Gazette*, September, pp. 380–5

Smith R. (1975), *Keeping Employees Informed: Current UK Practices on Disclosure*. British Institute of Management, London

Stern R. and McCarthy C. (eds) (1986), *The Organisational Practice of Democracy*. Wiley, New York

Storey J. (ed.) (1989), *New Perspectives on Human Resource Management*. Routledge London

Taguchi, G. (1986), *Introduction to Quality Engineering*. Asian Productivity Organization, New York

Terry M. (1983), 'Shop Stewards through Expansion and Recession', *Industrial Relations Journal*, vol. 14(3), pp. 49–58

Thomson F. (1983), 'The Seven Deadly Sins of Briefing Groups', *Personnel Management*, February

Thornicroft K. (1991), 'Promises Kept, Promises Broken: Reciprocity and the Scanlon Plan', *Employee Relations*. vol. 13(5), pp. 12–21

Torrington D. (1989), 'Human resource management and the personnel function', in Storey J. (ed.), op. cit., pp. 56–66

Townley B. (1989), 'Employee communication programmes', in Sisson K. (ed.), op. cit., pp. 329–55

Vista Communications (1989), *Britain at Work*. The fourth Annual Vista survey of communications between managers and their staff, Vista Communications, Croydon

Walker C. and Guest R. (1952), *Man on the Assembly Line*. Harvard University Press, Cambridge

Walker K. (1975), 'Workers' Participation in Management: Concepts and Reality', in Barrett J., Rhodes E. and Beishon J. (eds), *Industrial Relations*. Collier Macmillan, pp. 434–56

Wall T. and Lischeron J. (1977), *Worker Participation*. McGraw Hill, London

Walton R. (1985), 'From control to commitment in the workplace', *Harvard Business Review*. vol. 63(2), pp. 77–85

Webb S. (1989), *Blueprint For Success: a report on involving employees in Britain*. Industrial Society, London

Weitzman M. (1984), *The Share Economy*. Harvard University Press, Cambridge

Whitaker A. (1986), 'Managerial strategy and industrial relations: A case study of plant relocation', *Journal of Management Studies*. vol. 23(6), pp. 657–678

White J. (1979), 'The Scanlon Plan: Causes and Correlates of Success', *Academy of Management Journal*, vol. 22(2), pp. 292–312

Wilding P. and Marchington M. (1983), 'Employee involvement inaction?', *Personnel Management*, December

Wilkinson A., Allen P. and Snape E. (1991), 'TQM and the Management of Labour', *Employee Relations*, vol. 13(1), pp. 24–31

Wilson F. (1989), 'Productive Efficiency and the Employment Relationship – The Case of Quality Circles', *Employee Relations*, vol. 11(1), pp. 27–32

Winkler J. (1974), 'The ghost at the bargaining table; directors and industrial relations', *British Journal of Industrial Relations*, vol. 12(2), pp. 191–212

Wood S. (1986), 'The Co-operative Labour Strategy in the US Anto Industry', *Economic and Industrial Democracy*, vol. 7, pp. 415–47

Wood S. (ed.) (1989), *The Transformation of Work?*. Unwin Hyman, London

Index

Index compiled by Frank Pert